Invisible Forces

Invisible Forces

Motivational Supports and Challenges in High School and College Classes

PEI PEI LIU

SUNY PRESS

Published by State University of New York Press, Albany

For information, contact State University of New York Press, Albany, NY
www.sunypress.edu

Library of Congress Cataloging-in-Publication Data

Name: Liu, Pei Pei, 1982– author.
Title: Invisible forces : motivational supports and challenges in high
    school and college classes / Pei Pei Liu.
Description: Albany : State University of New York Press, [2023]. | Includes
    bibliographical references and index.
Identifiers: LCCN 2023015784 | ISBN 9781438495774 (hardcover : alk. paper) |
    ISBN 9781438495798 (ebook) | ISBN 9781438495781 (pbk. : alk. paper)
Subjects: LCSH: Motivation in education. | College preparation programs—
    Psychological aspects.
Classification: LCC LB1065 .L587 2024 | DDC 370.15/4—dc23/eng/20230714
LC record available at https://lccn.loc.gov/2023015784

10 9 8 7 6 5 4 3 2 1

Contents

Illustrations

Figure

Tables

Acknowledgments

I am indebted to so many for this work. First and foremost, I thank my participants, the educators I call Diane, Zachary, Liz, and Colin. The experience of original data collection with you, and then revisiting your classrooms through my field notes and reliving our conversations through interview transcripts and recordings, has been infinitely rewarding and enlightening to me. I am truly honored to have been entrusted with your teaching practice.

This book would not be possible without the mentorship of Mandy Savitz-Romer, Karen Brennan, and Sara Lawrence-Lightfoot, as well as the invaluable feedback and emotional support of Megan Powell Cuzzolino, Bryan Mascio, and Rebecca Wiseman Lee. For their help at various stages of the conceptualization and development process, I thank Treseanne Ainsworth, Sheldon Berman, Patricia Bizzell, Arria Coburn, Maria DiPietro, Dara Fisher, Amy Gonzalez, Steve Mahoney, Peter Nguyen, David Perda, Jennifer Plante, Meghan Rosa, Modhumita Roy, Daniel St. Louis, Adina Schecter, Stacey Sheriff, and Nancy Sommers. I am also grateful for the thoughtful commentary of my manuscript reviewers, the everlasting patience and counsel of editor Rebecca Colesworthy, and the team in design, production, and marketing at SUNY Press.

Finally, thank you to my parents, Triung Yueh Yang and Shih-Long Liu, who always put their three kids first and, in raising us outside of their birth country, conquered challenges that I did not fully appreciate until far too late into adulthood. I try to enact my gratitude for what you have given me by working for the benefit of others.

Grateful acknowledgment is made to the following for permission to reprint previously published materials.

The President and Fellows of Harvard College for appendix B. An unabridged version of appendix B, including portrait excerpts, was previously published as an article of the same title in *Harvard Educational Review* 90, no. 1 (2020), 102–26.

Coach House Books for excerpts from Christian Bök's *Eunoia* in chapter 4.

Introduction

The Invisible Ecosystem of Student Motivation

I am on hall duty when one of my students—I'll call him "Damian" here—is kicked out of algebra class for the third consecutive school day. On Friday, he apparently called the teacher a "fucking bitch." On Monday, he was thrown out as soon as he stepped through the door because the teacher was still angry about Friday and thought Damian should have been suspended (but had not drawn up the paperwork to initiate the process). Today—which is also the last day before the math MCAS[1] exam that Damian and the rest of the tenth grade will be taking—he was talking in class, Damian tells me as he shuffles slowly toward the hall monitoring table.

It is May 2008, and I am nearly through an exhausting third year in the Boston Public Schools. After teaching eleventh and twelfth grade my first two years, I was shifted to the lower school to fill a vacant slot that was initially supposed to be four sections of ninth-grade English. My school, however, had also just acquired a new headmaster, and student recruitment had fallen through the cracks during the transition,[2] leaving the ninth grade underenrolled and necessitating a dramatic intraschool restructuring two weeks into the school year. My unit's four sections of ninth graders were consolidated into two, and we acquired two sections of tenth graders from another unit of teachers within the school—who, somehow, were allowed to hand-pick which students they wanted to reassign to us. On their first day in the new configuration, my tenth graders looked around the room at each other and said, "Dang, they put all the bad kids together in here."

Though algebra class has been especially contentious, everyone has been struggling with these tenth graders all year. A month ago, I had it out with Damian myself when he would not stop wandering around the room, poking

1

his classmates, and not doing his work during my class—and then also refused to serve the detention I gave him until I threatened to suspend him in a heated exchange that I later regretted. I probably lose my cool a bit more than I should with Damian because his latent potential is so obvious to me. He reads the extra books I give him outside of class and seems to have a near-photographic memory for tiny details in them; we've discussed the ethical issues raised in Monster, Flowers for Algernon, The House of the Scorpion, The Kite Runner, The Bluest Eye. *Even when I handed him* The Sound and the Fury *on a whim, just because it's a favorite of mine and I wondered what he'd do with it, he gave it a fair shot before finally returning to me to ask, "Miss, what is this??"*

Damian is also an especially frustrating puzzle to me because he seems so self-aware. He surprised both of us during our suspension argument after I told him, "I am so sick and tired of having this conversation with you!" and he replied, "I'm tired of making you have to have this conversation with me." Nor is he defiant and confrontational with teachers by default; last week of his own volition, he hung out in my classroom with me and my coteacher after school, joking that he was going to crash her upcoming wedding. "You know that part at the end when they ask if anyone has objections?" he said. "I'm gonna stand up and start wilin' out: 'Hell no, I didn't approve this marriage—nobody even asked me!' They're all gonna be like, 'Who's that skinny Black kid in the front row?'"

Now, he perches on the edge of my table, all long limbs and natural hair and big eyes—he's always reminded me of a Simpsons character come to life—and suddenly says, "You know how when you're a little kid, they give you a ribbon or a prize no matter how you do? Like if it's a competition, even the last-place kid gets something because he tried? I don't think that's right."

I reply that some people believe that we're raising generations of people who never develop self-reliance because they are dependent on praise for everything they do. Damian nods emphatically: "I think that's true! And it makes the people who win less motivated because it's like, if you get a prize for coming in last, who cares about coming in first?"

The above is a scene that I documented in my teaching journal at the time and that has stayed with me, a dozen years later. It's an exchange that I hope resonates with other teachers who undoubtedly have their own Damians: charmers chock-full of potential whom we somehow, infuriatingly, just cannot quite seem to motivate consistently to attend to their schoolwork. After that year, I was shifted back to upper school and therefore ended up teaching Damian—and that whole cohort—for eleventh and twelfth grade. While Damian did become somewhat consistently more engaged in English, he jeopardized his graduation by very nearly failing a required class on a technicality that he stubbornly refused to rectify until the last minute. On graduation day, I took a picture with him, joking that I needed the photographic proof that he'd actually finished school. And high school graduation was the finish line for Damian; he did not pursue any further education.

I ultimately left the high school classroom after eight years to try to answer the motivational questions and puzzles underlying student interactions like these. What was I doing wrong, or what more could I be doing for students like Damian to get them to invest in their schoolwork? Was he right that "participation-trophy" culture diminished the appeal of working hard, or was he just making excuses? Why didn't his love of reading and his clear affection for at least some of his teachers transfer to school assignments? What was it about algebra class—or the algebra teacher—that resulted in Damian getting kicked out multiple times every week? Had we failed him by not pushing him harder to go to college? What would have happened to him if he had pursued postsecondary education? Would he have blossomed in a less regimented learning environment, or would he have struggled without daily attention and check-ins from familiar educators?[3]

While the research questions of greatest interest to me have always focused on what I and other educators could do differently, I also remain cognizant of the broader contexts that shape educators' responses to students like Damian. When given the opportunity, Damian's former teachers chose to ship him and the other self-identified "bad kids" out of their unit—a decision that infuriated me at the time and directly impacted my classroom experience, but one that I can now more fully recognize as a downstream effect of a vacuum in school leadership and the ensuing institutional chaos. Those teachers, like my algebra colleague, used a tool that had been made available to them to try to create a better learning environment for their remaining students. These are crude tools, but sometimes born of necessity due to teachers not knowing alternative strategies, perceiving a lack of support—or accountability—from school administration, or simply being at wit's end. Many of these teachers were, like me, young and idealistic but working themselves to exhaustion in an often-unforgiving large urban public school district.

Stepping away from the classroom myself has only strengthened my empathy for educators and the challenges of their work. This empathy has demanded a holistic approach in my classroom-based research: I analyze educators' pedagogical approaches but always strive to contextualize them within each educator's specific situation. I identify possible alternative instructional decisions that educators could make, yet I also explore the reasons why the educators are not pursuing those options and what supports they might need to do so.

This book is situated at the intersection of these questions and perspectives. It presents four detailed case studies known as "portraits" that explore how educators can influence student motivation through instructional practices in the classroom and how these motivationally supportive practices may look different in high school versus college classrooms. The portraits depict secondary and postsecondary classrooms as complex motivational spaces where dedicated and well-intentioned educators implement innovative motivational supports but also encounter challenges in the form of individual student needs, institutional expectations and constraints, the stakes and pressure of the transition itself, and their own limitations. My goal is for the portraits to evoke recognition, empathy, and identification in readers as educators, school leaders, instructional developers, and scholars. The portraits prompt readers to reflect not only on how to support student motivation during a critical period of transition, but also on the necessary parallel process of supporting high school and college educators' ability to enact motivationally supportive instructional strategies.

In this introduction, I lay the groundwork for the portraits that will follow. I first present a practitioner framework for defining motivation, followed by a brief discussion of classroom influences on student motivation. I then review research findings on trends in student motivation from late secondary school into postsecondary education and specifically within the discipline of writing, my primary focus here. I close by framing the unique contributions that portraiture methodology can make to classroom-based motivation research across the secondary and postsecondary sectors and providing an overview of the four educators spotlighted in this book and the development of their portraits.

Motivation as Mindsets

Motivation is commonly misunderstood as a relatively static personal trait or disposition (i.e., people either are motivated in certain areas or they aren't) and that quantity is its key property (i.e., people can be more or less motivated toward certain tasks). However, motivation is a dynamic psychological process that is constantly in flux, and contemporary motivation theories are just as concerned with the quality and nature of student motivation as with the quantity. From a psychological perspective, motivation is the process of initiating and sustaining behavior in service of a goal (Schunk et al., 2014). It is an internal energy that influences our behavior by getting us to start, and then persist at, a particular task. Because it involves the selection of a goal and directs different kinds of behaviors related to that goal, motivation has many components and many touchpoints where it can be influenced, for better or worse.

The University of Chicago's Consortium on School Research (UCCSR) synthesizes multiple theories of motivation into four "mindsets" that, together, express motivation as a kind of inner voice within students. The four motivational mindsets are: "I belong in this academic community," "This work has value for me," "My ability and competence grow with my effort," and "I can succeed at this" (Farrington et al., 2012). I refer to these in shorthand throughout the book as **belonging**, **value mindset**, **growth mindset**, and **competence mindset**. When students experience these mindsets in academic situations, they feel the confidence and desire necessary to begin and continue positive academic behaviors. By contrast, when students do not experience these mindsets, or experience a negative version of the mindset in relation to academic tasks, their motivation toward that task is undermined. I discuss the research underlying each mindset in more detail in subsequent chapters but provide a brief overview here.

"I belong in this academic community" reflects the feeling that one is seen, accepted, and valued at school, which is a critical prerequisite for wanting to engage academically (Goodenow, 1993). Rooted in attachment theory (Baumeister & Leary, 1995), social belonging has long been recognized in psychological research as a basic human need (Deci & Ryan, 2002). In school settings, a common indicator for sense of belonging is a student's answer to the question, "Does anyone notice—or mind—when I'm not here?" Research has consistently found a positive association between perceived belonging at school and motivational and achievement outcomes (Beachboard et al., 2011). Conversely, feeling a lack of psychological security and social connections in classrooms and schools can impede students' motivation for academic tasks; it is difficult for students to summon a desire to engage when they feel unvalued or are in conflict with the teacher and/or their peers.

While belonging is an important condition for academic engagement, "This work has value for me" expresses students' reason for wanting to engage in specific tasks or subject areas in school. The expectancy-value theory of motivation identifies three interrelated types of value that students can perceive in an academic task: 1) intrinsic value, the inherent interest or satisfaction a student gets from doing the task; 2) attainment value, the value of a task for a student's sense of personal identity, including its ability to help the student achieve personally meaningful and important goals; and 3) utility value, the usefulness of a task for an individual's daily life and future goals or its broader social utility (Eccles & Wigfield, 2020; Gaspard et al., 2015). Research has shown that students' perception of value toward a task or within a subject area predicts their academic performance and academic choices, such as choosing to enroll in similar courses or choosing to major in a related field (Wigfield et al., 2016).

"My ability and competence grow with my effort" articulates a theory of intelligence as malleable, in contrast to a "fixed" theory of intelligence as a static, innate trait (Dweck, 1999). Individuals tend to endorse one of these two theories of intelligence, which provide different frameworks for setting achievement goals and interpreting successes and failures. Individuals with a growth mindset tend to pursue mastery goals focused on learning and to view failure or mistakes are an inevitable part of development and an important learning opportunity. By contrast, individuals with a fixed mindset view both successes and failures as evidence of innate ability (i.e., either being inherently smart at or dumb/bad at something) and can tend to pursue performance goals rooted in social comparison (either looking smarter or avoiding looking dumber than others). A robust body of research demonstrates that individuals with a growth mindset and mastery goal orientation exert more effort in their learning, persist through difficulty, are more resilient, and achieve at higher levels than people who hold a fixed view of intelligence (Blackwell et al., 2007; Kennett & Keefer, 2006; Mangels et al., 2006; Yeager & Dweck, 2012).

"I can succeed at this" describes a positive self-assessment of one's own competence and likelihood of success that is central to many different motivation theories (Bandura, 1997; Deci & Ryan, 2002; Wigfield & Eccles, 1992). Evidence consistently shows that students who feel competent and are confident that they can succeed are more likely to engage and persist in academic tasks (Baier et al., 2016; Salanova et al., 2011). Competence mindsets also predict academic achievement as measured by both grades and test scores (Rosenzweig & Wigfield, 2017; Wigfield et al., 2016). Importantly, competence mindsets do not necessarily need to be accurate; research suggests that individuals' subjective judgments of their own ability influence their academic choices and behaviors in ways that are independent from their actual ability or skill level as measured objectively (Schunk & Pajares, 2005).

Identifying these four mindsets is helpful for understanding the distinct components of student motivation, but it is important to note that the mindsets interact with and influence each other. For example, the expectancy-value theory of motivation examines the relationship between the competence and value mindsets in predicting academic achievement and behaviors (Eccles & Wigfield, 2020). We may tend to be more interested in and hold more value toward tasks we know we can succeed at, but our valuation of a task may also help us persist when we encounter difficulty or are not feeling so successful at the task. Other theories examine how belonging can promote competence mindsets by providing positive peer models and social supports that help students feel more confident and capable (Bandura, 1991; Ryan & Deci, 2020).

Thus, rather than being concerned with amounts or degrees, high-quality motivation involves students experiencing all four mindsets in positive and mutually reinforcing ways. Conceptualizing student motivation as this set of mindset statements helps reframe the central questions for educators to consider about student motivation. Instead of questions with a yes/no or quantitative focus, like *Are my students motivated?* or *How can I increase my students' motivation?* it can be helpful to think in more descriptive terms. *What pattern of mindsets is each of my students demonstrating today, or for this particular task? What can I do to help each student get closer to the optimal mindsets for motivation and engagement?* While educators' practical expertise often provides them with good intuitions about students' motivational needs (Dja'far et al., 2016; Hardré & Hennessey, 2013), a primary goal of this book is to help educators practice thinking about student motivation through this more nuanced framework. As such, the chapters strive to provide both an in-depth look at a focal mindset through the educator's portrait and insights on the interplay between the mindsets in the interpretive commentary that bookends the portrait.

The Motivational Ecosystem in Classrooms

Even with a well-developed understanding of motivation, educators often encounter challenges with trying to support student motivation in the classroom. Motivation is an internal process, whereas educators can only control factors external to the student; the final step of fully endorsing and integrating the motivational mindsets will always fall to the student alone. Zachary, one of the focal educators in this book, describes motivation as one of the "invisible forces" in students that he tries to wrangle in service of learning but is never quite sure whether he's successfully snared. This intangibility may explain why educators often feel their influence on motivation is limited. In an interview sample of high school teachers, Hardré and Sullivan (2008) found a majority expressed doubts about the effectiveness of their motivational strategies, such as, "A lot of the time there just isn't much that we can do to motivate [students]," "For some of them, nothing helps," and "I keep trying . . . but I wonder if in the long run it makes any difference at all" (p. 2069).

In fact, educators have a great deal of influence on student motivation, though that influence may not always be intentional or in the desired direction. Borrowing a metaphor from Urie Bronfenbrenner's (1977) work in developmental psychology, we can view motivational mindsets as part of a larger, complex system of psychological processes operating in each classroom, akin to a biological ecosystem. Classrooms, like ecosystems, comprise many different interconnected relationships and cyclical processes among the living organisms and the environment. Seemingly insignificant events can have ripple effects elsewhere. Even when teachers may not consciously be trying to motivate (or demotivate) students, their reward structures, explicit and implicit messages, and other cues in the classroom supply information to students that can influence their motivational mindsets (Liu et al., 2023). In the opening vignette, Damian alludes to this influence when he identifies participation-trophy culture as a motivational deterrent.

What makes educators' work doubly challenging is that, unlike in a biological ecosystem, the downstream effects of these complex environmental processes are not observable, even at a microscopic level. The "invisible forces" of motivational mindsets ultimately hinge not on any objectively identifiable stimulus, but rather on an individual student's *subjective perception* of what is happening around them (Kaplan et al., 2002). A key motivational competency for educators, then, is perspective-taking: the ability to view their teaching practice through a student's eyes and motivational mindsets. While it is impossible for anyone ever to know and be able to experience the full complexity of another's experience, educators can endeavor to cultivate new ways of seeing that at least partially illuminate the invisible. Thus, in addition to promoting a reconceptualization of student motivation as qualitative mindset patterns rather than static quantities, another goal of this book is to use portraiture to help educators incorporate that new conception of motivation into a kind of motivational-perspective-taking "lens" through which they can examine, first, the focal educators and classrooms featured in the case studies, then ultimately their own practice. Honing this skill will enable educators to recognize more opportunities to enhance students' motivational mindsets in service of higher-quality motivation and learning.

I discuss the research on specific environmental influences for each mindset in subsequent chapters, but the metaphor of a psychological, partly invisible ecosystem is helpful for remembering that these are dynamic, living interactions, rather than automatic inputs and outputs. Motivating and demotivating influences can vary from classroom to classroom, and even from day to day or task to task within the same classroom. A student can therefore seem highly motivated in one class but not in another, or they can vary in motivation toward different tasks in a given class depending on how the task is presented and what supports are available to promote the student's belonging, value, growth, and competence mindsets in relation to the task.

Crucially, the motivational ecosystem includes a feedback-loop mechanism, such that the influence does not only operate in one direction, classroom event influencing student motivation. Students' motivational mindsets also influence how students behave and interact with others in the learning environment, such as their teacher or peers. Those interactions are new learning-related events that then inform students' motivational mindsets in future academic situations. For example, one of the strongest influences on the competence mindset "I can succeed at this" is prior mastery of a similar or related task (this is discussed further in chapter 4). Thus, prior learning experiences have already shaped the motivational mindsets that students bring to day 1 of a new class, and each new learning experience informs their subsequent motivation.

The cycle of this feedback loop operating over time means that although all classroom educators can promote positive motivational mindset development in students, they are also contending with students' entering mindsets. This is especially salient for educators working with older students, who have many years of prior learning behind them; I certainly felt at times that teaching Damian was like working in a closed system, where no new inputs were making any difference, even as the consequences felt increasingly high-stakes and imminent. However, the constant presence of that cycle of motivational feedback is also an opportunity for classroom educators to provide learning experiences that reinforce the positive motivational mindsets students may bring with them and disrupt the negative mindsets, creating a stronger foundation for future learning.

Of course, current and former classroom-based learning experiences are not the only forces acting on student motivation at any given moment. Other domains of life—family, friends, communities of faith, work—play a role in the attitudes and belief that students formulate related to learning. A student's motivational ecosystem also includes indirect influences from people, institutions, and policies with whom they have no direct contact. The classroom practices that students find motivating or demotivating may not always be a result of the educator's intentional design but rather are "baked in" to the overall fabric of a department, school, or system, or else are overt constraints placed on the educators, as we will see in some of the portraits. As with students' mindsets, though, the educator's *perception* of broader constraints or culture is the key influence on their practice. My hope is that cultivating a new lens on students' motivational experience can also help educators refresh their view on their own ecosystems and see new opportunities and affordances, even amidst the constraints. In doing so, this new lens on student motivation can support a parallel motivational process in educators, enhancing their own mindsets about their competence and growth potential in teaching and their feelings of membership in and value for the profession.

The portraits in this book aim to illuminate the motivational ecosystems created by the four focal educators in their classrooms. My focus at the classroom level is not meant to be evaluative of individual educators or to hold them solely responsible for student motivation, but rather to combat educators' perceptions of their limited influence on student motivation. I mean, in other words, to make visible the role educators can and do play in shaping those invisible forces by highlighting strategies within their sphere of control—that is, their classroom—that can make a difference for students. Though not their primary focus, the portraits also provide some insights into each educator's professional background, experience, and working conditions within their respective institution to illustrate how these contextual factors in the extended ecosystem can indirectly influence the motivational climate that students ultimately encounter in the classroom. The postportrait reflections in each chapter, the interlude between chapters 2 and 3, and the cross-case discussion in chapter 5 delve into these factors in more detail. My goal is for the portraits, as a collection, to help identify motivationally supportive classroom practices that secondary and postsecondary educators can enact, as well as supports that the educators themselves may need to implement these strategies.

Motivation at the College Transition

Creating motivationally supportive learning environments for students is especially challenging—but also especially important—when students transition from one school to another because students often confront different norms and expectations for learning at their new schools that can undermine their motivation (Farrington et al., 2012). By definition, sense of belonging is disrupted by school transitions, as students have to establish new adult and peer relationships. The change is especially stark at the college transition, as many students move from a localized K–12 educational system, where they may have had a consistent peer cohort and/or stronger connections to school through parents and siblings, to the far more varied options for higher education (Venezia et al., 2003, 2005), which they often embark on alone.

The college transition also coincides with a well-documented trend of decreasing perceptions of value and overall motivation for school over time in the K–12 sector (Jacobs et al., 2002; Spinath & Steinmayr, 2008; Watt, 2004; Wigfield et al., 2015). While young children are often enthusiastic about school, those feelings of interest and value tend to decline when they enter middle school and then further erode in high school. This pattern coincides with student perceptions of a greater emphasis on performance goals and competition in secondary school (E. M. Anderman et al., 2002), which can reinforce fixed mindsets and focus students on the demonstration, rather than actual development, of competence. Paradoxically, the elective nature of higher education overall, as well as the expectation that students declare a major, can lead college instructors to assume that students have a valued area of specialization that they are motivated to pursue and can recognize the value of the knowledge and skills they are acquiring in relation to that goal (Cox, 2009; Dja'far et al., 2016). There can be an overoptimism about students' ability to seamlessly adopt a fairly different way of doing school than anything they have previously experienced. Colin, one of the college instructors in this book, was bemused by his first-semester college students' enduring preoccupation with high school culture but seemed to have a moment of new insight when I pointed out to him that the difference between being a high school senior versus a first-year college student was a matter of a few months.

Finally, confronting more rigorous coursework and higher academic expectations in college can threaten students' growth and competence mindsets or further reinforce existing negative mindsets in these areas. In a phenomenon known as the big-fish-little-pond effect, studies have shown a consistent negative relationship between the achievement levels at a school overall and individual students' competence mindsets, such that students at higher-achieving schools experience lower feelings of competence, regardless of the student's individual achievement level (Marsh & Hau, 2003). Similarly, Kosovich and colleagues (2017) found that college students' competence mindsets in an introductory class generally declined over the course of the semester and that this reduced sense of competence was related to a decrease in perceived value for the course. Other research has shown that college students with fixed mindset can become defiant about the decreased academic performance and critical feedback that some of them inevitably experience (Forsythe & Johnson, 2017; Nussbaum & Dweck, 2008), potentially making it more challenging for college instructors to nurture growth mindset as well as the actual academic improvement that could strengthen students' competence mindsets.

Even as the college transition is a vulnerable time for student motivation, however, research suggests that positive motivational mindsets could be critical tools in helping students experience a smoother first-year transition and better academic outcomes in college overall (Greenfield, 2013; Venezia & Jaeger, 2013). For example, Han and colleagues (2017) found that high measures of perceived competence, belonging, and value in first-year college students predicted their first-year academic performance and retention between the first and second years. These findings are consistent with other studies on the importance of belonging and competence mindsets for college students' persistence (Baier et al., 2016; Wright et al., 2013) and academic performance (Chemers et al., 2001; Freeman et al., 2007; D. R. Johnson et al., 2007; Krumrei-Mancuso et al., 2013). Other studies of early college students have also demonstrated a relationship between academic performance and motivational factors aligned with the value and growth mindsets (Bong, 2001; DeFreitas, 2012; D'Lima et al., 2014; E. Jones, 2008). There is evidence that the big-fish-little-pond effect is short-lived and that being in a more challenging academic and peer environment eventually raises individual students' achievement levels (Stäbler et al., 2017), which would in turn be expected to promote their competence mindsets and sense of belonging in college. Attending to students' mindsets during this time could therefore support and strengthen similarly adaptive patterns in motivation and achievement.

The evidence suggesting that positive motivational mindsets could be important assets in students' adjustment to college makes motivational support a worthy target for secondary-postsecondary alignment efforts. Studies have shown that high school experiences, particularly relationships with high school teachers, influence students' relationship-building interactions with college faculty, potentially influencing their sense of belonging (Hudley et al., 2009; Hurtado et al., 2011). Research has also demonstrated that high school students who are better prepared academically for college tend to have greater perceived competence compared to their less-prepared peers (Melzer & Grant, 2016) and that precollege students' competence as well as value mindsets for a subject can predict their academic behaviors in college, such as college course selection and choice of major (Musu-Gillette et al., 2015; Priess-Groben & Hyde, 2017).

However, K–16 alignment efforts on motivational mindsets and similar skills have received less attention and investment than initiatives focused on academic expectations (Kirst & Venezia, 2004) and curriculum alignment (ACT, 2016; Alliance for Excellent Education, 2007). There are several possible reasons for this oversight. One is that the secondary and postsecondary sectors have historically operated quite separately in both practice and research (Venezia et al., 2003), creating obstacles for people trying to conduct research or provide instructional development that spans the two sectors. Another reason is that academic standards and curriculum are typically documented in some way, which facilitates large-scale and systematic comparison across sectors. By contrast, motivational support is a more nebulous topic, especially given the unique features of each classroom as a motivational ecosystem. Finally, instructional practices are far less researched in higher education compared to the K–12 sector, in part because of sector differences in pedagogical training and professional pathways for educators (Baum & McPherson, 2019).

The college classroom in particular has not received much attention as a setting where motivational mindsets can be promoted by the instructor of record. Efforts to promote positive mindset development in first-year college students are more commonly situated in student affairs, advising, or specialized first-year programming such as first-year seminars (Hyers & Joslin, 1998) and learning communities (Beachboard et al., 2011), rather than in core academic classes (Conley, 2015). This book aims to fill part of the gap created by these challenges by presenting portraits of twelfth-grade and first-year college classrooms and how the educators in these classrooms play a critical role in fostering positive motivational mindsets that can facilitate students' college transition.

A Focus on Writing

The portraits in this book are all set in writing-based classrooms: high school English classes and first-year undergraduate introductory writing classes that are not part of broader institutional first-year support initiatives like a learning community or first-year seminar. There are both methodological and substantive reasons for this choice. At a basic methodological level, focusing on a particular discipline aids in cross-sector comparisons that are already complicated by multiple contextual variables. Substantively, however, writing classrooms also offer unique affordances for this work as well as opportunities to contribute to the knowledge base on motivation at the college transition.

Writing is a critical academic skill for college readiness and subsequent college success (O'Neill et al., 2012), and it also socializes students in the academic culture of college (Sommers & Saltz, 2004). The intellectual work of college, across disciplines, is often carried out and demonstrated through academic writing, so learning to write in and for college is a central dimension of becoming a college student. The importance of writing is reflected in the prevalence of four-year English requirements in high school and first-year writing requirements in college (ACT, 2014; NCTE, 2013), making it close to a universal academic experience for students across the college transition, regardless of intended major: students write through their last semester of high school, and they have to write from their first semester in college. Examining the motivational opportunities and challenges in writing classrooms on each side of the college transition is therefore a key first step for understanding what educators can do to better support their students' college readiness and success.

In addition to its ubiquity and centrality in the college transition experience, writing is a complex task that draws heavily on students' motivational reserves (MacArthur et al., 2016). A dynamic and cyclical process of conceptualizing, planning, organizing, drafting, and revising is essential for developing an effective piece of writing (Downs, 2016; S. Jones, 2014). As such, the writing process also affords multiple opportunities for motivational mindsets to serve as assets or liabilities, depending on the students' entering mindsets and the extent to which the circumstances of the writing task promote positive mindset development. As with research on the college transition overall, however, the exploration of students' writing experience as they move from K–12 to postsecondary education has typically examined courses taken (Imbrenda, 2018) or contrasting expectations and beliefs about the purpose and nature of writing assignments (Addison & McGee, 2010; Patterson & Duer, 2006), but without a specific focus on motivational implications or pedagogical strategies per se. Indeed, studying motivationally supportive instruction within writing classes is a relatively new area of exploration, even though the separate fields of motivation research and composition studies have long and robust histories (Hidi & Boscolo, 2006; MacArthur & Graham, 2016).

Contemporary work that does aim to bridge the two fields typically takes a cognitive perspective by synthesizing motivational research on the constructs underlying the competence, value, and growth mindsets and aligning these with composition research on writing purpose, authenticity, and meaningfulness, as well as the management of writing processes (Boscolo & Gelati, 2018). For example, studies have shown that attending to mindset constructs such as self-efficacy and perceived value can improve students' writing performance (Pajares et al., 2007; Zumbrunn et al., 2014). However, scholars have also identified the need for greater attention to sociocultural elements of writing and writing classrooms (Boscolo & Hidi, 2006), which implicates the belonging mindset. Additionally, few studies have focused on the affective or emotional experiences of writing that implicate student motivation—such as when receiving and incorporating feedback, writing multiple drafts, and interpreting evaluation criteria (Ballenger & Myers, 2019; Callahan & Chumney, 2009; Cox, 2009; Feltham & Sharen, 2015)—rather than using writing performance as the main outcome of interest when examining motivationally supportive practices.

This book aims to bring the fields of motivation, college transition, and composition studies more directly into conversation with each other. My approach acknowledges the complexity of learning contexts in the K–12 and postsecondary sectors and the central role of participants' motives and meaning-making within those contexts. Although I ground my work in mindset constructs drawn from a synthesis of motivation theories, I embed the discussion of these mindsets within rich descriptions of the pedagogical puzzles that educators encounter when teaching writing on either side of the college transition. My goal is that readers who are well versed in educational psychology will recognize familiar constructs from the motivation literature but will come to see them in a more complex and textured way, while readers experienced in college transition work and/or writing instruction will recognize the classroom contexts depicted here but will gain a motivational lens for reflecting on their own work.

Developing the Portraits

I developed the case studies in this book using a qualitative research methodology called "portraiture," which aims to depict the nuance and complexity of human experience through rich narratives known as portraits (Lawrence-Lightfoot & Davis, 1997). While the foci of portraits can range in scope and scale—including schools (Lawrence-Lightfoot, 1983), concepts (Lawrence-Lightfoot, 2000), and processes (Lawrence-Lightfoot, 2012)—the methodology always attends to the "ecological context" of its focal subject or phenomenon (Lawrence-Lightfoot & Davis, 1997, p. 44). This made it an ideal vehicle for examining individual educators and the ecosystems—both experienced and created by them—in which they strive to support student motivation.

Educator developers have long touted the affordances of case narratives as a vehicle for teacher learning (Gravett et al., 2017; Heitzmann, 2008; Moje & Wade, 1997). In my own professional experiences working with secondary and postsecondary educators, I have seen educators' positive responses to text or video cases as helping to "make it concrete." During the study, all four of my participants expressed, on numerous occasions, their interest in reading the other participants' portraits. Though they did not necessarily have a model for what the final portraits would look like, they understood intuitively that reading portraits of other educators would lead them to a deeper understanding of their own teaching context and would contribute to their toolkit of motivationally supportive strategies to use in the classroom.

However, portraiture differs in important ways from both the teaching cases typically used in professional learning contexts and other qualitative research methodologies like ethnography. Portraiture affords the opportunity for a researcher to present the reader with analytic themes as in other qualitative research, but through more expansive and literary narratives. These narratives are also longer than typical cases used for educational purposes and incorporate more aesthetic features, particularly metaphors. The rich descriptions and use of metaphor in portraits are meant to invite and encourage the reader's active interpretation and response—as with literature or visual art—rather than positioning the reader as a more passive recipient of didactically transferred information. As a former teacher turned researcher, I have found portraiture uniquely suited to capturing the overall "feel" of a classroom: the overlapping voices and intersecting personalities, the spontaneous and improvisational elements, the delightful messiness, and—perhaps most of all—the humor. Given the subjectivity of student uptake of motivational influences, the conveyance of this classroom gestalt is essential for understanding the complexity and nuance of a motivational ecosystem that is perceived and experienced differently by each student.

Additionally, portraiture deliberately seeks to counter the "focus on pathology" characteristic of much social science research by rooting itself in a search for goodness that acknowledges that "the expression of goodness will always be laced with imperfections" (Lawrence-Lightfoot & Davis, 1997, p. 9). The methodology therefore takes a generous stance toward participants by seeking to illuminate the pursuit of goodness that drives their choices while simultaneously not papering over the imperfections, limitations, and mistakes that will inherently be found. Portraiture does not aim to label participants' thinking or actions as "good" or "bad" but rather to add texture to our understanding of human behavior in context. This makes it an appropriate method for exploring educators' approaches to supporting student motivation and providing educators with cross-sector depictions of classrooms across the college transition. As neither of these goals has received much attention in extant research or opportunities for educator development, the generous, phenomenological approach afforded by portraiture seems warranted.

Proponents of case method advocate careful attention to the composition of cases (Darling-Hammond & Hammerness, 2002; McAninch, 1993; Merseth, 1991); the mere presence of a case does not automatically ensure identification on the part of educators, nor are all cases suited to all teacher education or professional learning situations. Likewise, portraitists adhere to a rigorous methodological process that ensures that the work is empirically sound as well as aesthetically pleasing. In the following sections, I provide an overview of the portrait-development process, focusing on what I deem essential context for the finished portraits and anticipating likely reader questions about the educators, their schools, and key procedures in the research study. Readers who are interested in a deeper methodological perspective are invited to explore appendix A, which includes additional details as well as artifacts from data collection and analysis.

THE EDUCATORS

The data informing the portraits include classroom observations, course documents, and interviews with four classroom educators: two twelfth-grade English teachers and two instructors of first-year college writing. To facilitate within-sector comparisons, I selected high school teachers who worked at similar types of schools and college instructors whose institutions were likewise similar. Because postsecondary pathways vary widely, however, I did not try to align the institutional features of the high schools and colleges to project an "expected" or "typical" college for the graduates of the focal high schools. Nevertheless, all four schools were within a ninety-minute drive of each other in the same northeastern state and students from the two focal high schools were accepted to both focal colleges during the course of my data collection. The portraits therefore depict college writing instructors that students of the focal high schools might plausibly encounter following their experiences with the profiled high school English teachers.

The portraits introduce my participants and their schools in more depth, but table I.1 below summarizes key characteristics as well as the data collected in each classroom. "Diane Bauer" and "Zachary Kaplan" were the two high school teachers.[4] They taught at, respectively, "Riverside Academy" and "Oak Bridge School" (OBS), small public schools in separate urban districts of roughly 25,000 students.[5] Riverside served approximately 700 students in grades 6–12, while OBS served approximately 275 students in grades 7–12. Student cohorts generally entered both schools at the earliest grade level through lottery-based admissions, with few new students enrolling in the later grades. At both schools, the majority were students of color, and there was a high percentage of "economically disadvantaged" students.[6] Both schools also had impressive results on the state high school equivalency exam, with passing rates in each subject exceeding those of their respective districts.

My college instructors, "Liz Cartwright" and "Colin Zimmerman," taught at "Mayfield University" and "Abbott University," private institutions with selective undergraduate admissions. Mayfield served approximately 2,200 undergraduates, with a first-year cohort of about 540. Abbott served approximately 5,000 undergraduates, including 1,300 first-year students. Mayfield was rated "highly selective" under the Barron's classification, with a 55 percent overall admissions rate; incoming first-year students had average critical reading and mathematics SAT scores in the low 600s, and an average high school GPA of 3.65. Abbott was rated "most selective" by Barron's, with a 16 percent admissions rate and average incoming SAT scores in the low 700s. Both colleges were predominantly White institutions, posting similar percentages of domestic students of color (22 percent for both) and international students (Mayfield: 14 percent, Abbott: 12 percent), and had fairly low numbers of Pell Grant recipients (Mayfield: 22 percent, Abbott: 13 percent). Appendix A provides more detailed information about the four schools.

Each educator chose a focal class for me to visit consistently over the course of one academic semester. I collected data from January to June 2017 for the two high school classrooms, and from August to December 2017 for the two college classrooms. I observed each classroom roughly twice a week (for the college classes that only met twice a week, this was the majority of

Table I.1. Overview of Participants and Data Collection

Participant (Institution)*	Diane Bauer (Riverside Academy)	Zachary Kaplan (Oak Bridge School)	Liz Cartwright (Mayfield University)	Colin Zimmerman (Abbott University)
Personal background	— MA in teaching, EdD from Fairfield University — 29th year teaching (10th at Riverside) — Previously taught at comprehensive public high school in Connecticut	— MA in teaching from Mayfield University — 5th year teaching (all at OBS)	— MFA in fiction from "State University" — 5th year teaching (3rd at Mayfield) — Taught analogous course at "State University"	— PhD candidate in English at Abbott University — 5th year teaching at Abbott — Concurrently teaching same course at "Barton College"
Focal class	— AP English Literature and Composition — 22 students — Met on rotating schedule (57–65 min sessions), 5x/week	— Superheroes in World Literature — 25 students (11th and 12th graders) — Met from 12:23–1:23 pm, 4x/week	— First-year writing ("Expository Writing") — 18 students — Met from 9:00–10:15 am, 2x/week	— First-year writing ("English 101") — 16 students — Met from 12:00–1:15 pm, 2x/week
Data collected	— Feb–June 2017 — 19 observations — 5 interviews — course documents	— Feb–June 2017 — 17 observations — 5 interviews — course documents	— Aug–Dec 2017 — 25 observations — 4 interviews — course documents	— Sep–Dec 2017 — 21 observations — 4 interviews — course documents

*Participant and focal institution names are pseudonyms, as are "Barton College" and "State University" because of potentially identifiable information in the data when participants discuss their experiences at these institutions.

Source: Author provided.

the total class time for the semester), interviewed the educators periodically, and collected documents related to the course, including student work.

It is important to note that in selecting my participants, I did not seek educators who had earned any particular commendation for their teaching or received specialized training. Instead, I used the topic of the study itself—promoting motivational mindsets—to recruit educators who felt they could identify to me what they already did to support student motivation but were also interested in learning more. The educators profiled in the cases are therefore not meant to be "exemplars"—though I personally consider them extraordinary for their willingness and generosity in opening up their classrooms to me. Rather, I believe there is much to learn from "ordinary" educators like these, including the motivational challenges they face with students and their mixture of effective and imperfect strategies for addressing these challenges.

I used a combination of existing themes from motivation research and open-ended exploration to collect and analyze the data for the portraits. To reduce the obtrusiveness of my observations, I did not record the classes but rather took detailed field notes, guided by motivation theory and research about the types of instructional practices, teacher talk, and classroom features that can either promote or undermine the development of students' motivational mindsets. I used a similar framework to guide my analysis of course documents. The interviews occurred periodically throughout the semester and provided me with opportunities to learn more about each educator's thought process behind certain instructional decisions. Occasionally, I was able to share excerpts from my field notes and ask the educator to respond, explain his or her thinking in that moment, and verify my account and interpretation of the event. I recorded and transcribed all interviews.

At the same time, I examined my field notes, the course documents, and the interview transcripts to gain a sense holistically of each educator's approach to motivation support, independent of motivation theory. I wanted not only to use motivation theory as a lens for looking at educator pedagogy, but also to understand each educator's pedagogy in its own right and consider ways in which these real-life cases might provide new insights for motivation researchers about what supporting student motivation looks like in the classroom. I documented my emergent thinking, questions, and preliminary hypotheses in memos and eventually developed a set of ten to twelve codes for each participant that described the key characteristics of their teaching. I then mapped these codes onto my original observation framework derived from motivation theory and created a visual matrix of the key themes within and across each case. For more information about the coding process, see appendix A.

This thematic matrix provided the foundation for the portraits, including the decision to focus each participant's portrait on a focal mindset: Diane on belonging, Zachary on the value mindset, Liz on growth mindset, and Colin on the competence mindset. While this structure may seem suspiciously convenient, I did not embark on my analysis intending to pair off educators and mindsets. Rather, as I worked through the data, I began to see a resonance in these pairings: in addition to each mindset having a particular prominence in a particular educator's class, each educator's unique teaching style and approach illuminated new insights about the focal mindset I had paired them with.

Importantly, I do not mean to imply that the educators *exclusively* supported the mindset featured in their portrait. As noted previously, the mindsets work together synergistically, and all four educators supported all four mindsets in rich ways. Focusing on a particularly resonant mindset in each portrait, however, allowed me to achieve the level of depth and nuance I felt was necessary to truly understand the complex role of that mindset within that classroom's motivational ecosystem. In each chapter, I offer some reflections after the portrait that identify connections with the other mindsets. The cross-case discussion in chapter 5 elaborates on these areas of overlap and contrast. My hope is also that the portraits, like good literature, stand up to rereading and offer new insights into the synergy of the mindsets each time, especially after readers have gained new understanding and fluency with the mindsets and their supporting practices.

Indeed, reader endorsement is key to portraiture's standard of "authenticity" as its benchmark for quality (Lawrence-Lightfoot & Davis, 1997). Portraits should feel credible and resonant for three audiences: the portraitist, readers, and the participants themselves. While the portraits in this book depict particular educators working within particular contexts, they resonated with me as a classroom educator who has taught at both levels, and I hope that readers likewise recognize a certain universality of the depicted tensions and dilemmas in each classroom.

The portraits have also been reviewed by the focal educators themselves, a critical step in portraiture that extends its methodology beyond what is typical even among many qualitative research traditions. Portraitists consider participant response "a deliberate part of the research enterprise" (Lawrence-Lightfoot, 1983, p. 377), but it is also a potentially fraught process in which participant and portraitist alike are vulnerable. Yet this, too, drew me to portraiture as the appropriate methodology for this study, as a way to disrupt common research-practice hierarchies in which educators are "subjects" of research who are "analyzed" and then metaphorically discarded once the primary data have been extracted. Broadening our outlook on the motivational ecosystem includes embracing different paradigms for research-practice collaborations in the interest of supporting educator development and, ultimately, student outcomes.

Accordingly, I sent the four focal educators near-final drafts of their portraits, and all four affirmed the resonance of the findings and the narratives. However, the variation in their responses reinforced interpretations that I already presented in the portraits and accompanying analysis, bolstering my confidence in my conclusions but also introducing new methodological considerations and dilemmas. Though worthy of attention, these methodological questions strained the boundaries of my study and the intended primary implications for educators; additionally, the participants' responses fell outside the scope of the original data collection plan. I therefore wrote a separate conceptual piece to make sense of these "post"study negotiations, asking permission from the educators to use their responses for this new purpose. As Diane did not respond to this secondary request (and her original response was only a brief acknowledgment and endorsement of the portrait), I did not include her in the methodological essay, an abridged version of which is reprinted in appendix B. I encourage curious readers to seek out the full participant responses there; for the immediate purpose of establishing the portraits' third dimension of authenticity, I will summarize that Liz was the only participant to offer (very mild) pushback on the content of her portrait and the addition of a small paragraph of additional context satisfied both of us. Minor edits and factual corrections were the only other changes from the review drafts to the final publication versions.

Book Overview

This book is organized into five chapters with additional commentary provided in an interlude between chapters 2 and 3 and two appendixes. Chapters 1–4 comprise the four portraits, each of which depicts a focal educator grappling with a focal motivational mindset. Each chapter has three sections: an overview of the research underlying the focal mindset, the portrait itself, and a postportrait reflection that contextualizes the portrait more explicitly within the research outlined at the top of the chapter, the findings from preceding portraits, and relevant literature from college transition and writing-studies scholarship.

Chapter 1, "Making the Team," follows high school teacher Diane Bauer and how her experience of trying to cultivate belonging in her students differs at her current small, Expeditionary Learning school compared to her previous experience at a traditional comprehensive school. Chapter 2, "Choosing Your Adventure," depicts high school teacher Zachary Kaplan's ambitious curricular restructuring to promote the value mindset in his students by providing them with choice and stimulating interdisciplinary content. An interlude follows this chapter to mark the transition from the high school to the college portraits and to provide context for the shift in educational sector. Chapter 3, "Trusting the Process," presents college instructor Liz Cartwright's efforts to integrate a growth mindset in her first-year writing course and the challenges she faces in promoting *strategic* effort from students, rather than merely time spent, as well as countering some students' grade-driven motivations. A similar reckoning with grade fixation permeates chapter 4, "Mastering the Game," which explores the tension that college instructor Colin Zimmerman navigates in trying to help his high-achieving students recalibrate their expectations for academic success at a highly selective college while still promoting competence mindsets.

Importantly, the postportrait reflection in each of these chapters is not an *evaluation* of the educator; it provides the reader with one interpretation (mine) of how the focal educator's practices align with motivational mindset research. I also focus on what I see as the key takeaways for strengthening the educator's approach to supporting the focal mindset and the implications of this specific case for researching and developing other educators' motivationally supportive instruction, while acknowledging that there are any number of themes or questions of personal interest to different readers that I am unable to address directly. I encourage readers to pause after the portraits and/or the concluding reflections to mentally note their own reactions and ideas.

Chapter 5, "Illuminating the Invisible," presents a cross-case synthesis and discussion of the four portraits. I revisit and expand on key threads from previous chapters to propose strategies that educators can adopt to promote positive motivational mindsets in their classrooms. I also "zoom out" to provide a more expansive look at the motivational ecosystem, including a broader analysis of the institutional and systemic factors that comprise each educator's teaching context, the influence of the educators' own motivational mindsets, and recommendations for supporting educators in the challenging work of motivating students across the college transition.

The two methodological appendixes speak most directly to scholarly readers, inviting reflection on how we conduct and present classroom-based research, including the implications of those decisions on our relationships with practitioner participants. Research in the fields of motivation, college transition, and writing instruction alike can benefit from scholarship that contextualizes the study of teaching practice by acknowledging the complex ecosystem that every educator operates in. Additionally, I urge scholars in these fields to consider not only how to authentically reflect educators' realities, but also how to do better at "brokering" our own work (Joram et al., 2020; Neal et al., 2015) such that it reaches educators directly, rather than requiring a separate (most likely time-consuming) research-to-practice translation process. I hope that my collection of portraits in this book provides a worthy example of this model of research and that the appendixes illuminate the mechanisms of my approach to be extended and improved upon by others in future work.

Notes on Composition

I close with explanatory notes about methodological and aesthetic choices in my portraits. Readers may initially be surprised at how present I am in the portraits, both in terms of my first-person narration as well as the depictions of my interactions with the educators and sometimes their students. Portraiture endorses the researcher making herself visible as author and actor in the portrait itself, rather than attempting to convey a false sense of objective narration. It is important for readers to consider the potential impact of my presence on the educators, the students, and their words and behaviors.

My presence as an actor in the portraits also invites the reader to scrutinize me as much as the focal educators. As noted above in the explanation of the postportrait reflections, my interpretations are not pronouncements of truth, but rather one possible perspective on the educators' instructional practice through the lens of motivation theory. The reader's active questioning of the narrative and my interpretation is vital to achieving the goal of having the portraits prompt reflection and change in practitioner readers, and I strongly encourage readers to engage in that critical inquiry.

To facilitate readers' independent interpretation of the source data, I periodically use block text in the portraits as a technique for presenting a self-contained unit of data (a participant quote or an excerpt from my field notes) without interruption or interpretation from me. I am occasionally present as the observer in excerpted field notes to help convey the "feel" of the moment beyond the technical aspects of what people are saying or doing, but I refrain from providing interpretation until I exit the block text and return to the main narrative.

The educators are my focal participants, not their students; as such, I have fully deidentified students' written work. However, it is impossible to observe instructional interactions without observing the students. As such, I have made certain decisions about how to present students in the portraits. I give students pseudonyms if I deem it necessary for narrative clarity and then continue to refer to them by pseudonym if I feel a reader might gain insight into the educator's practice by seeing the same student's reactions to various instructional decisions or events. If identifying a student is not necessary for either of these two objectives in a given classroom scene, I refer to him or her generically ("student," "young man," "young woman").

Additionally, I do not provide any identifying physical descriptions of the students themselves, other than occasionally describing their clothing. I did not ask the students how they self-identify, so I choose not to make assumptions about their race and ethnicity, although for the sake of narrative clarity, I had to compromise on this standard with regards to gender identity and pronoun usage. As I composed the portraits, I also became intrigued by the idea of focusing on what the students were saying and doing, rather than what they looked like, and thus putting readers in the position of wondering how their own reactions to certain classroom events might change depending on the identity or appearance of the student(s) involved.

I have made certain formatting decisions within the portraits because of the language-rich environments and the centrality of writing as the core skill in all four classrooms. Within the portrait narratives, italics designate all written text; I use underlining (in narration) and capitalization (in dialogue) for emphasis.

Finally, other than redacting identifying names and making one edit for clarity in some of Liz's students' work that I explain in that chapter, I present all student work unedited; any mistakes in italicized text throughout the portraits should therefore be considered "sic erat scriptum."

Chapter 1

Making the Team

Cultivating High School Belonging through Collective Goals

Overview: "I belong in this academic community"

Starting with the child's attachment to the mother, the need to belong and relate to others is a universal psychological experience. Every individual is a member of multiple social groups, of which an academic community is just one—but an important one for the kinds of adult and peer relationships that are foundational to well-being, success, and motivation at school. Belonging at school is frequently defined as "the extent to which students feel personally accepted, respected, included, and supported by others in the school social environment" (Goodenow, 1993, p. 80). The emphasis on "others" in this definition is important: the onus is not on an individual student to summon feelings of belonging, as if on command. Rather, teachers and peers contribute to an overall social environment that can foster or undermine feelings of belonging in individual students through inclusive or exclusionary practices (Jansen et al., 2014). Like the other three motivational mindsets, belonging is a subjective perception within individual students that arises in response to the surrounding environment.

A sense of belonging at school is crucial for all students, but the processes that support belonging may look different for different students. For example, there is general consensus that positive, caring teacher-student relationships are a key mechanism for adults to help promote students' school belonging (Furrer & Skinner, 2003), but different students may hold different perceptions of what kinds of behaviors constitute caring. Most research on teacher-student relationships indicates that teachers can convey caring through being attentive to and involved with students (Raufelder et al., 2014), listening empathically (Noddings, 2005; Wentzel, 1997), speaking kindly to students (Alder, 2002; Valverde, 2006), and upholding established norms of behavior that foster feelings of trust and safety for students (Bryk & Schneider, 2002; Voelkl, 2012). However, there is also evidence that students perceive this kind of emotional support as intersecting closely with academic support (Liu et al., 2018). Research suggests that students—particularly those from minoritized groups—commonly identify teachers' academic help and assistance as a dimension of caring (Garza, 2009; Hayes et al., 1994; Nieto, 2004; Tosolt, 2010).

It is particularly important to attend to variations in what students perceive as caring because students of different backgrounds can have widely different experiences with social support at school (Bottiani et al., 2016; Brewster & Bowen, 2004; Decker et al., 2007; Fredricks et al., 2004; Garcia-Reid et al., 2005). An extensive body of literature demonstrates that educators can formulate distinctive beliefs about students based on the students' different racial/ethnic backgrounds, gender, language fluency, and special education status, among other identity factors. These beliefs then influence the kinds of teacher-student relationships that develop. For example, educators' differential perceptions of student conflict or aggression in minoritized youth have been linked to disproportionate disciplinary actions that convey messages to students about their lack of belonging in school (Ferguson, 2001; Saft & Pianta, 2001). Alternatively, it is common for educators to expect girls to be better socialized for school (Kesner, 2000; Silva et al., 2011), which may contribute to preferential treatment of girls by some educators (McGrath & Van Bergen, 2015; Timmermans et al., 2016) or extra efforts to engage boys in other cases (Francis et al., 2008; Marsh et al., 2008).

These kinds of patterns may pose obstacles to all students feeling "accepted, respected, included, and supported" in the same school spaces. Even if educators do not enact overtly prejudicial or exclusionary practices, students could still be affected by "threats in the air" due to their accumulated awareness of stereotypes and overall systemic inequities (Steele, 2003; Urdan & Bruchmann, 2018). For example, research demonstrates that adolescents are especially sensitive to teacher behaviors that suggest differential academic expectations for students across identity groups, such as gender-based stereotypes about ability in math and science or low expectations for Black and Latinx students. Regardless of the teacher's actual beliefs and behaviors, the perceived dismissal or exclusion of certain groups from achievement culture can become a self-fulfilling prophecy leading to lower performance and feelings of alienation from school for students affiliated with these groups (Brown et al., 2003; G. L. Thompson, 2004; Vega et al., 2015).

In response to these risk factors and threats to belonging, research is increasingly considering the importance of culturally relevant and responsive education practices (CRRE; Kumar et al., 2018) as an approach to promoting sense of belonging (Arunkumar et al., 1999; Bonner, 2014; Gray et al., 2018). CRRE practices support feelings of belonging and identification with school by allowing students to "maintain their cultural integrity while succeeding academically" (Ladson-Billings, 1995, p. 476). CRRE is not a codified set of specific practices but rather an approach that informs and infuses educator pedagogy. Common characteristics of CRRE practices include designing inclusive curricula that enable diverse students to see themselves reflected in the academic community (Oyserman & Fryberg, 2006), acknowledging students' cultural backgrounds as assets to learning (Hastie et al., 2006; Morrison et al., 2008), building relationships with students' out-of-school caregivers and community members (Bonner, 2014), and holding students to high academic expectations (Phillippo & Stone, 2013). Ware (2006) describes a framework for CRRE centered on the teacher as a "warm demander" who provides emotional support and warmth alongside "demanding" expectations for students' academic work and behavior. Holding students to high academic standards and expectations is central to CRRE as a direct counterapproach to the lowered academic expectations that many minoritized youth experience from their teachers (Ladson-Billings, 1995a; Morrison et al., 2008).

Some perspectives advocate for the importance in CRRE of teaching for social justice and seeking to dismantle systemic inequities (Durden et al., 2016; Kumar et al., 2018). Such practices can support the belonging of minoritized youth in particular by acknowledging students' life experiences and empowering them to engage in education as a mechanism for social change. A critical component of such approaches is educators' awareness of their own racial or ethnic identity and worldviews, as well as their ability to consider the role of race and power in the classroom as it implicates themselves as educators (Hill, 2012). The ability to identify and negotiate these tensions is central to an educator's cultural competence and ability to foster positive relationships among members of the classroom community to support belonging for all students (Howard, 2003).

The following portrait illustrates the foundational role that belonging plays in schools and many of the belonging-supportive practices described above. However, for something that makes such intuitive sense as a bedrock of school community, belonging is complicated. Readers will see Diane Bauer's active investment in Riverside Academy's distinctive school culture that seeks to encourage students' sense of belonging by emphasizing collective goals: she invokes the idea of recruiting students onto an achievement-oriented "team" that will help them "compete" within the educational system. Yet, there are times when Diane questions whether this mission-driven team mentality adequately considers the different "teams" that Riverside teachers and students are affiliated with outside of school. Her portrait depicts the challenges, dilemmas, and tensions that can arise related to fostering school belonging when there are key racial, socioeconomic, and cultural differences between educators and the students they serve. What tradeoffs, if any, should individuals—especially from historically disenfranchised groups—be asked to make in order to belong at school?

Making the Team

Team Spirit

The colorful banner hanging over Riverside Academy's high school entrance reads, *Work hard. Get smart. Be nice.* Each phrase is superimposed over a corresponding photo: students studying together, students staring down at a paper together, a student smiling. After being buzzed through the outer door, I walk past a metal detector that seems to be out of use (or order) but still takes up half the entryway, sign in at the main office, then continue down the main artery of the school. Slender flags displaying Riverside's "character traits"—including Perseverance, Responsibility, Self-Discipline, and Friendship—hang from the ceiling, spaced a few tiles apart. The cinderblock walls are painted in pastel neutrals and decorated with a combination of professionally printed posters and curated student work. Underneath a series of glass-encased bulletin boards, individual students' college acceptances are publicized on half-sheets of colored paper taped to the wall. Throughout my semester at Riverside, this display has expanded in an ad hoc fashion, presumably as students share their admission news with school staff: some students have three or four acceptances posted in close proximity.

Diane Bauer's classroom is off this front hallway, between the Respect and Cultural Sensitivity ceiling banners. As with other Riverside classrooms, a sign next to the room number placard spells out the teacher's name and degrees, which in Diane's case include an EdD from Fairfield University. The door itself is dominated by a large, laminated poster version of a slogan that has become familiar to me from recent political protests and rallies:

In this classroom, this is truth:

- *Black Lives Matter*

- *Women's Rights Are Human Rights*

- *NO HUMAN IS ILLEGAL*

- *Science Is Real*

- *A Person Should Not Be Judged by the Actions of Others*

- *Love Is Love*

- *Kindness Is Everything*

Inside the spacious, brightly lit classroom, the twenty-two students in Diane's AP English Literature class are buzzing. It's a designated Spirit Week at Riverside: the school uniform rules are relaxed to allow students to dress according to the daily wardrobe theme. Today is Decade Dress-Up, and the senior class has the 1990s. As the students compare outfits and chatter excitedly about the upcoming photo shoots in their advisories, I am amused—as a child of the nineties myself—at their hyper-stylized vision of a decade that predates most of their births; there are lots of pale-wash jeans, half-unbuckled overalls, and sky-high ponytails. The students continue talking through the morning announcements, ignoring the disembodied voice coming over the loudspeaker until it announces two recent college acceptances, including one from this class: Talia has been admitted to Mayfield University. Talia jerks her head and crinkles her brow, either in genuine surprise at hearing her acceptance broadcast to the entire school, or in an elaborate adolescent pantomime of exasperation at being singled out. The roughly one hundred students in Riverside's twelfth-grade cohort have been at the school together since the sixth grade, however, so Talia's classmates do not let the moment escape unnoticed: Zara makes soft golf-clapping gestures with her fingertips, and Will leans over from a nearby desk to give Talia a high five.

Diane, a White woman in her fifties with blonde pixie-cut hair and a wiry frame, sits at the school-issued laptop stationed at the front of the room, chatting intermittently with the students as she finishes typing out a Do Now prompt that she wants the students to discuss in pairs. She asks one young man if he's dressed on theme, and he affirms that he is, somewhat defensively ("I wouldn't dress like this normally!")—though, like Diane, I am uncertain how his light blue button-down shirt and khaki shorts are particularly evocative of the nineties. Another student interrupts to tell Diane how "sweet" her "ride" is, having finally identified her red pickup truck in the school parking lot this morning. Outside of working at Riverside, Diane prefers a rural lifestyle: she lives on several acres of farm land north of the city and keeps horses.

Diane draws the students' attention back to the prompt projected on the white board, which is mounted on the front wall of the room along with dozens of Riverside t-shirts commemorating past events and student cohorts dating back to the class of 2011: *Riverside JUNIOR PRIDE*; *Riverside 1st Homecoming*; *Congratula16ns, you played yourself.* The students have had time to discuss the Do Now, so Diane cold calls: "Marisa, baby."

"Yes, Mom?" Marisa says, swiveling away from her partner to face front but answering with her usual touch of sass.

"In your opinion, which character should feel the most guilty? Why?" Diane asks her, reading the Do Now prompt aloud.

"I said Dimmesdale," Marisa replies, "because he got Hester pregnant."

Nathalie, who is wearing a red bandanna tied over her hair, enormous hoop earrings, and an oversized T-shirt, offers Chillingsworth, "because he's always looking for revenge."

"That nineties look is so good on you," Diane tells her.

"Thank you."

"Just smashing. Is that Tupac?" Diane asks, gesturing at the enormous face printed on Nathalie's shirt. It is, and Diane nods. "I love that," she says.

"What decade are you, Dr. Bauer?" one of the other students asks. Although she teaches all four sections of twelfth-grade English at Riverside, Diane is not dressed like her students; she tells them that she is a tenth-grade advisor and is therefore assigned that grade's decade, the 1970s. She jokes that unlike the students, she could just rummage in her own closet to produce her look, which includes a flower-embroidered peasant tunic, striped wool poncho, ripped jeans, and moccasins. On most other days when I visit, I find Diane wearing some kind of Riverside apparel, including duplicates of the t-shirts that are stapled around the white board. A fanciful vision that struck me once of Diane pulling shirts directly off her classroom wall to wear is both amusing and not entirely unfitting: in her tenth year of teaching here, Diane thoroughly embodies all things Riverside.

Diane was looking for a school with a strong vision and identity when she decided to leave her teaching job of nineteen years at a comprehensive public high school in an urban district in Connecticut. Near burnout from the exhaustion of toiling in a school where "you go in your room and you shut your door," and colleagues resisted notions of student-centered pedagogy, collaboration, and professional development—even more or less "chas[ing]" out a principal who tried to implement them—Diane felt she was "fighting a losing battle. I was like, 'I can't do this anymore,'" she tells me. "If I was going to teach again it had to be somewhere different and cool, and this is how I found Riverside."

Founded as an Expeditionary Learning (EL) school in partnership with the experiential learning program Outward Bound, Riverside is part of an educational "movement" that blends character education with mastery approaches to authentic learning to engage students and teachers alike *in work that is challenging, adventurous and meaningful*, the EL website explains, helping them become *active contributors to building a better world*.[1] When she was initially hired as the ninth-grade English teacher in Riverside's second year of operation, Diane was finishing her doctorate in education "with a focus on progressive schools" and found Riverside's mission—including its stated commitment to providing a *small, personalized setting* to support students in learning *to care for themselves and others*—appealing as a different model for working with an urban student population very similar to her students in Connecticut. Forty-seven percent of Riverside students are classified as Hispanic, 25 percent Black, and 1 percent Asian, with 25 percent classified as White; 48 percent are classified as economically disadvantaged, and Diane identifies many of her students as first-generation college goers, meaning they will be the first in their families to attain postsecondary education.

Unlike the "losing battle" she was fighting alone in Connecticut, Riverside provides Diane with the opportunity to feel like part of a team of educators, working together to create a learning environment where students from historically underserved populations can likewise feel a strong sense of belonging in a culture of achievement. I notice that in contrast to how she talks about her former school, Diane often uses "we" when describing Riverside, positioning herself as part of a unified collective. With her students, she has "talked a lot about teamwork and us being a team," she tells me. "The community is the team; we're all trying to help each other." For

Diane, teams are defined by collectively working toward the same goals and rooting each other on in the process: "We'll psych ourselves up like a team" prior to the AP exam, she tells her class one day.

Indeed, much of Riverside's messaging around students' scholarly potential feels analogous to the kind of "psyching up" that occurs around athletic team competition. Like a stadium bedecked in championship banners and tributes to franchise legends, the school building is decorated with artifacts that remind students of their team membership and the legacy of success they are part of. Students see their own names lining the hallways they walk through every day, their community membership paired with exemplary work, honors and accolades, and college acceptances. For the seniors, graduation takes on a community meaning all its own, as the twelfth-grade teachers have coined the moniker "Operation Graduation" for their united mission to ensure that 100 percent of the students graduate.[2] Displays in the hallway report on target graduation benchmarks from each twelfth-grade advisory, and several of the tees on Diane's classroom wall are Operation Graduation shirts from previous years. The shirts also mark senior class identity more generally; the students are sometimes directed to wear them for grade-level events even when the event has nothing to do with graduation. These rituals of wardrobe coordination, like the Spirit Week dress-up themes, serve as a physical demonstration of team affiliation and belonging.

However, the more I talk with Diane, the more I realize that being part of the Riverside "team" actually comprises membership in multiple communities at different levels—the classroom, school, educational system, and a broader societal or cultural level. Each of these communities has different characteristics of and conditions for belonging and requires Diane to negotiate different challenges and dilemmas of authority, ownership, and responsibility for the team's function and well-being.

COACH AND CHEERLEADER

A birthday sign for one of the twelfth-grade advisors has been taped up next to the entrance when I arrive at Riverside one day—a detail that I initially register as insignificant until the bell rings for the start of third period, which follows advisory, and Diane's classroom is only about half full. A Do Now prompt projected on the board asks students to *Write down 3 strategies you would use when taking the AP multiple choice exam,* but the students are moving sluggishly, the low attendance conveying a lack of urgency to do anything and making it difficult for Diane to focus the students who are present on the task at hand.

"YOU don't have your notebook open. YOU don't have your notebook open," Diane calls out, pointing to individual students in a kind of reverse-Oprah routine as she weaves between the rows of desks to reach the phone at the back of the room. "What're you eating?" she asks one student who used the classroom microwave to heat up some food and is now chowing down at her desk. "It looks really good." When she reaches the phone, Diane dials the main office to request that they call the birthday teacher's room and have him send any of his lingering advisees to class. "Right now," she adds.

"And how is everyone today?" she asks the rest of the students, hanging up the phone and crossing back to the front of the room. The students answer in solo words—"good," "tired," "dead"—as Diane starts passing back a practice AP section that the students took last week. Janie gazes briefly at the score on the front of her packet before holding up a clear plastic folder stuffed full of papers and shaking it at Diane, saying, "This whole thing—it's full of 1s from this class!"[3]

"That's because you didn't try enough," Esther says, with just enough of a lilt in her voice to make me suspect she is ironically parroting an often-heard line.

"Apparently, I didn't!" Janie scoffs.

"Are you being sarcastic or serious?" Diane asks Janie. "You ARE improving; you just have to keep trying."

Diane understands that students' relationship with the course content influences their sense of belonging in a classroom. The AP class provides an opportunity for some students to enact a particular academic identity and join a community of learners they want to belong to. "I think it's kind of a cultural mindset that . . . there's a group of kids who are the 'smart' kids—" Diane curls her fingers into air quotes around the words—"and they naturally are going to go into AP because that's just where they're all going. And for one of them to not do that would probably be a difficult choice, like, 'I'm putting myself in with those other kids.'" Other students, though, may have been "pushed in" to AP by a well-intentioned teacher or counselor trying to challenge students "to do it just to see that they could do it," and may "feel like they really don't belong" because they are struggling academically. Affirming and deepening students' competence beliefs is therefore critical to their sense of belonging in the class.

In striving to build this community of confident learners, Diane occupies a hybrid role of team coach and cheerleader—the latter a role that she herself identifies playing for students, particularly struggling learners who openly say things like, "I suck at this; this is so hard . . . I shouldn't be in here," or otherwise draw attention to their poor achievement outcomes, as Janie does. Diane's efforts to "be much more of a cheerleader for these guys to help them feel like they belong" include countering students' negative mindsets by "remind[ing] them of our growth self-talk"—alluding to Carol Dweck's work on growth mindset, which Riverside teachers and students alike have learned about through school-wide initiatives. "You have to say, 'I can, and I will, and I'm going to,'" she says. She also models her own improvement process to show students that making mistakes is a natural part of growth and does not invalidate someone's belonging. Despite her decades of teaching experience, this is Diane's first time teaching an AP class, a fact she says she openly admitted to students at the beginning of the year, telling them, "I'm new at this, too. We're going to grow and figure this out together." In one lesson, she admits to the students that an activity "didn't work as well as I thought" and reassures them that "that's not your fault, it was my lesson idea." Likewise, she sometimes allows students the option of revising final graded essays, especially if she recognizes patterns across the class indicating that "we really haven't practiced this as much as maybe we should've, or maybe I need to reteach the lesson a little bit clearer." Such a revision policy is not without logistical challenges—including a sometimes-dizzying shuffle of multiple assignments being turned in or passed back at the beginning of class and Diane snatching precious minutes of class time to keep up with her piles of grading while students are working—but it is a key way to show students that she, too, is actively working toward self-improvement.

Diane knows, though, that verbal "cheerleading" only goes so far; she also has a coaching responsibility to guide students through exercises that will simultaneously build their efficacy and feelings of belonging. These exercises can be as simple as the Do Now prompt activating students' thinking about test-taking strategy for the AP exam, or they can serve as the guiding principle underlying classroom interaction. She invokes the notion of "teamwork and us being a team" again when it comes to collaborative learning activities like discussions, where "if I don't understand something, my classmates will talk about it and help me understand. And it's not like they know much more than me; it's that as a group we can all get this. Alone, maybe if I look at a poem, I'm like—" Diane blows out air between her lips in a "pffft!" of exasperation. But "as a group we start to talk and help each other out, so it's a lot of teamwork here again, too."

Joining the team at Riverside taught Diane about the value of pedagogical activities that position students as collaborators and co-constructors of knowledge. "When I taught in Connecticut, I had never even heard of any of this stuff," she tells me. "It was almost a new language" that she had to learn at Riverside, since EL Education "is all about protocols" that require active student participation and interaction. These activities "are hammered home" in professional development and EL institutes Diane has attended over the years. "That's one of the magics for me of coming to this school," she says. "It's like I learned to teach all over." That learning process was not without challenges. "The planning is so much harder," she says, because "there's just many more moving pieces" to constructing a meaningful student-centered learning activity instead of preparing a lecture. "My first few years here . . . it felt like I was juggling sixteen balls at the same time," but gradually she saw her planning efforts behind the scenes playing out in a new kind of classroom dynamic, one where "I could just sit back and watch" as the students collectively owned the responsibility for the work in class. "I think it's better teaching, you know?" she reflects. "It makes them more active and in charge of their own learning . . . If you get out of their way, they often do better." Diane recognizes that her coaching role is bounded; at a certain point, coaches have to step back and expect the team to execute.

I witness this dynamic at work one day when Diane divides the students into groups to "become experts" on one of the four novels they read this year (*Great Expectations, The Scarlet Letter, The Great Gatsby,* and *Things Fall Apart*); tomorrow, the students will form heterogeneous "jigsaw" groups—a student says the name along with Diane, revealing his familiarity with the protocol—where they will each be responsible for teaching their expert content to the new group, giving everyone a role to play in the collective learning experience. "Understand what you need to do?" she asks.

"Yes, Mom," a couple of students intone.

I am sitting closest to the *Great Expectations* group, and while I hear them oscillate between the assigned task and free-associative comments— whether there is a difference between a graveyard and a cemetery, college rejections, financial aid, glaucoma, backless bras for prom—they also regulate themselves. One student play acts a strict teacher at one point to get the team back on topic. "Everyone say a character," she orders. "Janie, go." When Diane adds another task, assigning the expert groups to read through a list of Q3 essay prompts dating back to the 1970 AP exam and choose four that could be answered with their assigned novel,[4] the group instantly strategizes, electing to divide and conquer the lengthy packet—essentially creating their own kind of minijigsaw protocol to accomplish the task as a team.

As Diane herself tells me, though, turning things over to the students can be "messier . . . way messier. And that's what's scary" about enacting pedagogy that commits to student-centered collaborative learning, rather than a teacher-centered model. Within the *Great Expectations* group, the students share out their ideas about the essay prompts and collectively choose the four that they feel work best, but they do so with minimal engagement with the text before quickly returning to their other topics of conversation, which they discuss for the remainder of the class period. Across the room, one member of the *Gatsby* group is turned around in her seat talking to Esther, whose *Scarlet Letter* group appears to have disbanded: Kirk's head is on his desk, and, in one of the only displays of student conflict I ever see at Riverside, Amanda has drawn her desk away from the others and turned it around so that her back is to them. When Diane checks in with the class a few minutes later, the *Scarlet Letter* group is the only one that reports not being finished with their work. "Why not?" Diane asks them. "Everyone in this room is finished except you—why is that?" I cannot hear the student responses, but Diane warns them that they must be caught up for the jigsaw portion of the activity tomorrow because "everyone else is gonna rely on you to explain *The Scarlet Letter.*"

"We got it," Esther assures her.

The moments when Diane, as cheerleader and coach, is relegated to the sidelines are crucial moments for the team's growth. Part of belonging to the team means contributing to the team's execution of a task, and collectively owning successes and failures. When reprimanding the *Scarlet Letter* group, Diane invokes their responsibility to the rest of their peers as the impetus to get the work done; they are letting the team down otherwise. She also does not offer them any assistance in solving their self-inflicted problem, leaving them to sort it out amongst themselves—which Esther assures her that they will do.

But as Diane notes, even these relatively contained hiccups in the team-building process are "messy" and "scary" for a teacher to leave up to the students. The anxiety only increases when the team is not performing on a larger scale, when the stakes are higher than the successful completion of a jigsaw protocol. Diane's sense of responsibility to student belonging extends to a definition of community beyond the walls of her classroom, which in turn raises different questions about her role in relation to the team.

FAMILY TIES

At the end of my second observation at Riverside, Diane tells the students she wants to use the last few minutes of class to share with them what the twelfth-grade teachers discussed in their most recent meeting about "HOWs." Ignoring the handful of audible snorts this acronym prompts, Diane points out that the twelfth grade has the fewest Scholars in the school, largely because of low homework completion.

Riverside designates homework completion as a "habit of work," one of four academic success behaviors that the school promotes;[5] collectively, the four "HOWs" are assessed as 20 percent of a student's quarter grade in each class and also averaged as a kind of alternative GPA. Students who reach a certain threshold on their HOW GPA each quarter can earn an additional team affiliation: recognition as a Riverside "Scholar." The Scholars bulletin board, which explains the selection criteria and displays the full names of the Scholars by grade level for each marking period, is directly across the hall from Diane's classroom and informs me that in addition to public recognition, Scholars receive rewards such as free admission to school events, extra dress-down days that relieve them from uniform requirements, and bathroom privileges: middle school Scholars are allowed to go to the bathroom *at their discretion* during lunch, while high school Scholars have access to a dedicated *Scholars bathroom*, the bulletin board explains.

Diane asks the students to help problem solve what to do about the low Scholar attainment in the twelfth grade; in the younger grades, she says, the teachers have decided to start giving detentions for missed homework.

The students groan en masse and then all start talking at once. My not knowing their names yet adds to the impression of general cacophony. Many students are incredulous that "We're getting ready for college" and teachers want to give detentions for not doing homework?! Diane agrees that a punitive approach may not be appropriate, but what about new incentives? Would those help? One young woman scoffs, "I'm still not doing it." Within a couple of minutes, Diane and the students are in agreement that neither punitive consequences nor incentives are preparing students for the reality of college, but if that's the case, Diane wonders, what should Riverside teachers do?

The students are talking partly amongst themselves and partly to Diane. "Just leave it." "It is what it is." "Think about it, if you go to college and don't do your work, you get a zero."

"Well," says Diane, "it gets nerve wracking when those zeroes become an F, and you don't graduate."

"That's our fault," someone says. Another student explains that it's a matter of prioritization. When multiple assignments are due, she takes care of the biggest or most pressing one; if the smaller assignments don't get done—"Oh well," she shrugs.

Diane observes that homework detentions are consistent with another recently announced policy: assigning detention to students after they are tardy to school three times.

A young woman near me speaks out so forcefully that her classmates fall silent to listen to her. She argues that the tardiness policy "ignores different socioeconomic situations," such as homeless students, and "target[s]" those students unfairly when they have legitimate reasons for not being able to get to school consistently on time.

Diane drags an empty student desk toward her at the front of the room and sits on the table portion, her feet on the chair seat, facing the students, perhaps signaling that she is pulling up a seat at the debate table, that this conversation is serious and worthy of settling into. Resting her elbows on her knees as she addresses the class, she acknowledges that there are students who face real obstacles and transportation challenges in getting to school, but "what about kids who just don't want to get up?"

"That's on them," the young woman retorts.

Another student observes that it'd be one thing if the tardiness policy had always existed, but "they can't just make up new rules at the end of the year." Her comment opens the floodgates again for the rest of the class. Someone bursts into a tirade about "certain teachers—not naming any names" who assign huge projects, but then say, "You can't text me past 8 p.m."—"SEVEN!" someone corrects—and how unfair it is that teachers can impose time restrictions on answering questions from students who are sometimes staying up all night to complete the work. "And then I'm punished for being late to school because I'm tired?!" the student exclaims. "OK, I'm just not gonna do it, then."

Diane is highly cognizant of the demographics of the Riverside student population and constantly negotiating what role she should assume in order to serve students best. She is aware that many of her students "have to deal with life on a very different level than wealthier students might," but at the same time, she recognizes that they need to find a way to overcome those circumstances and perform despite the obstacles. Many of the terms and conditions of community membership at Riverside are not just about creating a sense of belonging here and now, they are intended to equip student to belong to future academic communities. "My thinking has changed a lot from teaching ninth graders to twelfth graders," Diane tells me. "Like if I didn't teach ninth grade well, at least there would be tenth, eleventh, and twelfth[-grade teachers] that could possibly pick up where I left off." When teaching twelfth graders, "I need to give them a product that is going to help them when they walk out of here," she says, because "there's nobody after me to help fix it up . . . That's really scary on my part, you know." Diane feels a sense of urgency to try to give her students everything they will need to succeed in their post–high school lives—which, ideally, includes the ability to sustain membership in a college community. "Since college is our end goal here," she says, "if we're not preparing them then we're not doing a service . . . I say to my students at the beginning of the year, 'I have a responsibility to prepare you to be successful in your college classes, and I take that responsibility very seriously.'"

That seriousness manifests through Diane's enforcement of Riverside's rules and policies in a way that evokes a tough love, "my house, my rules" parenting approach. Diane says that Riverside—again using the school name to describe the collective behavior of the faculty—"pushes and prods and encourages and lifts and hugs and holds and cajoles" its students, conveying an intimate, familial relationship between teachers and students. It has not escaped me that some of Diane's saucier students call her "Mom" when she gives them a directive. Moms can nag and scold and punish, but they do it because they care about you and your future.

Indeed, Diane sees the role of family as critical in conveying a sense of investment in the current academic community in order to gain access to a future team. She often speaks about a difference in "cultural expectations"—"'cultural' meaning, you know, not necessarily skin color," she says, "but social expectations"—between Riverside families and those in more affluent communities. For example, in her own experience growing up in an "all-White, upper middle-class" New England town, Diane explains, "it was kind of like, you learn to walk, you learn to swim, you learn to ride a bike, and you go to college. It was just part of—there was just no NOT doing that. So, you did your homework." By contrast, "I'm thinking that where families have different kinds of expectations for their children, it's different," she says. "Our students, they don't do homework. They do not do homework. They won't do it; they don't do it; they don't care if they're gonna fail or not. It's like, 'I'm not doing homework.'" While she acknowledges that her students can face structural impediments such as having to work or take care of younger siblings after school that may not leave them "as much time to 'do school,'" Diane also sees schools and teachers as providing a kind of surrogate family acculturation of students into the importance of doing homework that is necessary for students to surmount those impediments and achieve on par with their more privileged peers.

A similar philosophy guides Riverside's policy of "sweating the small stuff" in service to the Self-Discipline character trait; the rules are intended both to create a certain kind of team environment in the present and to make students competitive for their future teams. For example, *School uniforms help to create a professional learning environment,* the Riverside student/family handbook proclaims, *and wearing appropriate attire is a good habit for the future workplaces that our students contribute to.* I also observe a common understanding of behavioral expectations that are not codified in official school policies, such as when Diane reminds students to "SLANT" when listening to a guest speaker. "What does SLANT mean?" she prompts, and after some temporary amnesia over some of the letters, the students are able to collectively piece together the acronym (Sit up, Lean forward, Ask and answer questions, Nod your head, Track the speaker).

Yet Diane expresses some reservations at the implications of this teacher-student dynamic when a predominantly middle-class White faculty is placing these conditions on low-income students of color. Riverside's full-time staff—a broader category than teachers alone—is 70 percent White,[6] making it slightly more racially diverse than the district and much more diverse than the state and country,[7] but Diane is aware that the inverted student-versus-teacher demographics can make a school's promotion of achievement culture seem like "paternalism"—a perversion of the idea of family. "Our guidance counselor—who is a woman of color—points out that it's interesting that mostly urban schools and kids of color have those tight rules," Diane tells me, whereas "if you go to suburban schools and White schools and districts, there's none of that. And I'm like, 'That's interesting, I wonder why teachers, urban schools feel the need to tighten up so much,' you know? And does it help or does it make things worse?"

"Do you have an opinion about that?" I ask.

"Well," she replies, "I just had a thought that could come from my, you know, very White upbringing and White privileged self: maybe it is White people's thought that students in urban settings don't have enough structure in their families and lives, so we have to make structure for them." She sees the problematic assumption of inferiority reflected in this perspective, but also insists that "it's never been like the Great White Hope, I'm going to go in and 'save' those kids." Rather, she recalls the explanation provided by Riverside's founding principal, the man who hired her and who is "White as White can be," Diane says. "Irish-Catholic . . . grew up doing the White upper-middle-class thing." She summarizes his philosophy as, "If we want students to be able to make their way in a White-dominated society, they need to have those skills to be able to code-switch in and out. And it's not necessarily taking away their culture, but we're not teaching them to compete with the dominant society if we're not giving them that ability.

"And, you know, that feels OK to me," Diane says, because "we still are a White-dominated society, so if a kid can find more opportunities there, then that's great." She muses briefly over whether she might have some "Black colleagues who might not necessarily feel that way" but ultimately concludes, "I think pretty much everybody here is on board with the philosophy." She also sees that collective buy-in from the staff as critical for "everybody in the building ha[ving] the same expectations" and creating a consistent school culture. "When I worked in Connecticut, there was no sort of unity," she says. "Everybody did their own thing; there was no set of common rules, and that place was insane." Diane views the enforcement of school rules and expectations as similar to the use of active learning protocols: the goal is that "do[ing] school" in these ways "becomes kind of second nature" to the students and teachers alike, creating a shared understanding of what membership in this community looks like.

Yet I wonder whether "unity" in a goal or mission must necessarily be enacted through behavioral conformity, especially given the discretion I see Diane herself exercising with regards to the rules. She admits to being "on the fence" about the merit of some school policies and can be selective in her enforcement of them. For example, until I perused the Riverside student handbook later, I was unaware of the rule that *students may not bring food or drinks to class, with the exception of water* because they are *a distraction from learning* since I never saw Diane enforce the rule by *throw[ing] away unauthorized food and beverages in the classroom*, as the handbook dictates; in fact, she lets students use her microwave during class and bonds with them over their food several times over the course of the semester. Neither does she mindlessly toe the company line even with the many school rules that she does enforce. She questions some of the "very insignificant" minutiae within the dress code, for example, as possibly not worth the "backlash" teachers sometime get from students, "escalat[ing]" minor infractions into major disciplinary issues and ultimately distracting from learning more than the original offense. "Is it more important to send a kid to in-school suspension for the day because they're out of uniform three times," she asks rhetorically, or to keep students in class as much as possible? Diane also tries to continue enacting her "team" mentality by inviting students into the teacher debate over homework detentions, giving them space to push back and express the conflict between school policies and their lived reality.

For their part, the students respond to Diane's invitation in complex, possibly contradictory ways. They simultaneously demand individual accountability ("that's on us") and teacher support via text message late into the night. However, they also highlight the difference in agency allotted to teachers versus students: teachers are allowed to set boundaries on their out-of-school time, but students are still beholden to school responsibilities even after leaving the building. This imbalance is a feature of all teacher-student relationships—teachers assign homework and control the pace of class—but there are additional power and privilege dynamics here as well. Diane acknowledges that many Riverside students "have to deal with life on a very different level than wealthier students might"—including after-school responsibilities that may delay their homework start time—and the students argue that the school punishes them for not overcoming these obstacles without providing equivalent support to help them meet those expectations or demanding reciprocal teacher accountability.

Indeed, Diane tells me that Riverside "kids I've talked to who have gone to college find it easier because they have more time. They're like, 'We have a lot of homework but we have more unstructured time to do our homework, even with jobs.' Because, you know, they spend a million hours a day in school here, no break—" As if to punctuate her point, the bell signaling the end of the period sounds over Riverside's PA system and interrupts her, and she trails off, losing her train of thought as students spill into the hall.

In Diane's comment, though, I hear the echoes of her insight from the student-centered active learning protocols: "If you get out of their way, they often do better." Like her experience leaning to facilitate those activities, Diane's efforts to create a unified sense of urgency around the team mission while also allowing space for students to occasionally direct the conversation can be "messier . . . way messier" than being entirely prescriptive. It requires finding a tenuous balance between promoting a strong team culture and recognizing and valuing counter-perspectives from team members' out-of-school lives.

THE "I" IN TEAM

Diane and I are discussing how she might handle ideological disagreements during her research paper unit—in which students are examining a "national issue" connected to the newly inaugurated presidential administration that "affects or will affect you or your family"—when she suddenly says to me, "I don't know if I ever told you about coming out in front of the kids."

"No!" I am startled not by the comment itself—Diane has spoken openly to me about being gay since I first met her, and all of her students know—but rather by its seeming nonsequitur from what we have been discussing.

Diane chuckles and leans back in her seat, settling in to tell the anecdote. "Oh, it was a trip," she says, recalling that it was early in her first year at Riverside, when she "barely knew" her ninth graders. The morning announcements over the loudspeaker that day included a reminder about a GSA meeting after school, which prompted some students to ask what the acronym stood for. When Diane explained that it was the Gay-Straight Alliance, the students erupted. "They were all like, 'blahhh, gayyyyy,' you know, like a lot of ninth-grade silly comments about gays," she says. "I couldn't shut them up." One student in particular kept insisting, "There's no gay people in this school!" to which Diane replied, " 'Yes, there are.' And he's like, 'WHO?!' and I said, 'I AM!' So then they were all like—" Diane sits up rigidly in her seat, eyes and mouth wide open, imitating the students' shock. "So I said, 'All right, let's talk about it. Go ahead and ask me anything you want to ask.' " Though relatively composed in the moment, she says she was "shaking a little bit" after class; "at my old school," she says, "it was don't ask, don't tell," so she had never before talked about her sexuality in a school setting. When the principal happened to walk by shortly after, Diane told him what she had done:

I said, "I just outed myself to the class."

And he goes, "Are you OK?"

"Yup."

"OK. Do you need me in there?"

"No, I don't think so."

"Well, that was a great teaching moment; get back in there and talk about it."

. . . So like the whole day was talking about being gay and answering questions. There was an adult in my room . . . I can't remember if she was special ed or whatever, and she went and complained to [the principal] that it was inappropriate, and he said, "No it's not. If you don't want her to talk about that, then go to your office and take down the pictures of your family and don't ever mention your spouse again."

So, you know, as I did that, more teachers did that and . . . it just became a nonissue. It's just not a thing, and that's made it really easy for gay kids to come out. We've had some transgender students, and it just becomes a "whatever" . . . And that's really what our school focuses on, is the staff just being OK with being who you are. Which is wonderful . . . We're people first, you know . . . There's never been a time where we've been told not to be who we are.

Although Diane then directs me "back to our questions," apologizing for being "off topic, I know," I find her story illuminating. She otherwise speaks so often and so seamlessly as part of the "we" of Riverside that it is fascinating to hear her retrospective on a time when she was still figuring out where and how she as an individual might fit into that "we." Embedded in her colleague's complaint is an implicit conception of what school is about and a belief that certain out-of-school group affiliations, that is dimensions of individual identity, do not belong in the fabric of the school's collective identity. In his rebuttal to the complaint, the principal stretches that fabric to include acceptance of diverse individuals as a condition of Riverside team membership—a sentiment that Diane echoes years later by posting a statement of inclusion on her classroom door, the words conveying the idea that you should not have to give up who you are to be part of the team.

At the same time, though, familiar messages remind us that being part of a team sometimes requires individual sacrifice. We might be told to "take one for the team" or that "there's no 'I' in team," encouraging us to be selfless in putting the team first and subordinating our needs and desires to the competitive goal or well-being of the team as a whole. The principal in Diane's coming-out story is the same one she quotes to me arguing that the school's goal of helping students "compete with the dominant society" is "not necessarily taking away their culture." Even if the school's intense focus on achievement culture and identity is "not necessarily" subtractive, though, I am curious about where teachers like Diane find space not just to tolerate individual difference, but actively to invite students' culture and individuality into class.

Diane herself identifies an ongoing tension around this question, especially in her AP class, where her deep sense of responsibility to prepare students for college sometimes conflicts with her inclination to provide more personally relevant learning experiences. She often refers to AP teaching as "teaching for a test, which is kind of a bummer," she tells me, "but it's the reality of the thing, and I'd like for them to pass it so they can have that credit bump" from receiving college course equivalency, saving them "time and money." Both to me and to the students, Diane often juxtaposes college readiness skills—and sometimes the prospect of college itself—with "real life." She tells me that she and other Riverside teachers have "brain-washed [students] to think, over the years, that [their school work is] really important for college. Like [with] a research paper, I'll get, 'Why do we have to do this? What does this have to do with life?' And you know, it might not have anything to do with the job you hold ten years down the road, but it's gonna help you in college."

In addition to the pragmatic benefits of earning a high score on the AP exam, Diane believes the AP curriculum itself helps students to "keep up better" in college by training them to "tak[e] a piece of literature and [do] New Criticism, sort of just sticking with the text and talking about the elements of literature. Those are skills I know that they're gonna need in college," she says, "as opposed to more of a reader response, like 'What does this make you feel?' 'How does this relate to your life?'" The perceived imperative to teach classic literary criticism skills in AP persists for Diane no matter what the focal text is. In her first year teaching AP, she has prag-matically adopted the previous teacher's reading list of what she derides as primarily "the White male canon," so when she tells me she "want[s] to add an African American–authored book and . . . something more modern" to the syllabus next year,[8] I expect her rationale to be increased representation and personal relevance for students. The main justification she gives, however, is that "in college, [students are] going to be exposed to a much greater variety of authors and styles and time periods," so "being able to manage some different genres . . . will be helpful" for them. For Diane, trying to maximize students' college readiness and achievement outcomes constrains her ability to personalize the curriculum. Without that pressure to prepare students for college, "my lessons would be more kind of character, real-world focused," she says. "Like, what can we take out of this literature that might relate to you or the society we live in . . . you know, really getting at life issues as opposed to literature-focused elements."

Despite these perceived constraints, Diane does manage to carve out some space to "get at life issues," even within the AP class. She reframes the research unit she teaches in all four sections of twelfth-grade English to allow students to write their papers on a national issue that matters or relates to them, setting up a grade-wide "expedition"—the eponymous interdisciplinary, project-based learning that is a cornerstone of EL Education—on citizenship and activism. The expedition officially launches on a "kickoff day" that Diane and the twelfth-grade teaching team organize: instead of regular academic classes, students hear invited speakers in keynote and breakout sessions, and then they engage in discussions as well as individual reflection before forming groups to begin thinking about their topic of choice for an activism project. On the morning of the kickoff day, Diane reminds the students that ultimately each project group will get to decide what their activism will look like, "so you have voice and choice. It could be a march; it could be writing a public service announcement; it could be a letter-writing campaign to senators; it could be fundraising for an immigrant center." The goal is for the group to decide on an "organic action" rather than the teachers telling them what to do. Later, Diane tells me that this expedition is "the kind of stuff that has life-time value" for students. It also clearly holds personal value to Diane: many of the invited activist speakers are friends of hers, and partway through the semester I notice she has acquired and started wearing a rectangular pendant on a silver chain that reads, "Nevertheless, she persisted" in block letters, connecting her to the current activist movement of woman-led resistance.

As the longest-tenured teacher on the twelfth-grade team, Diane takes a central role in planning and coordinating the expedition kickoff, and throughout the day I see evidence of her efforts to make the day inclusive of identities and lived experiences that differ from hers and the majority of Riverside teachers'. The photo slideshow that plays as students filter into the auditorium for the keynote session intersperses iconic images of Ruby Bridges, Rosa Parks, César Chávez, Harvey Milk, suffragettes, and college students protesting the Vietnam War with images of a Black Lives Matter T-shirt, a "die-in" protest, Kobe Bryant and teammates wearing *I can't breathe* warm-up shirts, and a kneeling Colin Kaepernick (a student near me murmurs his name when the image appears). The breakout session that I randomly choose to attend is led by a youthful-looking Puerto Rican man who grew up in the city and is now a Riverside parent and community organizer for criminal justice reform. He minces no words when describing the overlapping context of his work and personal background:

> The U.S., he tells the students, was founded on principles of white supremacy, and this oppression continues today through ongoing rhetoric and policies aimed at being "tough" on people of color, such as the disparate sentencing for crack versus cocaine in the 1980s. Contrary to "the media narrative that we're all lazy," he says, it is these kinds of racist institutional policies that criminalize communities of color and entrench them in poverty. He has lived this pipeline himself. Growing up in a segregated neighborhood—several students nod in recognition of the local zone he names—and attending an underresourced public school that disciplined him harshly for being "a hyper kid" caused him to "internalize that I was stupid. You guys know labeling theory, right?" he asks, explaining that he "started acting really tough" to counter the "really low self-esteem" he developed from absorbing explicit and implicit messages about his ability and worth. He was incarcerated twice on drug charges, the first time at age eighteen. When he was released, he struggled to get a job, "even at McDonald's," he says, even though "I'm light-skinned, right, and I can dress up real nice and look professional."
>
> Eventually, the speaker says, he was able to turn his life around in part because he began taking community college classes and realized for the first time that "school was fun." He could go to the bathroom whenever he wanted and study topics that genuinely interested him, like Malcolm X and Puerto Rican history. He'd never known from his K–12 experience that education could be like this: "The school system sold me a lie," he says. Around the same time, he landed a job as a janitor at a "prep school," where he learned that "hyper kids" there were diagnosed with ADHD and given resources because "rich kids get taught" while "poor kids get tested" and pushed out. Wealthy

students, he realized, are taught to think critically and feel a sense of agency over their lives. To do the same for "poor kids," he argues that schools should "give them a true understanding of the systemic oppression of Black people to support the top tiny percentage of White people." Without this critical understanding of systemic injustice, he says, poor communities of color can easily lapse into self-hate.

This speaker presents quite a different image of the "White-dominated society" than the one in the principal's philosophy that Diane recalls: rather than a largely agnostic default academic culture that students should strive to be accepted in, the speaker depicts an actively hostile and oppressive hegemony to be challenged and changed. One by one, he takes aim at ideologies and practices that Riverside itself espouses through its "sweating the small stuff" policies: strict discipline, bodily control over students, the equalizing power of professional dress. (Diane shares with me that "sweating the small stuff" is rooted in broken windows theory, whose loaded history she is unaware of until I describe its connection to the overpolicing of poor communities of color—though she is then able to link it conceptually to her own doubts over disciplining minor infractions.) Yet the speaker also sends his own daughter to Riverside—she is a tenth grader—and later in his talk credits "a White liberal woman" with "sav[ing] my life" by knocking on his door one day and introducing him to the idea of community organizing. Likewise, one of the keynote speakers—an African American eighth-grade teacher at Riverside whom Diane introduces as "an activist by virtue of being a teacher"—delivers a similarly complex message, describing the experience of her eleven-year-old son asking her about Tamir Rice as a clarifying moment when she realized she had to start thinking about "what I could do to change the way the world sees my son and sees all of you," to "prevent you from becoming the next hashtag." She implores the students to "not just get accepted to college, but graduate, and take your rightful place on the throne of change."

Both of these speakers present students with a stark perspective on the structural and systemic challenges that many of them face as members of urban, low-income communities of color. They speak from a place of solidarity with students, a solidarity rooted in shared identity and lived experience. Some of the students' notes on the day—a mandatory assignment that was collected for a grade—suggest the personal resonance of these perspectives; of the eighth-grade teacher, one student writes, *She reminds me of my mom . . . has to have hard conversations with [her kids] long before she thinks she has to. Story of life in Black America.* Yet the speakers also include Riverside in that solidarity, endorsing the school as an institutional ally through their choices to work and enroll their children here. It is a solidarity Diane has enacted by inviting them to speak at this event and privileging their voices above her own, at least for the day: other than introducing the speakers, she barely speaks in the keynote session and is not present in my breakout room.

I am left wondering, though, how these diverse and multifaceted perspectives might play out in a more sustained and systematic dialogue across different school stakeholders about what goals, hopes, and beliefs unite them as members of the Riverside community even while they may also have widely divergent philosophies that stem from their membership in different out-of-school communities and identity groups. As one student writes in her notes from the kickoff event, *People have an obligation to question societal systems.* Another student similarly observes, *We have the right and obligation to question the authorities.* It is unclear, though, what avenues at Riverside exist to continue fostering that spirit of critical questioning—and to allow it to be directed at local "systems" and "authorities" as well as national ones.

Achieving this kind of dialogue likely requires institutional commitments beyond the efforts of individual educators like Diane, who already struggled to balance what she saw as the "completely separate" curricular strands of AP and the activism expedition throughout the semester. She freely admits to me that she had to shortchange the expedition in her AP class because of time constraints. Her individual juggling act mirrors the larger institutional trend she perceives of Riverside "becom[ing] more traditional" over time as it straddles the tension between the EL ideal of personally meaningful and relevant work and the perceived imperative to promote individual student attainment within the existing educational system. While these two goals are not inherently oppositional, Diane says that in practice it is hard to sustain an educational model that effectively balances both. "The ideal and the practical are two different things," she tells me. "You can't be a unique school and be part of a district or necessarily be competitive . . . It's just good practice to have our kids be able to keep up with kids in other schools. And get them into some better [colleges]," she adds. "A lot of our kids go locally into state schools," but "it would be great to have a bigger chunk of high-reaching kids. And I think AP does that."

Engaging students in the "real-world learning" ideal of EL Education has therefore taken a backseat to the pressures of the state accountability exam, adopting Common Core standards, and expanding AP offerings. Riverside ninth graders no longer attend Outward Bound, the founding partner of EL Education and "one amazing thing that made us unique" as a school, Diane says, but she accepts the sacrifice because, in the end, "was that going to make them get into colleges as easy as kids who were taking five AP courses at Western?" she asks rhetorically, naming one of the larger comprehensive high schools in the city that has drawn some students away from Riverside because of its broader range of offerings. "I think offering more AP classes is important. I think our kids want it and deserve it," Diane says. "They deserve that opportunity"—even if it hampers teachers' ability to design and implement more innovative curriculum that allows students to bring more of themselves into the classroom.

The irony here is that many elite high schools are increasingly moving away from AP and toward curricular approaches that resemble the EL model; eight independent schools recently announced that they are abandoning AP classes in favor of *a curriculum oriented toward collaborative, experiential and interdisciplinary learning* that *will not only better prepare our students for college and their professional futures, but also result in more engaging programs for both students and faculty . . . We expect this approach will appeal to students' innate curiosity, increase their motivation and fuel their love of learning.*[9] While this announcement came a year after my Riverside data collection concluded, I recall an interview in which Diane alluded to socioeconomic disparities in which students are generally allowed to be themselves and develop as individuals at school. She mused that it would be "wonderful to have places that . . . speak to kids" who are not interested in traditional academics and/ or "are great doing other things," but added, "Who gets to go to them, you know? Rich people probably get to send their kids to these cool schools, but will low-income families get to do that?"

Diane was originally drawn to Riverside as a "cool school" for these "low-income families," but in enacting its mission to field a competitive, college-ready team, Riverside has shed some of the "cool-school" attributes that Diane loved about it—which in turn forces her as an individual teacher to conform to systemic pressures as well. She admits that "philosophically" she experiences "a great tension around that," but she sees change as "ha[ving] to start, really, from the top down." Unless "testing companies" magically "go away," she says, or stop being so financially lucrative, "the whole school 'thing' that we've always known would have to be completely revamped" in order for educators to be genuinely free to build the schools they want for all students. And because "that's not possible," she says, "if you're gonna be a public school, you have to play by those rules. Until the entire education system changes from colleges on down, you have to keep doing what everybody else does." Faced with what she perceives as an inequitable and intractable system, Diane sees conformity as the only viable strategy, even as it constrains the ability of teachers and students alike to fully "be who we are" in making a strong school team.

Reflections on Promoting a Belonging Mindset

The intersection of academic support and teacher caring is discussed in the literature on school belonging broadly but is particularly salient to the experiences of minoritized youth who may encounter lower academic expectations from teachers, as well as more contentious relationships borne out of negative perceptions or stereotypes. To counter this trend, many models of CRRE practices incorporate high expectations and "academic press" as dimensions of teacher caring (Phillippo & Stone, 2013), such as in the notion of teachers as "warm demanders": "warm" in the more traditional emotional definition of caring and "demanding" in their high standards and expectations for both student behavior and academic work (Ware, 2006). Warm demanders demonstrate caring and build relationships with students through authoritative—and sometimes authoritarian—upholding of classroom order through exacting standards for students' academic behavior and discipline; they clearly define what it means to be a member of the current classroom community so that students can succeed in the future.

While she never uses the phrase itself, I see Diane striving to enact warm demander pedagogy; she uses similarly oxymoronic language in talking about teacher-student relationships at Riverside when she says that "Riverside *pushes* and *prods* [demanding] and *encourages* and *lifts* and *hugs* and *holds* and *cajoles* [warmth]" its students. In her vision of her class as a "team," Diane emphasizes the mutual encouragement and social support that team members offer each other. She herself takes on head "cheerleader" duties, striving to replace students' negative self-talk ("I suck at this; this is so hard; this is terrible; I shouldn't be in here") with positive affirmations and verbal encouragement ("I can, and I will, and I'm going to"). She participates willingly in goofy school traditions like Spirit Week and adorns her classroom with Riverside paraphernalia promoting a team culture of achievement.

Beyond these verbal and visible messages of encouragement, Diane also "assume[s] responsibility for implementing strategies that enhance student learning" (Ware, 2006, p. 441) as a way of showing her support for students. She embraces the challenge of "learn[ing] to teach all over" again in order to enact Riverside's student-centered, "progressive" pedagogical philosophy, modeling her own learning, development, and mistake making for her students. These pedagogical strategies and protocols themselves often relegate Diane to the metaphorical sideline by design; the emphasis is on the students' performance, with Diane offering support, encouragement, and guidance from the periphery.

However, warm demanders also provide a "tough-minded, no-nonsense style of teaching" (Ware, 2006, p. 436). Diane's acceptance and enforcement of most of Riverside's "sweat the small stuff" rules reflect her belief that such structures are a way of showing her students the tough love they need to overcome out-of-school adversity and achieve academically. Even when she experiences doubt over the merit of some rules, such as the potential to be suspended over dress-code violations, she is able to embrace the overall guiding philosophy and spirit of the rules as a mechanism for helping students find success. The students jokingly calling Diane "Mom" echoes Ware's (2006) depiction of a warm demander who functions as an "other-mother" by providing a "cultural bridge" between the "middle-class, mainstream expectations of schools" and the students' home communities (p. 445). Diane invokes the cultural divide between school and home often as a context for her work and responsibility as an educator; she sees herself and the other Riverside teachers as playing the role of surrogate family in acculturating students to college-going aspirations and expectations. Moreover, Diane's framing of Riverside's mission as social-justice activism and her blending of the activism expedition with AP instruction geared toward making students "competitive" echo historic perspectives on the importance of education for political and economic success in Black communities (Walker, 2001). There is a directionality and an intended outcome in "other-mothering"; Diane wants her relationships with students to promote their achievement motivations and outcomes, giving them greater economic and life opportunities.

However, it is critical to note that studies of "warm demanders" primarily center on African American teachers of African American students (Ladson-Billings, 1994; Ware, 2006); these warm demander traits and practices are therefore contextualized within a sense of shared racial and/or cultural identity and *out-of-school* community membership between teachers and students. White teachers face different challenges and considerations in trying to enact warm-demander pedagogy with minoritized students (Ford & Sassi, 2014), such as the different valence of strict discipline policies coming from a teacher vested in sociopolitical systems of power, rather than authority stemming from shared community with students (Sleeter, 2008; Villegas & Lucas, 2002). Diane invests her energies in cultivating a sense of "team" within the walls of her classroom—including posting a statement of inclusion prominently on the door—but she and her students simultaneously hold other team memberships that they do not relinquish once they enter school. Diane demonstrates her caring and recognition of the high stakes for her students through her decades-long commitment to urban education and ongoing efforts to improve as a teacher, but she does not share in those stakes in the same way as do members of Riverside students' various home communities. Beyond enacting certain practices, CRRE practices also entail developing a deep understanding of racial identity and affiliation, which can be particularly challenging even for committed White educators (Hyland, 2005; Matias, 2013).

In many ways, Diane's recognition of her own multiple team memberships primes her to do this work. Out of my four participants, she is by far the most frank and forthcoming about racial dynamics within her classroom and school: she readily identifies as White and names her Whiteness several times in our interviews as she mulls over the intersection of school policies and racial identity (e.g., her awareness of the danger of seeing oneself as "the Great White Hope" or a White savior). She is not a rule-enforcing automaton: she allows her students to challenge the teachers' proposed new consequences for not completing homework or being late to school and air their grievances over the disconnect between school policies and the realities of their lives. She and her colleagues also demonstrate intentionality in the speakers they invite for the expedition kickoff: the Riverside parent activist and eighth-grade teacher both appeal to students from shared experience and community membership, and they endorse Riverside as an allied institution.

However, Diane and the twelfth-grade team seem to have taken these actions on their own, and the issues raised by these speakers are not sustained in conversations beyond the special event. There does not seem to be the same institutionalized support for Riverside teachers to engage in reflections and discussions about racial dynamics in the way that there clearly has been to achieve consistency in instructional and disciplinary approaches. Thus, Diane is left on her own to muse and speculate about whether she has "Black colleagues who might not necessarily feel that way. I don't know. I think pretty much everybody here is on board with the philosophy."

What would it look like to promote students' sense of belonging in a strong school community that simultaneously acknowledges and affirms their other out-of-school identities and team affiliations? This question is not unique to Riverside—nor only to White teachers. The fact that the national teaching population is overwhelmingly White does make the issue particularly salient for that group (Zumwalt & Craig, 2008), but teachers of color are not automatically equipped with culturally relevant methods simply because of shared racial identity with students (Villegas & Davis, 2008). All schools and teachers should be engaged in this question.

Riverside's existing culture and the buy-in and continued effort it inspires from veteran teachers like Diane presents an especially promising institutional context, but more research is needed to bridge cultural perspectives with the motivational and psychological scholarship on belonging (Gray et al., 2018; Kumar et al., 2018). Such cross-disciplinary research could help schools like Riverside develop institutional practices like daily routines, building norms, and teacher professional development focused on cross-cultural relationships and valuing of students' authentic selves (Jansen et al., 2014). Prioritizing these dimensions of school culture as much as "sweating the small stuff" could help promote students' sense of belonging in a unified achievement culture that recognizes and endorses the individual differences of all team members.

Chapter 2

Choosing Your Adventure

Promoting Value Mindsets in High School through Personal Relevance and Self-Direction

Overview: "This work has value for me"

A major component of students' motivation is their answer to the question, "Do I want to do this and why?" Research has shown that valuing an academic subject area is related to students' engagement and persistence in that subject, as well as academic choices such as declaring a college major or pursuing a career path (B. D. Jones et al., 2010; Wentzel, 2000).

However, the "value" expressed in the value mindset statement can mean many different things to different students. Expectancy-value theory, a common framework for thinking about value, identifies three main types of value: 1) intrinsic value, the interest, enjoyment, or satisfaction an individual gleans from doing the task; 2) attainment value, the importance of a task to a particular individual, including its relationship to the individual's identity; and 3) utility value, the usefulness of a task for an individual's everyday life, future goals, or society generally (Eccles & Wigfield, 2002).

Of these three types of value, utility value is the most commonly studied and is often used interchangeably with the term "relevance," though some researchers define utility value as having a more personal component (i.e., useful/relevant *to me*), whereas relevance refers to a broader recognition of relationships or interconnectedness between topics or ideas (Hulleman et al., 2017). The idea of relevance is also prominent in youth-development literature, which identifies the importance of allowing students to make choices in academic work that allow them to pursue topics and skills that feel relevant to them, helping them to integrate academic work with their sense of self (Nakkula & Toshalis, 2006). Research has also examined the role of relevance in helping students to develop a sense of purpose for learning and academic work (Yeager, Henderson, et al., 2014).

Intrinsic value is related to theories of interest development that describe a continuum between the short-term or "situational" interest that students might feel when they are "hooked" by a task or activity in class, and the more enduring individual interest in a subject that leads students to seek out opportunities to continue learning even outside of assigned class work (Renninger & Hidi, 2002). Obviously, not every subject is going to develop into a deep-seated interest for every student, but research has shown that even sustaining student interest beyond the initial "hook" is beneficial for engagement. For example, interest is related to engagement, academic choices, and achievement (Beymer et al., 2020; Harackiewicz et al., 2016).

Attainment value has not received as much attention to date in motivation research, in part because it is difficult to measure and potentially harder to influence than utility or intrinsic value (Eccles & Wigfield, 2020). Attainment value includes the extent to which engaging in a task aligns with key aspects of identity that an individual may not even be fully conscious of. For example, a substantial body of research examining the underrepresentation of certain groups in STEM fields has found that many students still hold a mental representation of scientists as White, male, and "clever" or "geeky"; students who do not personally identify or want to identify with these attributes may therefore rule out a career in science without necessarily being fully aware of how they are constructing their identity through these choices (Archer et al., 2015). While all three forms of value are dependent on individualized perceptions of the task, attainment value's connection to personal identity can make it a more challenging—but also possibly an especially important (Perez et al., 2019)—target for educators to try to influence.

Across all three types of value, the classroom relationships and community that support belonging mindsets are a critical tool. In chapter 1, Diane and her school leveraged a team-building mentality to promote students' endorsement of college preparation as a source of utility value. A key tension in her case, however, was whether that top-down imposition of a hegemonic utility value overshadowed opportunities to encourage students to act agentically on salient dimensions of their identity and cultivate intrinsic or attainment value for school. Diane's purely utility value justification for wanting to include more diverse authors in her AP course ("in college . . . being able to manage some different genres . . . will be helpful") revealed the limitations of so heavily prioritizing pragmatic rationales; she never mentioned the impact that a more diverse canon could have on students' interest in and feelings of identification with course content. The commentary from the two speakers of color at the expedition kickoff revealed potentially powerful intersections of utility and attainment value, as the speakers spoke of the complexity of endorsing traditional, utilitarian achievement goals within the existing education system but as a means of disrupting that system to better serve their communities ("get accepted [to college] . . . graduate . . . and take your rightful place on the throne of change").

A helpful practitioner-oriented organizing framework for these approaches is Brophy's (2008) three-step model for cultivating students' "appreciation," or perceived value, for what they learn in school. The first step of Brophy's model charges educators to consider *what* students are learning. Educators can influence students' perceived value through the design of academic tasks, which are more likely to be valued by students if they include clear and relevant learning goals (Assor et al., 2002; Jackson et al., 2016); provide students with variety, choice, and autonomy (Hafen et al., 2011; Patall, 2013); and promote collaboration and active, higher-order thinking (Carr & Walton, 2014). Of these criteria, the second seemed to prove the most challenging for Diane when applied to curricular content, the "what" of students' learning. She was able to incorporate choice and autonomy in students' in-class activities and in the premise for their research paper, but she struggled to balance competing value demands in a more cohesive way within her AP Literature class.

The second and third steps of the model describe *how* educators can "frame" and "scaffold" student appreciation. Beyond task design, educators can further promote a value mindset by modeling their own academic interests and speaking explicitly about the relevance of academic tasks to students' interests (Green, 2002; National Research Council, 2004). Studies of utility-value interventions have also shown that teachers can promote students' value mindsets by inviting students to identify and articulate the value or relevance of what they are learning, either verbally or through a reflective writing prompt (Harackiewicz et al., 2016; Hulleman et al., 2010, 2017; Kafkas et al., 2017). On this front, Diane's case very much embodies the challenge that some teachers face in identifying the "affordances" in their subject matter that will allow students to perceive it as valuable and relevant, especially when they inherit curriculum whose original intended value may be obscure to them (Pugh & Phillips, 2011).

However, little research has been done on educators' understandings of the value of their own course content. One analysis found that two elementary teachers held different views not only on what was relevant and valuable about their curriculum, but also on what "relevance" itself meant, which in turn influenced how they supported relevance in their classes (Green, 2002). For example, one teacher enacted relevance by "choosing tasks that involved activities relevant to student concerns and interests (e.g., games, hands-on activities)" whereas the other enacted it through verbalizing rationales for "more traditional classroom activities" (Green, 2002, p. 1001). Likewise, in a study of middle school science teachers, Schmidt and colleagues (2018) found that teachers who perceived less-complex connections between science and students' lives also talked less about the relevance of science to their students during class.

Zachary Kaplan's portrait presents a counterpoint to Diane's approach. While both teachers work in small schools and emphasize relationships and belonging in the classroom, Zachary leverages those relationships in very different ways from Diane when it comes to curricular choices and considerations of value. Notably, his approach is likely supported by two key structural flexibilities: he does not teach an AP course, and though his small school is also mission-driven like Riverside Academy, the institutional goals seem less pervasive in Zachary's experience compared to Diane's. Many of Zachary's approaches to curriculum design map onto Brophy's (2008) model for developing students' appreciation for their course content, but they also demonstrate the tension between allowing students' autonomous pursuit of what they find interesting versus more intentionally guiding the "invisible forces" of perceived value and relevance in service of student learning.

Choosing Your Adventure

CLEARING A PATH

TESTING is hastily scrawled in green marker on a piece of scrap paper taped to the glass panels of Zachary Kaplan's classroom door. Though the glass, I can see the telltale signs of a waning standardized exam session: desks spaced apart in rows, a handful of students lingering noncommittally over their papers, a bored proctor ambling around and looking at the wall decorations in someone else's classroom. It is about a month into my observations at Oak Bridge School and the first of three days of the English Language Arts portion of the high school equivalency exam being administered statewide to tenth graders this week. The test's disruption of normal routines is familiar to me from my own time teaching in the Boston Public Schools, and I am just turning away to continue my search for Zachary when the proctor comes to the door, having caught sight of my unfamiliar face peeking in. (In a school of 275 students and 18 teachers, it is easy to identify who doesn't belong.) He advises that I ask about Zachary's room reassignment in the main office.

Housed in a red brick building built in 1885, OBS does not have hallways in a traditional sense; on each floor, the classrooms open onto a spacious central area as large as the classrooms themselves. On the first floor, this central landing area serves as the "main office" but reminds me more of a youth hostel than a school because of all the people—mostly students, but sometimes staff—who are usually chilling around the large semicircular secretary's desk during my lunchtime arrivals for Zachary's class. One time I had to shift a tray of celebratory cupcakes in order to sign in at the visitor log that no one seems to check. Today is especially busy, as students displaced from their regular lunch rooms by the testing have congregated here. I wait my turn for the secretary's attention behind a soft-spoken ninth grader who is updating her on his recent academic and personal progress. I am in no rush; I know OBS is, as Zachary conveyed in an early email, "so small" that in the worst-case scenario, I could probably just wander the building until I found him.

In fact, it is Zachary who finds me as he crosses the first floor on a lunchtime trek around the school to attend to miscellaneous tasks. In his early thirties, a self-described "Jewish American male" with a narrow face and curly brown hair and beard, Zachary moves through the school with an easy-going energy, tossing back "Hey"s as students greet him in passing. The seniors call him just "Kaplan" out of both affection and an assertion of their respective statuses at OBS; in his fifth year here, Zachary is an established entity whom twelfth graders respect but also a ready participant in banter about NBA players and pop culture.

Zachary tells me that he has been relocated to a classroom on the third floor—grinning at the gasps of horror this announcement elicits from two nearby seniors who do not want to climb extra stairs—and sends me up ahead of him while he grabs laptops from the technology cart. The ninth graders who are eating lunch there are slow to vacate, and Zachary's twenty-five students are slow to arrive, but since OBS has no bells signaling class transitions, the 12:23 p.m. start time has always been a little flexible. Today this gives Zachary some extra time to arrive with an armful of laptops, which he deposits on the front table before marking out six sections on the whiteboard with headings (table 2.1).

Table 2.1. Critical Theory Lenses in Zachary's Class

Psychoanalytic	*Gender/Queer*
Jungian	*Critical Race Theory*
Feminist	*Marxist*

Source: Author provided.

Apropos of nothing I can discern, a few students start singing "This Land Is Your Land" as they settle in at the unfamiliar desks, followed by a song I don't recognize but with the similar cadence of an elementary school choral selection. Zachary doesn't visibly react to this as he adjusts his tie, then unbuttons and rolls up the sleeves of his light blue dress shirt, combatting the overbaked, lunch-saturated air and also perhaps symbolically preparing to get to work. His unflappability extends to the two teachers who normally occupy this classroom staying seated at their desks and conversing with each other at regular volume throughout the entire period, even while Zachary is delivering whole-class instruction fifteen feet away. This is maddening to me, but if it bothers Zachary at all, he doesn't let on. Instead, he launches class by telling the students he wants to give them a quick overview of the six critical theories written on the board, so that students can choose the "lens" they want to use for their two-part final project on the whole-class text: the 1982 X-Men comic *God Loves, Man Kills*.

A class of older high school students reading an X-Men comic book directly above the room where younger students are taking a high-stakes standardized test may seem incongruous, but the juxtaposition feels familiar to me, as does the outsized impact of testing on an urban public school. Standardized testing seemed to suck up all of my former school's energy and resources: it dictated ninth- and tenth-grade teacher assignments, scheduling, and learning objectives. In a manner reminiscent of Diane's framing of the AP test, "passing MCAS" was understood by teachers and students alike to be the driving purpose of many class activities. Meanwhile, teachers in the older grades were given little instructional guidance, apart from AP curriculum; no one seemed to know quite what to do with students once the testing hurdle was cleared.

As the ninth- and twelfth-grade English teacher at OBS, Zachary experiences life on both sides of the testing divide. He can share in the pride of OBS's results on the state exam, which are impressive for any school, much less one with a historically underserved student population. All but two students passed the previous year's English exam, and OBS's passing rate on each subject exam exceeds that of the state as well as the district, even while 57 percent of OBS students are classified as low income by the State Department of Education, and 88 percent are students of color (54 percent Hispanic, 20 percent Asian, 12 percent Black, 4 percent other). Zachary knows, though, that passing the test is not synonymous with being prepared for rigorous academic work. OBS students may do well on the relatively "closed questions" on the state test, he says, but when it comes to the question of, "Are my kids producing college-ready work?" Zachary admits that "oftentimes I find myself thinking, 'No.'"

Zachary sees his students as "really bright kids . . . really good thinkers" who just need to be given the opportunity to "channel" that raw intellectual talent toward something meaningful to them in order to develop higher-order skills. That opportunity was missing in the existing twelfth-grade English curriculum outlined by the district: a traditional British literature chronological survey course starting with *Beowulf* and working up to *1984*. Zachary saw that students were not "fully engaging in" the material because of a lack of perceived relevance, a key component in the value mindset that can help motivate student effort. "Teaching *The Canterbury Tales* to a bunch of inner-city twelfth graders is difficult," he chuckles. "Like, 'why are we reading this thing that's a thousand years old?' And I wasn't really enjoying it either," he adds. "I love Orwell, but teaching *1984* is a SLOG. You know there's like 70 pages in the middle where it's literally a textbook?" Zachary laughs heartily at George Orwell's audacity. "And these kids who are already barely, BARELY interested are like—" he furrows his brow in an expression of adolescent incredulity—"now I gotta read this history textbook?!"

The uninspiring curriculum also exacerbated what Zachary sees as a uniquely twelfth-grade brand of disaffection and lack of perceived value in their remaining high school tenures. "By the time senior year starts," he says, students are "already counting down the days. Lethargy kind of sets in." Seniors are "kind of burnt out from junior year, and they're applying to colleges, and when that ends their brains kind of shut down." Some seniors loaded up on AP classes and used Zachary's non-AP English class as their mental break. The "lethargy" is particularly marked at a grade 7–12 school as small as OBS, Zachary says. Though he sees many more benefits than drawbacks to the small school size overall, one drawback is that twelfth-grade students have been in "the same classes with the same forty people for six years," creating a feeling of "stagnation" in the cohort.

Assignment completion rates "were terrible," he says. "Every year around the end of the quarter, I was tracking kids down about grades and stressing out about, you know, this kid has a sixty-four, and I don't want to give them a sixty-four on their transcript for colleges . . . It was really hard to get good work out of them."

Zachary's solution was to reimagine not just his own curriculum but the entire structure of eleventh- and twelfth-grade English at OBS. Rather than the traditional year-long grade-level English classes, eleventh and twelfth graders would be pooled together and given the opportunity to choose from semester-long electives. The principal approved the plan ("That's the nice thing about being here," Zachary says; "it's a flexible place to work, and if someone has . . . a good idea, a good effort is made to implement it"), and the new class offerings went into effect for the 2016–17 school year. Zachary offered two electives each semester: American Literature and the class I observed, Superheroes in World Literature. His colleague who had formerly taught both eleventh-grade English sections now taught Gender and Shakespeare as well as AP English Literature, which remained a full-year course.

The new courses still mapped onto district curriculum guidelines in broad strokes—the Superheroes class still reads *Beowulf* and excerpts from *1984*—but in addition to freeing the teachers to think more thematically about curriculum, the restructure allowed students to opt in to their classes. All of the new electives are considered "honors" level, just as the previous grade-level courses were—there is no tracking at OBS, apart from AP[1] and a couple of specialized courses—so there are no prerequisites or other barriers to student entry. The goal, Zachary says, was to "emulate" the "beauty of college," where "you have a lot more freedom over what you study" and "a whole range of classes you can choose from." His own high school experience in Madison, Wisconsin, provided him with a model for this kind of self-directed learning at the secondary level; by employing a similar mixed-grade elective structure in its upper English classes, his school had helped make the transition to college "so natural for me."

Zachary wanted to achieve the same effect at OBS, where despite the school's success on the state exam, "I didn't feel like we were doing our kids a service, telling them what classes they should be taking and telling them what they're studying." Instead, Zachary seeks to prepare his students for future academic success by making them feel like they are on a learning adventure of their own choosing, thus strengthening their sense of agency in school. Through his careful consideration of what curriculum and activities will feel relevant to students, as well as how to help students engage with content and with fellow learners in a self-transforming way, he seeks to promote students' perceived value of the class content and learning overall.

KINDLING A SPARK

In contrast to his relationship to the former upper-school English curriculum, Zachary aims to design his new curriculum to kindle students' value mindsets toward school by tapping into existing interests, opinions, and personal experience so that students see the work as "relevant to their lives or society today." He explicitly tells students during a class early in the X-Men unit that he "want[s] to bridge between real life" and the comic. "Yesterday we talked about allegory, right?" he reminds them. Then he rattles through some of the examples they covered, including *Animal Farm* as allegory for the Russian revolution and *The Lorax* as allegory for environmental activism. I notice there are also allegorical representations on some of his classroom decorations, such as a poster advocating the purchase of war bonds that shows Captain America punching a cartoon Hitler in the face. Reinforcing the *Animal Farm* allegory, a hand-drawn student project features an anthropomorphized pig advising, "Don't Be Beasts of England."

The X-Men, Zachary says, have often been interpreted as allegory for certain social issues "because they're a small group of people who are persecuted and feared for how they were born." He is going to play a couple of clips from the films *X-Men* (2000) and *X2* (2003), and he wants to hear what real-world connections students can make.

The students shift around in their seats to get a better viewing angle, in a manner I recognize from whenever I showed video in my class, no matter the topic. Their desks are scattered haphazardly around the room in what Zachary affectionately calls "amorphous blobs"; even when he directs the students to form more orderly configurations for group work, he is not a stickler about the furniture arrangements, and I never see him assign seats. The students are therefore sprinkled randomly around the room, the only real pattern being the absence of desks in an area where the view of the white board and pull-down screen is obstructed by a floor-to-ceiling support pole and the large wheeled cart that holds a document camera, projector, and Zachary's laptop. He uses that laptop now to play two *X-Men* clips in quick succession. First, the fictional Senator Kelly announces the need for a mutant registry in a campaign commercial. Then, he pushes back on anti-registry testimony from Jean Grey—a mutant herself, unbeknownst to

Kelly—on the Senate floor. In both clips, Kelly argues that mutants are dangerous and a registry is necessary for national security.

"If we're looking for allegory here," Zachary asks the students, "what could we look at?"

"Immigration," says Nia. "The way they keep saying, 'they're taking jobs.'"

"That's my family!" Veronica pipes up, with what sounds like pride. Zachary tells me later that Veronica wrote about her undocumented father's border crossing in her final paper for Zachary's fall-semester American Literature class—one month before the district announced, after the 2017 presidential inauguration, that teachers should not allow students to write about their immigration status in school assignments.

"Also segregation," Nia adds; "that part about 'who your kids go to school with.'"

After soliciting a few more comments, Zachary moves on to the *X2* clip, which shows the teenager Bobby Drake revealing to his family in the living room that he is a mutant. "It's like coming out," I hear someone mutter. At the end of the scene, the younger Drake boy sneaks out to call the authorities on his mutant brother, prompting a student near me, Eric, to hiss, "Snitch!" at the screen before asking Zachary, "Can we watch the fight scene?" Zachary declines this request but later indulges Eric in conversation while the students get started on their homework at the end of class:

> Eric has been asking/talking about the new X-Men movie *Logan* for virtually the entire class to anyone who will listen, and when Zachary draws near on a meandering lap around the classroom, Eric asks him if they can watch it in class. Zachary deflects the question—it's not (legally) possible given that the film is currently in theatrical release—but tells Eric that they will be looking at the character Wolverine more closely in class and will watch a fight scene then. "Which one?" Eric asks eagerly, rattling off several possibilities, and then both of them are off in a rapid-fire riff about the origins of Wolverine—or Weapon X, as Zachary calls him. "When he joined the X-Men, he became Wolverine," he tells Eric, then chuckles a moment later when Eric tries to dispute another piece of X-Men lore. "Don't listen to the movies," Zachary says. "The movies aren't canon." When Zachary moves away, Eric uses his school laptop to pull up the

Wikipedia page of X-Men characters and then searches "Weapon X" on Google.

In many ways, Eric embodies the vision and intent behind Zachary's curriculum restructure: he clearly has an existing interest in comic books, saw an English class that matched that interest, and opted into it. In Zachary, he finds a partner in *nerding out*, as I jot down in the margin of my field notes on the Wolverine discussion. Later in the spring, Zachary describes to me a whole-class discussion on *V for Vendetta* in which "Eric was super involved—to the point where sometimes he would only just talk to me," he laughs. "He was sitting next to me and just talking to me." The topic of the class and Zachary's support for his interest provide the necessary hook to engage Eric in the coursework; at the end of the semester, Zachary describes him as "a much more academic being than he was three months ago."

Zachary is aware, though, that his Superheroes class is not composed entirely of Erics. "So many kids," Zachary says, "within the first couple of weeks were like, 'I don't like comic books. I don't know why I took this class.' And I'm like, 'Well, **I** don't know why you took it; you had other options.'"

"Did you ever ask them that?" I ask him.

"Yeah," he says. "They took it 'cause their friends took it. Or 'cause they like me," he admits, "but like—don't do that! You know?" His wry chuckle conveys the mix of flattery and exasperation he feels at students' shallow decision making.

However, because OBS only has two high school English teachers, and one teaches AP English as a full-year course, even students who approach course selection with what Zachary sees as purer motives have only three options, from which they ultimately have to choose two to fulfill a year of English. For the students who do not bring to class an existing interest in the course theme, Zachary works to earn their "buy-in" by encouraging them to connect course content to their own lived experience as well as real-world issues that they recognize, as with the X-Men video clips. When parsing religious imagery and archetypes in a Superman comic, Zachary projects the Lord's Prayer on the board and asks students to "raise your hand if you've heard this in church, or seen it in a movie, or you're familiar with it in any way at all." Then he asks them to examine the text and consider, "What is it that you're actually praying for?" In the ensuing discussion, several students rattle off the prayer in Spanish—the language of their church services—and link their textual interpretations to the accompanying church rituals. ("That's why we hold hands when we say it.")

In another lesson, to activate students' thinking about rhetoric in messaging, Zachary shows them video clips from "real life" that he warns "are hard to watch, so I want to remind us to be respectful to other people. I don't mean that you have to be respectful to the views you're going to hear—which are disgusting," he adds after a beat, as if considering whether to say it, "but be respectful in your responses." The students, in turn, react strongly but without "disrespectful" language as they watch footage of Pat Robertson equating Islam to Nazism ("Catholicism was just as bad!" someone scoffs) and Megyn Kelly interviewing Carl Higbie about a proposed Muslim registry ("They ruled that constitutional?!" Nia squeaks in shock when the interview touches on *Korematsu v. United States*). Zachary also centers his American Literature elective curriculum on a question that positions students as experts in American identity and values: *What does American literature say about who we are and what do you want American literature to look like in the twenty-first century?* The final paper, he tells me, then becomes a way to include students' personal histories among the class texts, as students "writ[e] about their place in American literature and American history," expanding on themes and ideas from the course "in the context of their own story or a family member's story."

Zachary believes that inviting these kinds of personal connections and reactions gives every student an "entry point . . . like a doorway, where even the lowest[-skilled] kids have something valuable to say about whatever it is we're studying." It also results in higher quality work, he says, because the students are personally invested in the final product; Veronica's paper on her mixed-status immigrant family was "the best piece of writing she's ever done."

Beyond his curriculum design, Zachary's verbal responses to students in class reinforce the notion that their way of engaging with the curriculum is valid and welcomed; whatever point of connection, interest, or relevance they hit upon is entitled to at least a small amount of classroom airspace. He is strikingly open to students' spontaneous questions, even when they divert attention from the curricular topic at hand. I never saw him knowingly ignore a student's inquiry; over the course of my observations, he responded to questions that included:

"Are you responsible with your money?"

"Does the Bible ever say, where is heaven actually?"

"What's the name of that song from *The Breakfast Club* when the kids are running through the halls at the peak of finding themselves?"

"What's the ACLU?"

"Is that how cults start?"

During the discussion of the Pat Robertson video, someone asked what the literary term was for a word like "televangelism," and Zachary praised the student who interrupted him a few minutes later with the correct answer (portmanteau) after openly using her cell phone—technically a violation of school rules—to look it up. ("How do you know she's right?" the other students pressed, relentless.) The unfiltered questioning culture was so deeply entrenched that a student even turned to me one day during a brief debate over the word "connotes" and demanded, "You go to Harvard—how do you pronounce this word?"

Zachary also routinely affirms students' declarative comments to validate their contributions to the classroom discourse. "That's really interesting," he often says, or simply, "Nice!" He praises students' vocabulary ("great word!") and points out when students are using higher-order thinking ("I like the connection you're making") or introducing new ideas ("I never thought of that before!"). He encourages students to expand on their thinking, either through follow-up questions (in response to Zachary's frequent rejoinder, "Can you say more?" a student one day replies, "No," but then elaborates anyway, as if unable to help himself), or by giving them his undivided attention during individual consultations—even if this means temporarily not responding to anyone or anything else:

> Zachary heads over to a student at the side table with his hand raised. I hear him say, "Good . . . good . . . that would be a great quote." I scan the room. A few students are writing. Veronica is not; she starts making a soft high-pitched noise with her mouth wide open, then curling her lips in different ways to manipulate the sound. I don't time her precisely, but she does this for far longer than I'm expecting: maybe thirty seconds. A classmate near her jokes about someone or something from *Spongebob Squarepants*, and the laughter from that soon escalates into loud joking and some squealing. Zachary is still conferring one-on-one and does not react to the other students.

"I mean, to be honest . . . I get really into their stuff," Zachary laughs when I ask him about his unbroken focus on the student in front of him. "Like they'll give me an idea, and I get really wrapped up in it." He realizes that there may be trade-offs in not monitoring everyone else's behavior, but for him the opportunity to validate a single student's thinking is always worthwhile. "Get[ting] five minutes of intellectual conversation with their teacher . . . is important for each kid," he says, not only for affirming their thinking but also for "building relationships, even outside of the academic work."

Those relationships are key to the overall learning atmosphere that Zachary is trying to create. In our interviews, he uses the word "fun" nine times to describe classroom-based experiences—both his own as a student, and what he hopes as a teacher to create for his students. He is unusual among my participants in how frequently he mentions fun and how foundational it seems to be in his philosophy of teaching and learning. He recalls that, "knowing what I know now about pedagogy," his own high school English teachers weren't "amazing, uh, teacher-teachers, you know what I mean? But they were just really fun and inspiring, and it was great sitting in a class" with them. For Zachary, relevance, interest, fun, inspiration, and classroom community are intertwined—and, I think, central to students choosing his class even when they hold no existing interest in the course theme. Zachary expresses a preference for students not to make socially motivated course choices, but it seems plausible to me that the opportunity to learn with Zachary is as much of a draw as the content, especially given that every OBS student has had him as a ninth-grade teacher. They know that in his classroom, Zachary will make learning fun not only by actively kindling students' interests, but also by being kindling for them: his positive, affirming relationships with students provide the fodder to feed the initial spark into an enduring flame.

Becoming Explorers

When I arrive at OBS on an unusually cool day in May, all the seniors are wearing the college gear of the school they'll be attending in the fall; the flagship state university is well represented, as is a nearby public university. Zachary himself is wearing a Mayfield University Class of 2007 tee over a long-sleeved shirt and jeans as he stands in the center of the room, cuing up multiple videos and documents on his laptop before class begins. Today's lesson is packed, with Zachary trying to conclude a paragraph-writing task that students began yesterday and then start a new activity, but everything is taking longer than planned. Though Zachary told the students to "come to class with your paragraphs ready to rock," many students seem to be starting from scratch. In the only sign of any impatience on his part, Zachary gives them many time checks—"Let's make this literally take, like, three minutes"—saying he wants to have enough time in the second half of class to introduce them to "an incredible study of social psychology" that is "gonna Blow. Your. Minds," he teases. "Your lives will be forever changed."

Although Zachary is being jokingly hyperbolic here to try to motivate the students to speed up, his words, in a way, also very much reflect another guiding principle of his curricular design for the Superheroes course. He stressed to students during the elective sign-up process that the presence of comic books on the syllabus did not mean that they would be allowed to "just sit around all day, talking about our favorite superheroes, and that's that." He does not want to cater solely to students' existing interests and personal experiences, letting them study only what is pleasing or familiar so that they will perceive the content as relevant according to their current understanding of themselves and the world. For Zachary "relevance also means—I think kids just want to feel like they're learning something," he says, even if that means that not every class is "fun" or "enjoyable" in the traditional sense. "I think as long as kids come in understanding that this class is meaningful in a way that there's a tangible measurement for. That I go in, and I leave, and I am somehow . . ." He pauses briefly, considering the word he wants, before ultimately deciding on "changed."

What Zachary categorizes as an alternative definition of relevance, I see as his reframing of relevance from an abstract noun to a dynamic, cyclical process. In his view, relevance and value are not just static qualities that students can either perceive or not, with the design of curriculum and learning activities the only leverage points for teachers trying to activate those perceptions. Rather, the process of engaging in learning can change students and enable them to recognize value and relevance that they would not have previously. Moreover, Zachary believes that that personal change process is itself valued by students. While Zachary describes these processes as linked to different dimensions of relevance, in practice they blend together in his instruction as he seeks to tap into students' existing interests and values while simultaneously engaging students in a transformative process of becoming a different kind of learner with a different kind of relationship with academic content.

The transformation that Zachary talks most about involves a change in perception: students coming to see the world differently as a result of their learning. This focus on personal perspective shifts dovetails with Zachary's own preferences as a consumer of literature and culture and his perceived strengths as a teacher. He self-deprecatingly assures me that, unlike some of his teachers who "could go on and on and on for a whole class period just about the beauty of the language and, you know, more traditional stuff," he is no brilliant literary scholar. "I'm much more suited to, can we find relevancies in our world today, or in human behavior, or human nature, or psychology, or philosophy." These topics "interest me more," and he likewise believes that "most kids have a natural attraction" to them that goes unmet in many high schools. Thus, even before Zachary initiated the new elective system, he was trying to incorporate philosophical and psychological theories into his traditional twelfth-grade English class, believing that "any way that you think about how you think, kids are really interested in that, or how you behave." There is something tangible and satisfying for students in possessing a possible explanation for human processes that are otherwise invisible.

With the greater freedom afforded him in the Superheroes elective, Zachary is able to center his curricular units more fully on questions of culture, belief systems, and human nature, pairing the more accessible and high-interest comic books with difficult supplemental texts that students would not naturally seek out themselves. He gives his students excerpts from the Book of Revelation so that they can identify religious allusions in a Superman comic and discuss it as an example of "cultural mythology." He assigns excerpts from Plato's *Republic* to engage students in questions of morality and ethics. On that cool day in May, the "incredible study of social psychology" turns out to be Stanley Milgram's 1962 experiment on obedience, prompting students to consider the psychological underpinnings of the dystopian authoritarian regimes in *V for Vendetta* and *1984* in preparation for a final essay. The students' draft thesis statements for that essay show them trying out some of these new perspectives on human behavior and governance:

> *All three texts show that humans can be slaves to authority.*
> *Authority can have a very negative impact on people, by restrictions, cognitive dissonance, or Authority fallacy.*
> *In every totalitarian government, a resistance rises. Normal citizens are brainwashed and follow the flow. Those who don't are considered crazy.*

*Surveillence changes the way a person acts based on the surveyors
desires. Therefore obedience to authority requires an individual
to feel like there are "Eyes" on them at all times.*

The final assignment for the X-Men unit is an encapsulation of the transformative learning goal for students, as Zachary asks them to use Freudian, Jungian, feminist, Marxist, critical race, and queer theory as "lenses" through which to see the text and in turn, the world, differently. When Nia asks during the theory lens presentations whether there is such a thing as a "bad" lens, Zachary tells her that the criteria for a good lens is that it "opens doors that you've never seen before." While Zachary laments to me afterwards that he "wasn't convinced that they knew what they were saying" during the presentations—"and a lot of it went over the class's head anyway"—the students nonetheless do describe real world phenomena through the lens of theory. The critical race theory group names mass incarceration, the wealth gap, and housing policies as examples of systemic racism. The queer theory group talks about "heteronormative structures in society," such as assumptions about what a couple or a family looks like and arguing that the absence of openly gay characters in the X-Men comic is a form of erasure that is common in media because producers "don't want people feeling uncomfortable in any way." The feminist theory group points out that the 1982 publication date of the X-Men comic closely follows the "second wave feminism" of the 1970s, when women who fought for equal rights were viewed by some as unnatural "mutants" for rebelling against established order.

Zachary likewise hopes that his teaching overall will help his students to "see the world in a much more academic lens," and in particular to see themselves as belonging to that academic world, broadly defined. Students shouldn't feel like "their interests have to be divested from academics or school," he says; they should recognize that critical theory helps them think differently about their favorite Japanese anime or that blockbuster movies rely heavily on narrative tropes and archetypes to trigger certain emotions in the audience. Zachary believes that developing a new way of seeing can "legitimize school" to students as a mechanism for informing and deepening their personal interests. He himself experienced such a perception shift in high school, once he reached the elective English classes in the upper grades:

Once we started getting to more specialized classes, that was
when I really loved [English] . . . When I started to put together,

"Oh, I can write about pop culture in an academic way"—when I made that connection, that's when English really took off for me. And that's why this change in these courses was important to me because I think our kids don't get that sense [that], "You love Pokémon? You can write about Pokémon—academically, you know, and that can be your bridge into academics in college, that you didn't know existed before."

Such an "academic lens" can help give students agency by showing them new ways to use their learning, but also by "just mak[ing] them feel intelligent," Zachary says. He tells me about a student who "ended up sending me a photo through text at 9 o'clock one night, when she was driving home from work, 'cause someone had a *V for Vendetta* mask as a bumper sticker. And—there was no comment, you know," he laughs. "Until the next morning when she was like, 'Mister, you get my text?' But like, that's cool! You know?" A moment of recognition or insight in the outside world can be "a really empowering moment for a teenager," Zachary says. He recalls another former student who "came from a really, really rough home, really poor family. And she was going to Middlebury next year, which is, you know, very White and very—she was White, too, but . . ." Zachary trails off, looking at me knowingly, then finishes the sentence as if stating the obvious: "There aren't going to be many people from her background at Middlebury." This student had learned about Freudian analysis in Zachary's old *Macbeth* unit, "and that really stuck with her. And she sent me a text a month into her first semester at Middlebury, telling me that she told her whole class about the wandering uterus, and no one had ever heard of it. And she was, like, super pumped." Zachary smiles at the memory. "And I think that's a really important step. If you can give them those little things to latch onto, I think it really validates that in terms of, 'Oh, I'm on the same level as these people and I deserve to . . . you know, my interests and my academics are just as valid as whatever else anyone else is bringing to the table.' "

The wandering uterus story positions school content that students can "latch onto" as a kind of knowledge capital that can transform not only how students see themselves, but potentially how others see them. "I think that legitimizes them too, socially, in a way that's really powerful," Zachary says. "I remember in high school and middle school, I felt like my best friend was just heads and tails above me, intellectually. And I thought that was really neat, and it made me want to do really well in school so I could kinda 'battle' him back." The ability to hold one's own intellectually, "enjoying that kind of discussion, that kind of engagement with people around you" was also a crucial part of Zachary's experience in college, where he "made really good friends because I loved the conversations that we had."

Zachary recognizes that this kind of "social legitimization" might be especially important for his students, who are "from a poor neighborhood and an inner-city school" and often have to contend with other people's "misconceptions" about them. "I would love to have our seniors go off to school and just, you know, blow people's minds," Zachary says. "They should go to college and show that they're just as capable of being there as anyone else and have things to say and things to think." Even for his students who do not attend—or stay in—college, Zachary maintains that an "academic lens" is "important for their quality of life in the future . . . I think it makes them more keen observers of the world. It lets them into the world more than they would otherwise be," he says. "Wherever they are, whoever they're with, when they're thirty, when they're forty-five, when they're fifty . . . I want these kids to value knowledge and information, and just talking about it . . . Being able to talk to anyone about anything I think is an important skill in our world."

Zachary himself embodies this ethos in his own continued pursuit of transformative learning. When I ask him about how he handles the (self-inflicted) challenge of teaching brand-new classes filled with content that is less readily available in traditional K–12 teaching resources, he tells me:

> I like the challenge. I mean, I loved being in school because I loved learning stuff. Teaching the same things for four years . . . I think I was just kind of looking to be inspired by doing something else. It's a lot of work, but it's fun. I've learned way more about this stuff than I ever would've had I not taught this class, right? Like I didn't know anything about the Bible or the Book of Revelation before last semester. I never thought my class would be a class where we'd be discussing Plato's philosophies. I'm learning a lot more about philosophy and things like that because I'm trying to tie all that stuff into the class.

The new curriculum therefore provides Zachary with inspiration, perspectives, and a renewed appreciation for learning, just as he hopes it does for his students. "I'm sure good teachers can do that in no matter what English class they have, but I was not doing that," Zachary says, in his customarily self-effacing way. "And now I am, I think . . . And I think that [my] excitement and engagement transfer to the class."

GUIDED VERSUS SOLO NAVIGATION

"It's like a sweathouse up there," Zachary warns when he sees me signing in at the main desk. Indeed, I find both of his classroom doors flung open, the lights turned off, and a wire-frame fan thrumming noisily in front of one open window. It's nearly 90 degrees outside, after similar weather yesterday, and the building is holding the heat like a brick oven. Standing next to the laptop and projector, Zachary takes a long draught from a condensation-laden water bottle and announces, "Here's the plan for today."

"I can't really hear you," Jessica calls out, pointing at the fan.

"HERE'S THE PLAN FOR TODAY," Zachary tries again. He wants to start by reviewing the writing process since he's finished grading the students' previous assignments "and there are some trends I'm noticing" that he hopes they can address for their upcoming essay, the last of the semester. He explains that he will make a statement, and he wants students to raise their hands if they feel "Yes, this applies to me." Since it's clear to me that the statements will be about writing, I am amused that the students are all looking at Zachary as if they are anticipating a game.

"First statement," Zachary begins. "I plan my essays out ahead of time."

Not a single hand goes up, and the students laugh as they survey the room.

"Well, it depends on what you mean by 'plan out ahead of time,'" Jessica says. "Like, does ten minutes count?"

Zachary revises the statement: "I think of my essays like a road trip, and I plan out where I'm going and how I'm going to get there."

There are still no hands. "I write like three sentences, and then I expand it," Jessica offers. When Zachary prompts her for further explanation, she says that she writes the first paragraph, and then she picks her evidence, "and then I just expand from there."

Zachary decides to elaborate to help Jessica relate her process description to his. On a road trip, he says, you generally have a destination in mind first, and then you figure out which highways to take and in what direction—all before setting out. That way, even if your plans change along the way, you can modify from that foundation, rather than starting anew. "Jessica, tell me if this is what you mean," he says. "Instead of that road trip, are you saying it's more like, 'I wanna go somewhere, I'm not really sure where, and also I'm just doing it because my teacher told me to, so I'm going to just go out and hope that I hit it eventually'?"

"Yes, that's it!" Jessica says, grinning.

Zachary appeals to the rest of the class: "How many people approach their writing like that?"

About four students raise their hands. "It's like I'm blindfolded and throwing darts and just hoping I hit the target," one young man says, cottoning on to the metaphor game.

"My goal is to have you understand that essays have a logical structure," Zachary says. "Before we sit down and write, we have a map of where we're going."

By the end of the semester, this scene is a familiar one to me; in writing lessons in particular, Zachary often tries to coach students in this kind of meta-awareness of their own cognitive processes. To borrow from his favorite road-trip metaphor, he wants students to know both that a map exists and that successfully completing the journey will require them to interact thoughtfully with that map and monitor how they are using it. Ideally, students will internalize this process so that they can replicate it on their own, as more experienced writers like Zachary know to do. "When I write," Zachary tells me, "I still outline things, you know, I have a general sense of where I'm going with things." This process awareness and self-regulation means that writing "typically doesn't take very long" for Zachary. His students, however, still need prompting both to think of writing as a systematic process and to complete the steps of that process. "They don't understand how quickly these things can go if you know what you're doing beforehand," Zachary says. "Even when I try to force them to outline things, that typically doesn't help . . . they still have a hard time seeing that as the skeleton to an essay. And so my next step is, how do I figure out getting them to see it like that."

Zachary is describing the pedagogical work of scaffolding, or providing students with supported learning experiences that will extend their skills beyond their current capabilities. Zachary is scaffolding the students' writing on two levels. At the more immediate level, he sometimes "force[s]" students to outline their essays, making them participate in the interim steps that will ultimately lead to a better product. But he is also aware that he needs to scaffold their metacognitive processes: how they think about the outline they are making. Being tasked with outlining an essay does not necessarily mean that students understand why they are outlining or that outlining is a transferrable strategy they can apply to other writing assignments; they may simply write the outline "because my teacher told me to."

Zachary recognizes the critical role that teachers play in scaffolding student learning; he sees the "next step" of his growth as a teacher as "figur[ing] out" how to strengthen students' metacognitive awareness of the writing process. Asking students to describe their individual approaches to a task, as he does in the road trip discussion, is one strategy I see him use for reading comprehension as well as the writing process; once before class when I ask him how he saw students making sense of the dense biblical excerpts they read the previous day, he readily tells me, "I actually don't know. Want me to ask them?" and goes on to facilitate a brief class discussion on strategies for tackling difficult texts. He revisits this topic later in the semester by again having students identify their own strategies before reviewing "techniques for reading long texts."

Yet while Zachary explicitly scaffolds his students' academic skill development and has clear metacognitive takeaways he wants them to understand, he takes a more inductive approach to their value mindset toward the course content; he seems to view student perceptions of value or relevance as ideally arising somewhat organically or naturalistically. "I heard somewhere recently that one of the worst things a teacher can actually say to a kid is, 'This is important,'" he tells me. "No one likes being told why something is important, you gotta come to it yourself." He is therefore restrained about making explicit statements about value in the classroom, wanting students to "come to [the] conclusion" that the content is "helpful, or good to know" through their own engagement with it, "without me saying it. I mean," he chuckles, "I've planned for them to come to that conclusion, but it's better if they get there on their own."

Thus, while Zachary designs thoughtful curriculum and transformative learning experiences that he hopes students will find meaningful, he does not want to be overly prescriptive to students about how they engage in the course content or what ultimate meaning or value they glean from it. He invokes the NPR podcast *Invisibilia,* a show about the "invisible forces that we don't see or understand shaping us," to describe what he sees himself doing in relation to student mindsets. Thoughtfully designed curriculum and positive relationships with students are the mechanisms through which Zachary tries to "get those invisible forces to work to my benefit" by getting students "bought in" and personally invested in their own learning. Once he sees evidence of those positive invisible forces at work, though, he intentionally takes a light touch to allow students the freedom to navigate that experience on their own. He nods in agreement with my observation that some students occasionally spend the entire class period reading the whole-class text instead of participating in the lesson. "There are days where

I've noticed Alicia isn't doing what we're doing, but she is reading the book, and—that's great! You know? Like, OK," Zachary laughs. "I don't mind. She's absorbing what we're saying somehow, a little bit, and if she loves this book so much, the content of the course so much that she can't stop, I don't want to be the person to chastise her to say—" he adopts a stern, pedantic Teacher Voice—"Stop reading the book [because] we're TALKING about it." Rather than mandating that Alicia comply with an activity—even an activity that he deems valuable and important—he prefers to let her, as an agentic individual, follow her own passion in that moment, accepting that ultimately the mindsets and forces that move students are unseen, unknown, and not always aligned with a teacher's carefully laid plans.

However, Zachary himself concedes that "it would be great if I could find a way to actually incorporate" more "tangible" and "deliberate" strategies for influencing the "invisible forces" within students. Out of the four mindsets, he names the value mindset as one of the hardest "because I think even sometimes our brightest kids are like, 'Why are we bothering with this?'" He takes on that difficulty by "work[ing] double" to craft meaningful curriculum and lessons for students, but muses aloud that he may be putting "too much faith" in the invisible forces to respond in the desired way.

It strikes me that Zachary already has some deliberate strategies for building a stronger bridge between students' engagement with his curriculum and their mindset development: the metacognitive discussions and explicit instruction he uses for students' academic skill development. When it comes to writing, Zachary recognizes that he cannot just assign an outline; he must also build students' understanding of the outline's usefulness—yet when it comes to the value mindset toward course content, Zachary invites the students to make connections to the material but does not generally layer on that additional metacognitive awareness, perhaps out of deference to his ideal of student discovery and agency in the learning process. And indeed, a spontaneous student question in the aftermath of the critical theory lens presentations sparks the one occasion of Zachary taking a stronger declarative stance about the relevance of course material that is more analogous to how he talks about the writing process and reading strategies:

> "I have a question," Shay announces. "Do people dedicate their lives to doing this? And if so, then like why do they decide to use a particular lens?"
>
> Zachary tells her that literature professors do this kind of textual analysis. He says that they're interested in how a lens applies to a particular text. "The lens helps us filter our own

ideas," he says. "It makes what we study a little more relevant to the society we live in. It might not feel relevant to you at first—we don't live in a Marxist society right now, and Marx himself died something like a hundred years ago—but using the lens gives us an interesting way to see how his ideas are reflected in a fictional society. And how does that relate to our own society?"

Zachary tells me afterwards that that discussion "was probably the first time in a while I've done any sort of metacognitive reflection, self-reflection kind of stuff" with his older students. He does more reflection with his ninth graders, "but in that class, no," he says. "If it was a full-year class, there probably would be. I'm starting to realize how much dropping from a full-year course to semester courses is just—you lose a ton of time," he says. "I only have this short amount of time to get through all this content, so I can't spend as much time doing self-reflective stuff."

This time crunch is one of the only downsides to the curricular restructure that Zachary mentions, and it is ironic that what gets cut is a potential mechanism to activate students' value mindsets toward the curriculum that has been so thoughtfully designed to encourage feelings of relevance and perceived value. But Zachary's prioritization seems to be more than just logistical, especially since he makes time in class to engage the students in shorter process reflections for their academic skills. His choice is also partly philosophical as he wrestles with finding the right balance between providing guidance and allowing students their own individual experiences of interest, relevance, or value in school content. In searching for this balance, his own road-trip metaphor may provide some insights: students can autonomously set their own course and undertake their own learning adventures while still benefitting along the way from both material resources and an experienced traveler who can help them make the most of the journey.

Reflections on Promoting a Value Mindset

In keeping with Brophy's (2008) model of developing students' "appreciation" for school learning, Zachary demonstrates deep intentionality in both *what* his students are learning and *how* he tries to promote their value mindsets toward that academic content. Concerning the *what*, Zachary found few affordances for perceived value in his traditional twelfth-grade English curriculum and altered both the curriculum itself and the school's course assignment procedures in order to open up more affordances, including the affordances offered through students' ability to choose their courses. Beyond that structural overhaul, Zachary presents students with day-to-day content that is worth learning and activities that are worth doing. He retains some texts from the old curriculum, like *Beowulf* and *1984*, but he makes their affordances more transparent to students by pairing them with high-interest comic books—which then reciprocally take on added significance and weight themselves when juxtaposed with the canonical texts. The video clips he plays in class are not just diversions to hold students' situational interest; they illuminate larger questions about society and the nature of human interaction for students to unpack—as do his course assignments. Through these "wise choices about what content and learning activities to include" (Brophy, 2008, p. 138), Zachary engages in a process of "artistically crafting" a curriculum that students can value (Pugh & Phillips, 2011, p. 287).

Building on Brophy's (2008) proposals for *how* students should interact with material in order to develop appreciation, Pugh and colleagues (2017; 2011) discuss the importance of framing content not as "some more school stuff to master" but rather as "possibilities" that "generate anticipation about what may be experienced, solved, or understood" (2011, p. 289). Zachary embraces the notion of curriculum as possibility through his intuition that students are "naturally attracted" to philosophical and psychological topics that help explain their world. His desire to "blow students' minds" informs his framing of the content's explanatory or curiosity-satisfying value through questioning and "entry point" strategies that invite students to make personal and real-world connections to the material. By invoking and then validating students' insights and lived experience, he casts them as experts who are entitled to interrogate the content's relevance and value—even when that interrogation manifests as questions that many other educators would perceive as tangential distractions or annoyances.

Zachary's teaching goal of leaving students "forever changed" is also consistent with Pugh and colleagues' (2017) construct of "transformative engagement," which comprises students' autonomously "motivated use" of learning in " 'free-choice' contexts," the "expansion of perception," and "valuing content for how it enriches everyday experience" (p. 370). Zachary's work with students on critical theory lenses and philosophical/psychological approaches in general embodies all of these components, as he seeks to give students new ways of seeing course texts that they can apply to future "free-choice contexts" in college assignments as well as "everyday experiences" like driving home from work, watching movies, and joshing with friends. Indeed, his goal for students parallels my own objective for this book to provide educators with a new lens on their own classroom practice.

Importantly, Zachary is not prescriptive about what interests and values students "need" to endorse, from a utilitarian perspective. His acceptance and affirmation of students' questions and other verbal contributions are key components of his approach to building relationships with students *through* as well as *for* interactions over course content. He is willing to meet them where they are to facilitate their engagement in the content at whatever level they can currently access; his "artistically crafted" curriculum feeds the teacher-student relationships, and vice-versa. Zachary envisions school-based learning shaping students' social interactions and thereby their feelings of legitimacy in academic settings ("My interests and my academics are just as valid as whatever anyone else is bringing to the table") as well as broader self-satisfaction ("I think it just makes them feel intelligent") that seem to align more with the definitions of attainment and intrinsic value than with the more commonly studied utility value. Zachary articulates a personal theory of transformative engagement that identifies social interactions and relationships as mediators in the development of the more personalized and individually variable types of perceived value.

Zachary's areas for growth may lie in making his well-developed aims more transparent to students and then providing the necessary supports for students to optimize their efforts toward those aims. Zachary can discuss at length the design and intent behind his curriculum restructuring, but because he also believes that "no one likes being told why something is important, you gotta come to it yourself," it is unclear both to me and to him how much of his intentional design is visible to students and how much remains an "invisible force" that he merely hopes to channel, rather than actively works to influence. His framing strategies reveal his intentionality in considering how to introduce students to new material, trying to set them up to "discover . . . value through firsthand experience," but he sometimes neglects to "scaffold their engagement so as to help them to notice and appreciate the activities' empowering affordances" (Brophy, 2008, p. 138). Research suggests that students whose teachers more frequently articulate the value of course content are more likely to perceive that content as valuable themselves (Schmidt et al., 2018), but Zachary prefers a more hands-off approach, such as when he avoids intervening when he sees students like Alicia having a positive "firsthand" experience with material.

Yet subjective learning experiences such as the internalization of perceived value "usually do not emerge spontaneously upon mere exposure" (Brophy, 2008, p. 137). Alicia might be "hooked" on the text in the moment and feeding her situational interest by continuing to read it during class, but she is also potentially missing out on an opportunity to develop a more sustained interest in the book, the book's themes, or the genre more broadly through discussing it with her classmates and teacher.

Zachary seems to assume that trying to target students' perceptions of value would mostly take the form of pedantic lectures to students about what is important, but teachers can verbally convey value to students in many different ways, not just didactic statements about importance (Green, 2002; Kafkas et al., 2017; Schmidt et al., 2018). Modeling is a strategy that Zachary already uses, such as when he tries to demonstrate his own "excitement and enthusiasm" for the material as a less intrusive strategy for conveying value to students. He could take this further by modeling not just intrinsic value but attainment and utility value too, demonstrating to students why skills or concepts from class are important and useful in his own life. Zachary partly does this when he explains how scholars use critical lenses, but he is prompted to do so by Shay's question rather than a deliberate plan to share a personal application that might resonate more with students. Studies on utility-value interventions also demonstrate that providing time and structure for *students* to articulate the value and importance of what they are learning can be an effective strategy (Hulleman et al., 2010, 2017). However, there may well be scenarios where students, as relative novices in a discipline, lack the perspective necessary to articulate the relevance or value of school content. Shay's question about real people's use of critical lenses would likely be difficult for students to answer themselves through an inductive or Socratic process; it is Zachary's broader experience with and expertise in literary studies that enable him to answer.

In fact, Zachary demonstrates a greater willingness to take a more guided approach when it comes to developing students' writing skills versus their perceptions of value. He initiates the extended discussion of the road trip as a metaphor for writing because he recognizes that even when he "force[s]" students to engage in strategies like outlining, "they still have a hard time seeing that as the skeleton to an essay." He diagnoses the need for additional scaffolding to help students grasp the relevance of different prewriting tasks to a writing goal, rather than viewing them as more assignments to do "because my teacher told me to." He also demonstrates an openness to expanding his use of this practice, such as when he took an inquiry approach to my question about students' strategies for reading difficult texts ("I actually don't know. Want me to ask them?").

Thus, Zachary has the foundation for strategies that would promote students' value mindsets without imposing his own. In the metacognitive class discussions about both essay writing and reading difficult texts, Zachary first solicits student input on the developing skill before offering a metaphor or strategies as a scaffolding structure to support students' evolving understandings. Applying this strategy to discussing students' motivational mindsets would avoid the didacticism that Zachary fears, of "telling" students why something is important, but it would also go beyond his current approach of exposing students to stimulating learning experiences and hoping the spark catches on.

It is notable to me that the belonging and value mindsets emerged so powerfully in the high school teachers' portraits because these mindsets mutually reinforce each other in important ways. A strong sense of belonging can make you likelier to adopt the group's values, and conversely, perceiving value in academic work can promote feelings of belonging in school. Diane seems to focus primarily on the former—believing that the strong school culture at Riverside helps students come to endorse certain educational values—in part because she feels constrained in her efforts to achieve the latter, either through institutional barriers or her own perceptions of misalignment between different types of value. Recall, for example, that she draws a striking distinction between "life issues" of personal relevance and college preparatory skills that hold utility value. Though she tries to incorporate both types of value, even in her AP class, she struggles to reconcile what she sees as their contradictions, and her ways of enacting support for belonging belie that inherent tension.

The relationship between the belonging and value mindsets is more consistently bidirectional in Zachary's case. Students' feelings of relatedness with Zachary likely contribute to the value they perceive in his class (which, in the case of students who "don't even like comic books," may otherwise be nonexistent). However, Zachary also internally rebels ("like, don't do that!") against the idea of students using their relationship with him as a proxy for actual interest in the course. He seems to view the autonomous development of personal interests and value for learning as a tool that students can use as a way to find and build relationships through "being able to talk to anyone about anything." He also sees valued content as key to motivating students' higher-order skill development which will equip them for college study. Zachary understands one goal of the value mindset to be giving students "little things to latch onto" that give provide "social legitimization"; he attributes his former student's "wandering uterus" triumph at Middlebury to his approach. For Zachary, strengthening the connections between college and things that matter to students is an essential element of college preparation.

Yet both high school teachers confront classroom tensions that stem from a lack of transparency around these mindset-related goals. I have discussed some of the missed opportunities for transparency and scaffolding in Zachary's classroom above. At Riverside, the rules themselves were highly transparent, but less so were the complex dynamics around race and culture, the intersection of in-school and out-of-school identities, and the teachers'— and students'/families'—potential questions, discomfort, or resistance. Diane sat down of her own accord one day to talk with her students explicitly about some of the rules that governed their belonging in the Riverside community, but it was unclear how common or sustained this practice was. Greater transparency from educators about their instructional design and intent could facilitate better alignment between educator actions and student interpretation of those actions. This is a theme we will continue to see in the college portraits and which I discuss again in chapter 5.

I conclude by noting that the intersection of the belonging and value mindsets—and perhaps a challenge with being fully transparent about these mindset goals—may feel especially salient to twelfth-grade teachers who view themselves as serving what they consider a "disadvantaged" student population. Both Diane and Zachary view the belonging and value mindsets as essential precursors to students being able to "do school" successfully according to White middle-class norms and expectations, now and in the future. Diane talks about high school as a setting where grade-level colleagues "pick up" where the preceding teacher left off, whereas after twelfth grade, "there's nobody after me to help fix it up"—a "really scary" prospect. She perceives a yawning chasm between the secondary and postsecondary sectors—and accompanying pressure to prepare her students for that future unknown. Leveraging the "team spirit" built starting in sixth grade at Riverside to give students a sense of value for college and the ability to conform to college expectations may therefore be a strategy she views as critical to carry students through the "scary" handoff. Zachary expresses a similar sentiment when he describes colleges like Middlebury as not having many students who share a background with OBS students and the pressure on his students (and, implicitly, on him as their teacher) to combat other people's "misconceptions" about them.

At the same time, the high school teachers view the postsecondary sector as dictating the terms of students'—and, indirectly, their own—success. In all of Zachary's reflection about how to change his own practice and OBS's to "legitimize school to students," he never suggests that colleges needed to undertake a similar process. To both him and Diane, the pressure is squarely on them as high school teachers to give students "a product that is going to help them when they walk out of here," in the form of a comprehensive academic and mindset toolkit. They are also aware that their efforts fall short ("Are my kids producing college-ready work? Oftentimes I find myself thinking, 'No'"). I now shift to the postsecondary sector and the educators who are waiting to receive students on the other side of that divide, to examine the contexts in which students' high school belonging and value mindsets, as well as their academic preparation, are put to the test.

Interlude

Transitioning from High School to College

Before resuming with the next focal mindset and educator, I feel a pause is warranted. We have reached the midpoint of the manuscript and the transition from high school to college portraits, paralleling the transition that students make across the sectors—indeed, we are currently in the textual equivalent of the post–high-school no-man's-land gap that Diane finds so "scary." As such, I seek to cast some light ahead of us to see what awaits us on the other side.

As discussed in the conclusion to chapter 2, the belonging and value mindsets remain important considerations as students enter college, and readers will see Liz and Colin's approaches to both embedded in their portraits, even though they are not the focal mindset for either. In addition to being aware of the broader socialization role that writing plays in helping students acclimate to college (Sommers & Saltz, 2004; Sternglass, 1997), both instructors also articulate a desire for their students to feel a sense of belonging within writing itself as a disciplinary practice. Implicit in this cultivation of belonging is the goal for students to be able to transfer their writing skills beyond the first-year writing class, a prominent focus area of composition studies (Nowacek, 2011) and a potential source of perceived value for the students. Thus, again the belonging and value mindsets are linked in the educators' pedagogical thinking: when students feel a stronger sense of belonging in an academic setting, they are more likely to endorse messages of value (including transferability) from the instructor, and conversely when the value of their work is apparent, students are more likely to buy into the class and invest in community membership.

However, while both college instructors do try to promote students' value mindsets toward writing through assignment design, positive affective experiences (for Liz), and transferable frameworks and principles (for Colin), they do not explicitly talk—either to me or the students—about their efforts to convey the value of their course content as much as the high school teachers did. Much as Diane and Zachary were keenly aware of their "underserved" student populations and mission-driven schools, Colin and Liz perceive the students at their highly selective private colleges as achievement-oriented, goal-driven, and self-motivated; like many college faculty members, they seem to assume their students have reasons for being in college (Dja'far et al., 2016; Wallace, 2014). Instead, both instructors' mindset prioritization—and therefore my choice of focal mindset for each of their portraits—seems driven by their perception of the academic transition from high school to college-level work as the most salient experience for their students.

Even for students who have earned admission to selective colleges—and therefore, presumably, demonstrate a baseline level of "preparedness"—the transition from high school to college in the domain of writing presents unique challenges that can implicate student motivation. Reviews of misaligned writing expectations between high school and college have generally focused on large-scale patterns in the lack of substantive writing assigned in high school (Addison & McGee, 2010; Applebee & Langer, 2011; Ransdell & Glau, 1996), though neither Diane's nor Zachary's classroom fell into this category. Evidence also suggests that high school students perceived to be "college-bound" or in higher academic tracks, such as those who would matriculate at places like Mayfield or Abbott, tend to receive writing and reading tasks that better align with college-level work (Patterson & Duer, 2006). However, composition scholars have long noted qualitative differences between writing in college versus in high school. In contrast to highly standardized, rule-driven writing in high school, college writing is theoretical and exploratory (Fanetti et al., 2010); it interacts with thinking to construct complex understandings rather than being a formulaic reporting of what is already known (White, 2010). Relatedly, approaches to the writer's voice also differ; whereas considerations of voice tend to be reserved for creative or narrative writing in high school (Acker & Halasek, 2008), authorial voice is expected in college writing as a way of claiming a stance (Strachan, 2002).

These differences make competence and growth mindsets highly salient as students encounter new expectations for writing in college and possibly new practices around feedback, revision, and grading that align with those expectations. Accordingly, these are the focal mindsets for the two college portraits. I begin with Liz and growth mindset as the deeper-seated phenomenon theorized to be the psychological precursor for the endorsement of different types of achievement goals and beliefs about competence and control. Colin's portrait focuses on the competence mindset as the closely related but slightly downstream phenomenon. Both portraits demonstrate the need for educators to attend closely to the tension in trying to promote the competence and growth mindsets simultaneously, as Liz and Colin search for ways to show students how much they still have to grow as writers while not crushing their belief in their potential to succeed.

For example, readers will notice both instructors grappling with similar challenges related to these mindsets, especially with regards to grading—a topic with deep roots in both motivation and composition scholarship. Both instructors use conventional letter grades, but they both struggle with the impact of letter grades on genuine engagement in the writing and revision process, a focus on personal improvement, creativity and risk-taking in writing, student anxiety, and writing quality. Their pedagogical dilemmas in this area reflect ongoing debates in composition over alternative evaluation models like contract or labor-based grading (Cowan, 2020; Elbow, 1997; Farber, 1990; J. A. Smith, 1999). Similar to Diane's conflict over enforcing potentially paternalistic school rules, Liz also wrestles with the power dynamics in assessing and grading students' academic writing (Inoue, 2019, 2020). Interestingly, however, though Liz and Colin share similar reservations about grades, the grading policies they choose to enact are essentially inverses, as readers will see.

Finally, the competence and growth mindsets are also highly salient to the college portraits because of the role they play in the *instructors'* motivation for and approach to teaching. Beyond changes in the students' experience, the transition from high school to college brings a shift in educators' identities, professional training, and institutional roles. Whereas public school teachers like Diane and Zachary earn certification through coursework and practicum experiences focused on instructional design and delivery, college writing instructors comprise a much broader range of backgrounds. They may be faculty members in English, MFAs, graduate students from assorted humanities or social science disciplines, or, increasingly, nontenured contingent instructors who may be part-time or adjunct and sometimes hired at the last minute (Schell, 2017; Wardle, 2013). They may therefore have very little training in writing pedagogy upon entering the classroom, and the precarity of their positions within the institution may preclude the opportunity to engage in meaningful professional development (Vander Kloet et al., 2017). As such, their own competence and growth mindsets toward teaching deserve attention both for the impact these mindsets can have on the learning experiences the educators provide students in class and for identifying the supports that the educators themselves need to enable them to focus on the valuable work of teaching and learning. I discuss some of these larger systemic issues across sectors in chapter 5, but readers will notice the way they manifest in Liz and Colin's reflections on their instructional choices, and I encourage readers to consider the "parallel mindsets" of students and educators throughout my review of the remaining focal mindsets and the accompanying portraits.

Chapter 3

Trusting the Process

Embracing Growth Mindsets in a
First-Year College Writing Class

Overview: "My ability and competence grow with my effort"

Multiple motivational theories outline the importance of individuals endorsing both a desire to learn and the belief that effort, persistence, and the effective use of learning strategies are the key mechanisms for learning and personal development. These theories underlie the motivational mindset "My ability and competence grow with my effort." My shorthand for this mindset is growth mindset, which is itself one of the key theories behind the mindset statement, and which has received a considerable amount of attention in contemporary popular psychology. However, the nuances of growth mindset, including its relationship to other key ideas in motivation theory, are often not well understood, leading to an oversimplification or even misapplication of the theory to practice. I elaborate on these ideas here to make clear to the reader that my use of the term "growth mindset" goes beyond colloquial understandings of the phrase and instead encapsulates a large body of interlinked motivational constructs.

Growth mindset builds on prior work on the causal attributions that individuals make to explain the sources of their success and failure. These causes have three dimensions: internal to the individual versus external, stable versus changeable, and controllable versus uncontrollable (Weiner, 1986). For example, a student might fail a test and think, "My teacher is always just trying to get us with these super hard tests that nobody can do well on." This student is exhibiting an external attribution for the failure (the teacher and the difficulty of the test is the cause of failure, not the individual student) that is stable (the teacher "always" does this) and uncontrollable ("nobody can do well"). By contrast, a student who fails the same test but thinks, "I really didn't study hard enough for this test—I'll have to do more next time," is attributing the failure to internal, changeable, and controllable causes.

Growth mindset, then, is the more global "self-theory" about intelligence and ability that gives rise to certain attributions (Dweck & Molden, 2017). Students with a growth mindset believe that intelligence can develop through effort and effective strategy use, and therefore they are more likely to attribute both success and failure to internal, changeable, and controllable causes. Students with a fixed mindset believe that intelligence is innate, and therefore may attribute their academic outcomes to internal but stable and uncontrollable causes (e.g., "I'm just not a math person"). Or, like the sample student above, they may attribute their failures to external causes to avoid confronting the possibility of an internal cause because under a fixed mindset, an internal cause of failure signifies innate incompetence or lack of intelligence.

The implications of such attributions can lead students with growth versus fixed mindsets to pursue different kinds of achievement goals, which in turn predict their behaviors (Dweck & Leggett, 1988). Holding a growth mindset is associated with endorsing a mastery goal orientation, where students are motivated to engage in academic tasks in order to develop competence; these students understand that mistakes and failure are a natural part of that learning and development process. Holding a fixed mindset is associated with performance goals (also sometimes called "ego goals"), which are more focused on maintaining an appearance of competence and comparing favorably to peers. Generally, research demonstrates that mastery goals are related to greater interest, perceived competence (discussed further in chapter 4), and engagement, while performance goals are related to more negative academic outcomes such as anxiety, learned helplessness, and decreased engagement (Linnenbrink-Garcia & Patall, 2015).

Researchers of growth mindset and achievement goals have always been interested in the social processes that promote the development of certain kinds of mindsets and goals in classrooms (Urdan & Kaplan, 2020). Some of this work has focused on the benefits of explicitly teaching students about growth mindset (Wiersema et al., 2015; Yeager & Dweck, 2012) and training students to shift their attributions, often by sharing examples of older students describing how they overcame struggles (Haynes et al., 2009). Apart from these specific interventions, however, educators can also promote growth mindset and mastery goals during the course of regular instruction. Indeed, motivational work in this area increasingly emphasizes the need to attend to the interactions between students' mindsets and the psychological "affordances" within a classroom environment that mediate the relationship between mindsets and outcomes, rather than focusing exclusively on changing mindsets (Hecht et al., 2021). In other words, it is not enough for students simply to have the "right" mindset; optimal outcomes occur when students who endorse a growth mindset also find learning environments that provide opportunities for them to exercise that mindset to its full potential for motivation and learning.

One body of research examines the nature of educators' praise and feedback as related to students' growth versus fixed mindsets and mastery versus performance goals. Studies show that students' growth mindset and mastery goal orientation are enhanced when teachers attribute students' success to effort or strategy ("process praise") over praising individual characteristics such as intelligence ("person praise"; Mueller & Dweck, 1998). Conversely, educators' responses to student mistakes, whether through written feedback on assignments or during live classroom instruction, can similarly reinforce students' mindsets and goals. Educators may focus on an incorrect answer over the student's reasoning or disproportionately comfort students about failure in ways that imply that mistakes are to be avoided because they reflect poorly on a student's ability (Rattan et al., 2012; Sun, 2018a), instead of framing mistakes as an inherent part of learning and/or an opportunity to think differently (Kazemi & Stipek, 2009; Santagata, 2005).

Additionally, evaluation practices can convey implicit messages to students about the relative value of mastery or performance goals in a classroom, which can promote or inhibit the cultivation of growth mindset (Cimpian et al., 2007; T. Smith et al., 2018). For example, grading on a curve or conveying an expected distribution of grades can promote performance goals in students by highlighting their relative standing and competition with each other. By contrast, using rubrics that convey clear standards for quality work, providing specific feedback, and allowing students to revise their work to demonstrate improvement can promote mastery goals and growth mindset (Patall et al., 2022).

Beyond evaluation, feedback, and praise, foundational classroom practices that seem less obviously tied to success and failure can also influence students' beliefs about intelligence, attributions for success and failure, and achievement goals. For example, support for belonging and positive social relationships in class have been shown consistently to predict students' endorsement of mastery goals and recognition of mastery-supportive classrooms (L. H. Anderman et al., 2011; Patrick et al., 2011; Turner et al., 2002, 2013), perhaps because they create a psychologically safe environment in which to struggle and receive feedback. However, a warm classroom climate may not be sufficient to optimize motivational patterns, especially for students who are already highly mastery driven and confident (Liu et al., 2023). Somewhat counterintuitively, challenging tasks are important for promoting mastery goals, as long as there is sufficient support for students (Liu et al., 2023; Turner et al., 2002). Academic work that is too easy or that demands only surface-level engagement can promote the desire to perform competence rather than genuinely develop mastery, or it can be interpreted by students as evidence of the educator's lack of faith in students' ability to handle more difficult work (Chmielewski et al., 2013). Supports for the value mindset, such as giving students meaningful choice and honoring student preferences, can also encourage students to pursue mastery goals over competing against classmates (Ciani et al., 2010).

However, despite the popularity of growth mindset and a healthy body of research on how to promote it in classrooms, there is wide variability in educators' own growth mindset beliefs, their growth mindset-supportive practices, and the alignment between the two. In most cases, instructional practices in a given classroom do not promote either fixed mindset or growth mindset in a perfect dichotomy; rather, practices fall at different points along a continuum between fixed and growth mindset, and they also fluctuate as educators respond to different circumstances (Sun, 2018b). Recent work also suggests that instructors' own mindsets may influence the effectiveness of growth mindset interventions (Yeager et al., 2022), though there are lingering disputes within the field about whether the contextual factor driving those differences is teachers' mindsets or their use of instructional practices that may or may not fully align with their mindset beliefs (Park et al., 2016).

The following portrait of Liz Cartwright reflects the complex implications emerging from contemporary growth mindset research about the importance—but difficulty—of targeting both the student's deep-seated beliefs about intelligence as well as the instructional practices *and*, potentially, intelligence mindsets of the instructor. Liz embraces the idea of shifting students' beliefs about their writing ability as an intuitive part of her approach to first-year composition. Like Diane (who received professional development on growth mindset), Liz attends closely to students' emotional experiences, insecurities, and sense of belonging in the classroom and the school as a whole as potential impacts on their intelligence and ability mindsets. She also employs many of the practices described above as growth mindset and mastery supportive: she champions personal improvement over grades, endorses the writing process and revision as key mechanisms for developing mastery, and encourages student choice and voice in the authorship of their writing pieces. However, Liz's case also demonstrates a tension between her strategies for trying to shift students' ability mindsets and the affordances available in her classroom for students to actually use those mindsets to further their motivation and writing skills.

Trusting the Process

DEVELOPING A PRACTICE REGIMEN

Turn left as you exit Oak Bridge School and then right when the street intersects the main road, and you will reach Zachary's alma mater, Mayfield University, in three long city blocks. The main campus is on the north side of the street—a classic green-lawned academic quad opens directly onto the busy road—but the university also spills across the street, with shiny new construction buildings and parking lots tucked in between churches, nail salons, a Tedeschi minimart, and tiny mom-and-pop ethnic restaurants. As I wind through the main campus, passing the five-story university library, the noise of the main road fades quickly; nestled among quiet side streets, I might be on any suburban college campus. Door-to-door, it is half a mile—ten minutes' walk—from OBS to the building where Liz Cartwright convenes her first-year undergraduate writing class.

Liz's classroom is at the end of a second-floor hallway that primarily houses the modern languages department: colorful posters of far-away locations, Japanese calligraphy, and French versions of Marlon Brando movies line the corridor walls. The classroom itself, though, is a neutral and nondescript rectangular space: a wooden teacher's desk sits at one of the short ends, in front of a brown chalkboard, a wall-mounted projection screen, an outdated technology cart with a box television and VCR shoved into one corner, and the newer version with a sleek flat-screen monitor in the opposite corner. Occupying the student desks that line the remaining three walls in an angular U-shape are eighteen students, all of whom arrived scrupulously early for the first meeting of the 9 a.m. expository writing class—although doing so may have required some hustle from one young man who is wearing Christmas-patterned fleece pajama pants. The class is a mixture of, in Liz's description, "a lot of White kids from tiny towns in New England somewhere who've never met a person of color before, and then all these international students" who often come from "really wealthy families." This year, there are only two domestic students of color in the class; the other non-White students have all spent significant time living overseas.[1] Mayfield's typical first-year cohort is around 14 percent international students and 22 percent domestic students of color; 22 percent are Pell Grant recipients.

The students have just concluded the opening activity of interviewing and then introducing a partner to the class, and Liz is now ready to deliver her overview of the course. She stands up from the teacher's desk where she sat listening to the introductions and paces a little in front of the chalk board as she talks. A slim, White woman in her thirties, she has traded the t-shirt and cotton shorts she wore for our first interview last week for discernibly "teacher clothes": a mustard-colored blouse, pencil skirt, and black flats. Her long brown hair hangs straight down her back as she tells students, "I'm hoping this class shifts your way of thinking about writing from how you may have thought about it in high school." During college and beyond, she says, "you will always have to write and communicate with your writing," whether they are chemistry majors or interested in economics, as some students mentioned in their introductions. She picks up a piece of chalk and writes the numbers 1 through 5 vertically on the board, which cues a rustle of notebook pages rippling across the room as the brand-new college students diligently prepare to take notes.

As she introduces the class to the students, Liz fills in the numbered list with the five principles underlying her course design: *1) Process; 2) Awareness; 3) Tools; 4) Practice;* and *5) Community.* She stresses to students that "there's no such thing as a perfect essay, a perfect finished product." Instead, the class is going to be "focused on different ways we write and revise to get to a product YOU like. Like most things," Liz says, "writing is very responsive to practice. The more you practice, the better you get." She assures the students that by the end of the semester, after all the writing they do together, "you'll get better. It's impossible not to. And you'd be surprised at how much better you get with practice."

Overall, Liz tells the students, "I hope this is not a super stressful environment." She alludes back to the partner interview prompt, *What are you nervous about?* to which half the class responded with academic concerns: five students articulated worries about getting bad grades, "not being successful," and failing; four were worried about time management and balancing classes with sleep. "We'll do a lot of writing in class," Liz continues. "We'll do everything in incremental steps. There are no exams. There are no surprises." The syllabus lays out all the paper deadlines and expectations, "so you'll be able to plan."

She pauses to take questions, and there are several: students ask about laptop use in class, the typical length of papers, homework assignments, the nature of the final paper, and then, with a boldness that surprises me from a college freshman in his very first class, Ben asks, "How many times have you taught this class? Like, is this your first time?" Unfazed, Liz answers the question just as she has all the others, pausing only to search her memory and do the mental arithmetic: every semester for the past four years—two at the flagship state university, two so far at Mayfield—and sometimes multiple concurrent sections, "so . . ." she calculates aloud, "like fifteen times?" The students seem surprised and, I think, impressed—or reassured. "Yeah, lucky for you, I get better every time," Liz chuckles, echoing her earlier point about writing.

Although Liz tells me that she initially "found English to be super easy" as a student herself, and interpreted that perceived ease as a reason to major in it—"some people said that it wasn't easy for them, and I was like, 'Oh! Well then, maybe this is what I'll do, since it's easy for me' "—she got "so psyched out" and "paralyzed" over writing in her MFA program in fiction at the flagship state university that she could not resume "writing things I really really liked" until after she graduated. As a professional writer now as well as a writing instructor, she firmly believes that students should focus more on personal growth rather than trying to achieve a mythical "perfect finished product." She also espouses other core tenets of growth mindset: writing skills are malleable, and "the best way to get better at writing is to practice." Liz particularly emphasizes that what she calls "brute force" practice "is sort of the only—or," she clarifies, "the best way, I think, to get better. Like, just to do it as much as possible, over and over again."

Engaging students in a "brute force" practice regimen is therefore one of the main underlying design principles for Liz's class. She assigns five papers over the course of the semester—a personal essay, an analytic essay, a research paper, a creative analysis of place, and a final reflection—with multiple drafts and supplemental writing exercises accompanying each one. As she pledges to students on the first day, she reserves time in class for them to produce the volume of writing she asks for, a strategy she carries with her from the pedagogical training she received at the state university, where MFA and PhD students teach undergraduate writing courses—often their first experience leading a classroom. To counter the pressure that Liz and many other instructors felt to devise endless activities to fill class time, the instructional supervisors assured them, "This is a writing class. [Students] should be writing a lot of the time in class." Now in her fifth year of teaching, Liz continues to adhere to this philosophy: I observe all twenty-three sessions where her full class meets during the semester, and seventeen of them include several minutes of independent writing time for students during the seventy-five-minute session.

In addition to believing fundamentally that practice is the primary mechanism for writing improvement, Liz recognizes that mindsets around ability and effort may be particularly vulnerable for first-year college students. "Their status is completely changing from being sort of the top of the class, the big, important, know-it-alls in high school, as seniors," she explains, "to being terrified," feeling like "no one knows them, and they don't know anything." The recalibration of students' self-concept may be especially stark at a school like Mayfield, with its highly competitive admissions standard; students who were high achievers at their respective secondary schools—recall Talia's acceptance to Mayfield being worthy of the morning announcements at Riverside Academy—are suddenly just part of the crowd. On top of that, Liz notes, "for the first time a lot of them are away from home," which introduces new challenges that can interfere with students' ability to establish academic routines, including managing their time for sufficient writing practice. First-year students often "don't have a lot of time to focus outside of class," she says. "They have all these other things they're doing, all these other tests they're studying for, clubs that they're involved in, their roommate's having sex in the middle of the night and keeping them up," she laughs. "And so, part of the class is like, defending some time there for them to actually try to concentrate and write." She restates it for emphasis: "Defending that time for them in class, I think, is really valuable." Liz views the allocation of class time as a strategy for conveying to students the importance of continued writing practice and supporting their overall adjustment to college; the two processes are complementary and mutually reinforcing.

Leveraging class time to support students' mindsets around and approach to writing and the overall college transition may be especially vital for relatively lower-performing students, a category that includes Liz's students in the domain of writing. Although Mayfield itself is highly selective, enrollment in the first-year writing class is reserved for the lowest performers on a summer writing assessment that all incoming students must complete unless they have received a 4 or above on the AP English Literature exam. According to Mayfield's director of undergraduate writing, about one-sixth of the first-year cohort—approximately one hundred students—typically place into the class as an additional step before they are allowed to enroll in a writing-intensive disciplinary course, which is required of all Mayfield students for graduation. Liz's students are therefore also confronting an institutional message that they are among the minority of students who are not yet ready to tackle a baseline requirement. For some of them, placing into Liz's class seems to affirm their existing negative mindsets about their writing ability. *It actually seemed kind of embarrassing when I did get my placement results,* one student writes in her final reflection. *I didn't really want to tell anyone that I was taking Expository Writing.*

Liz is therefore trying to promote a growth mindset toward writing among students who are already adjusting their academic self-concept as part of the college transition and who potentially feel embarrassed and stigmatized as bad writers. Her decision to engage students in a "brute-force" practice regimen is an important first step in implementing growth mindset principles, but the specific choices she makes about what that practice looks like and how to incentivize students' participation reveal both the opportunities and challenges that educators face in trying to enact truly growth mindset-supportive practices.

CULTIVATING VOICE

The Mayfield English Department offices are housed in a gorgeous pale yellow Victorian house, one of several on a side street at the edge of the main campus. Wooden floors sheathed in worn carpeting creak under my feet as I mount the very narrow stairs to Liz's third-floor office. The air is warm and vaguely dusty. Several copies of a sign congratulating a faculty member on earning tenure are posted throughout the building; other flyers advertise clubs, courses, and the new creative writing major debuting this fall. At this hour of the morning, most of the doors are closed, and I can see small faux-wood nameplates screwed on each one, just above eye level. The office at the end of the third-floor hall does not have a nameplate; instead, *Liz Cartwright* and three other instructors' names are printed on a piece of beige cardstock with a red border. One of Liz's office mates, an early modern specialist, has tacked an additional piece of paper to the door that features her photo and a brief biography. Above these identifiers, a bumper sticker advises visitors to *Be the person your dog thinks you are.*

Liz's office is long and narrow and sparsely decorated, as if none of the four occupants wants to claim too much ownership of the space. The wall-mounted shelves are largely empty other than four stacks of writing books piled on one and some personal trinkets on another, including felt finger puppets of medieval figures (a princess, a king, a knight, a priest). A Mayfield campus map is taped up next to the door. The desk faces the middle of the long wall opposite the door, and Liz has pulled a wooden chair up alongside it for students to sit in when they arrive for their twenty-minute, one-on-one writing conferences on their Unit 2 analytic essays. Students have the choice of responding to one of two essays on race, identity, and language—James Baldwin's "If Black English Isn't a Language, Then Tell Me, What Is?" or Richard Rodriguez's "The North American"—in *a "conversation" between you and the author—one that takes your own ideas and the writer's seriously,* Liz's assignment sheet explains.

Alexander, Liz's third appointment of the morning, strolls in promptly when the previous student vacates the office. Other than his open-toed black athletic slides and a pink Nike cap slung backwards on his head, he might be wearing the clothes he slept in: a rumpled t-shirt, sweatpants, and tube socks. He returns Liz's greeting politely and hands her a printed draft.

"How'd this go?" Liz asks him as he settles into the chair.

"'S alright," he says, and then he confesses that he had several other assignments to do last night, so he ended up writing this draft "in like an hour and a half."

"Oh man," Liz chuckles, flipping through the three typed pages in her hand. "I wish I could write that fast!"

Liz invites Alexander to begin, having told students previously in class that they would be reading their drafts aloud in the conferences—a "useful" practice "because you catch things you don't otherwise." Indeed, Alexander notices and comments on several of his own typos and grammatical mistakes, even as he is reading so fast and with so little inflection that it is hard for me to follow along. Liz has an easier time as she scans the printed copy, a pen held loosely in one hand, occasionally nodding or making a note on the page. As she has done with the previous students, she murmurs, "Great," after the last sentence in the introductory paragraph, and then she praises Alexander when he finishes: "Awesome. Great job. I really love the quotes that you were able to pull out." She tells him his paper is "on track" and that he is able to "explain what Baldwin says and why you agree with it."

However, she calls his attention to some vaguely stated claims, pointing out that the lack of clarity often seems to happen in "places where you're trying to avoid saying 'I.'"

"My teachers always told me not to," Alexander explains. "I don't even mean to do it; it's just what I was taught."

"Yeah," Liz sympathizes. "It takes time to get used to using 'I' and not feeling like you're doing something wrong."

Coaching students into using first person in their writing is a common experience for Liz and represents more than just a grammatical or stylistic change; it is a perspective shift for students "to see themselves as having a valid opinion and a valid voice in the conversations they're entering into," which Liz sees as an important motivator for the "brute-force practice" required to improve. "Up until college," she says, "I sense that they aren't taught that they are the expert or that they have valid ideas . . . They're not really taught to trust themselves." Instead, she believes that students are often taught "to write in this style that connotes a 'truth,' like you're proving something scientifically, and it has to be this airtight argument. It can't just be, 'This is my experience and this is valuable.'" As a result, she thinks many students enter her class thinking, "What does it matter what I think about this? I'm an eighteen-year-old college student." Liz wants to impress upon them that "it's time to start thinking that what you think matters because it does."

Liz therefore wants to show students that they will be expending effort in her class in service of creative, open-ended assignments that they can personalize and use to cultivate their authorial voice. Like Zachary, she hopes that validating students' ideas and lived experiences will help them feel more invested in the assignments and motivated to exert more effort. She encourages students to incorporate personal experiences as evidence to support their claims in their responses to Baldwin or Rodriguez. In the personal essay, she asks students to identify and reflect on a "seeming con-tradiction" in their identity. The MLA-formatted research paper is required by the department, but Liz gives the students free choice of topic. In Unit 4, students compose a written piece that can take any form—most students write fairly conventional essays, but one writes a letter to a friend; another, a play—and deliver an accompanying oral presentation that analyzes *a piece of media from, describing, or representing your hometown, or the place you're "from"* and discusses *how your hometown helped shape . . . the way you think about things, your experiences, beliefs, actions,* according to the assignment sheet. In the final assignment, a personal reflection on their growth as writers over the semester, several students share the effect of Liz's assignments on their mindsets and effort toward writing:

> *I have found that I am much better at writing essays that are more personal. I am able to write more fluidly, the word float out of my mind and onto my paper. There is a personal connection that makes the paper almost more important to me as well. I feel like there is a larger desire to do well on it. I actually enjoy writing it as well. In high school, we did not do as many writing assignments that were personal . . . Once we got to Mayfield, it was nice to be able to write about something more personal for once.*
>
> *Rediscovering one's curiosity is no easy task. . . . In high school, I was always told what to do my research on, and it always had to be formally written. There was no such thing and choosing your audience, or adding in personal anecdotes . . . I used to like writing, but in my later years of high school, it became something that I dreaded. Thanks to this class, I've rediscovered something that was such a huge love of mine. I truly felt like I could be myself and was able to express myself freely.*

Throughout her course, Liz aims to encourage similar feelings of free expression in all her students by imparting a core belief that she repeats to me multiple times in interviews: "In writing, there's not a 'Truth' with a capital T." She wants students "to start thinking about there not really being a right or a wrong answer or a way to get an A." Instead, she wants to validate their personal subjectivities, get them to think "more deeply about ideas," and to lower their psychological barriers toward writing. I see Liz employ this tactic at the beginning of the writing conference that follows Alexander's:

"How'd it go?" Liz asks, accepting the printed draft that Vera hands over.

Vera sighs a little with a self-conscious smile. "I don't know; I feel like I'm just doing what I did in high school, so I don't know if I did it right."

"We'll see," Liz says in a mock-ominous tone, and then laughs. "No, I'm sure you did, and there's no right or wrong anyway."

Consistent with her philosophy of rejecting capital-T "Truth" and notions of right and wrong to encourage students' exploration and growth, Liz tries not to assert herself as an omniscient authority and arbiter of "Truth" for her students. She is judicious about intervening in students' interpretive process; while she will correct what she sees as major misconceptions or oversights, she tells Vera later in the writing conference to "focus on what you're most interested in" from Baldwin's essay and "if there are other things in this essay that are unclear to you . . . just leave it out." Likewise, she does not give student guiding questions with their assigned course readings because "I sort of just want them to read and see whatever jumps out at them," she tells me, "to give them a little more freedom in just what they like or what they pick up on . . . It's just like reading for pleasure."

Liz also seeks to mitigate her authority by using peer review to disrupt many students' preconceived notions of the teacher as the only useful source of feedback; a corollary to students recognizing their own expertise is recognizing their peers' expertise as well. Peer review often constitutes the major activity for a given session of Liz's class, as students trade papers multiple times with different partners and different prompts aimed at validating the reactions of other students as discerning readers of a work-in-progress. With the personal essays, Liz directs students to search for a line that could serve as a new opening; with the research papers, peer reviewers report back to each other what they learned about each other's topics to test the clarity of the writing. The frequency of Liz's peer review activities normalizes the practice of sharing imperfect drafts and ensures that students are doing a high proportion of the work: both important mechanisms in the development of growth mindset. Liz also tells students that peer review is an authentic part of writing in the real world, a fact that a couple of students comment on in their final reflections:

> As I am planning to be a biochemist and would probably want to publish my research, I am going to peer review others' works and be peer reviewed by others, and [this class] prepared me for that. It is a process that I will need to hold close to my heart even after I have stepped out of college and into the real world.
> Many of the things I learned are not only useful in writing but are also useful in many other aspects of learning. . . . The greatest writers in the world still get their work proofread. The greatest pieces of literature in human history have been reviewed by at least one person.

These students have made an additional inference relevant to growth mind-set: they recognize that biochemists, researchers with advanced degrees, and "the greatest writers in the world" still seek out feedback to improve their work; the second student also recognizes that this principle applies to "other aspects of learning," not just writing. In any domain, being "great" is not synonymous with automatic, effortless perfection.

Importantly, however, growth mindset fundamentally requires students to adopt an internal attribution for their own development: students must think about their improvement in first person, just as they learn to use first person in their writing. An instructor can craft compelling writing tasks, set writing exercises, and mandate peer review, but students must recognize that the responsibility for growth ultimately lies within. This is not an easy process; in his final reflection, one student describes the eventual shift in his attribution of responsibility from Liz to himself over the course of the semester:

> You[2] were a little bit disappointed. . . . Your professor gave you some exercises to do in class, but . . . all the exercises in class did not seem to help you in your writing career . . . "Will this be a waste of a course?" you asked yourself.
>
> No. I am writing this to tell you that you will learn some-thing. . . . Although your professor would help you a lot in the future, the person who would contribute the most to your improvement is, surprisingly, yourself . . . She did not help you do those exercises; you did all of them by yourself. . . . What you finally learned is that you are the only one who can improve your writing skills by practicing more and more throughout your life.

I see in this student's reflection the echoes of Diane recognizing the power of "get[ting] out of [students'] way" sometimes, and Zachary's belief that "no one likes being told why something is important, you gotta come to it yourself." The design of Liz's assignments and exercises and her commitment to "defending time" for students to write in class have provided this student with the right balance of external structure and adequate freedom and space for internal mindset development. Finding this balance for all students is the paradoxical challenge for instructors in mindset development work. They cannot directly influence students' internal psychology; they can only set external conditions that they hope students will interpret in the desired ways. As we will see, this tension is particularly evident when it comes to students' internal interpretations of external incentives and reward structures.

PRACTICE INCENTIVES

I arrive about five minutes early to the second class of the semester, and there are far fewer students here early—about half the class—though they all end up on time and sitting in almost exactly the same seats as last time. "I'm so tired," Dee tells her neighbor, Rafael, who nods in sympathy. "This is my only class today—I'm so glad," he says.

Liz wants to review the syllabus in more depth today, after the high-level overview last time. She opens the document on the classroom computer, projecting it onto the screen behind her desk as she talks through it in order, reaching the section on grading a few minutes in:

Your course grade will be broken down the following way:

Unit I: 10%

Unit II: 20%

Unit III: 20%

Unit IV: 20%

Final Reflection: 10%

Writing Community Membership: 20%

Total: 100%

Your grade for each unit will be based on process (that is, assignments that help you produce your final draft, like exploratory writing and initial and revised drafts) and product (the final draft).

Liz explains that the process and product grades are "sort of blended together" in the calculation of the final grade for the unit. Elaborating on the written description, she tells the students that the product grade is the quality grade they receive on their final essay in the unit, while the process grade is assessed through a unit portfolio, containing all of their drafts, peer-review comments, writing exercises, and other in-class activities. Students will submit these portfolios at the end of each unit, along with their final essay.

Derek raises his hand for clarification: "So, if you complete all the steps, your process grade is fine?"

"Yeah," Liz agrees. "If you do all the steps, you'll get an A on the process grade, and then the product grade is whatever you get on the final essay." (She qualifies this description to me slightly afterwards, explaining that she might vary the process grades on technically complete portfolios if one student "[wrote] a sentence where someone else is writing a page," but in general, her policy on the portfolio assignments is, "You did it or you didn't do it.") Derek seems satisfied and doesn't ask a follow-up.

Feedback and grading policies play a critical role in classroom messaging around ability and growth mindset. For the most part, Liz determines her own grading scheme; Mayfield has few departmental grading policies, other than that students who fail must retake the course. (Both Liz and the writing director, however, express the sentiment that "you have to really try hard" to fail, either by simply not showing up to class or not turning in work.) Nor are there departmental standards for evaluating student work: although there is a rubric for the placement exam essays, neither it nor the exam itself is automatically shared with the course instructors.[3] When I interview the writing director, she muses that "we should do a sort of norming session" with the instructors on assessing student writing, but that "we don't pay them nearly enough" to justify requiring part-time faculty to attend department meetings on their off days: to do so would be "unethical," she says. For her part, Liz tells me that she "would love to have more meetings with other teachers and talk about things and hear their ideas," having found that a professional learning community made her instructional training at the state university "a really valuable environment" for pedagogical growth. "The change from that to adjuncting—and I don't think it's adjuncting specifically at Mayfield; I think it's just adjuncting in general," she clarifies, "—is pretty stark. Like, no one knows my face" at Mayfield. The department is "pretty hands-off, unless you come to them with a problem."

Thus, left mostly to her own devices, Liz finds grades a source of major tension when trying to deliver a course focused on the writing process and individual improvement. Ideally, she says, "I wish that there weren't grades in a writing class. I just see it as, we're all there working on this thing together, practicing and practicing, and getting as good as we each can individually." Her written feedback to students conveys a sense of how she would prefer to engage with them over their work. She invariably begins by identifying the piece's positive qualities: *Great idea development!* she writes on an A– paper. *Great revision—I just wanted a little more on some ideas!* she tells a student who earned a B+. *Good observation in the middle!* she notes on a B paper. In the margins of student drafts, she brackets off sections of text to praise with *yes!* or *good*. Upon receiving drafts back in class one day, two students delight in Liz's use of *LOL* in the margin. Liz also chooses to begin the semester with a personal essay in part because she feels this genre presents the best opportunity to "draw out the things that [students are] already doing really well in their writing and to point out to them, 'Look at how you're engaging with the audience in this way and how impactful it is.'" By emphasizing students' strengths in her feedback, she hopes to combat the psychological barriers of distaste, resentment, and/or insecurity toward writing that impede the mindset to improve.

Likewise, Liz views grades as potentially reinforcing student anxieties and inhibitions, so she does what she can in her own class to neutralize their negative impact. "I don't know if this is the best philosophy," she admits to me, "but I want [the students] to not be worried about this class . . . not feel dread, and not feel fear, and not feel like they're doing a bad job. And I think that that actually makes them better." She names a student whose papers "technically aren't interesting . . . Like, all of his sentences sound the same; it sounds like he's just on the phone talking to his friend," she chuckles. "But if he feels good about it and wants to keep writing, then his writing will be WAY better than if he feels bad about it, you know? So I feel like grades in writing classes should just be encouraging. 'Cause there's no way for someone to improve if they don't write, and the only way to get them to write is if they like it."

Incentivizing students' writing production by reducing their anxiety and getting them to "like" and "feel good" about their writing is therefore the guiding principle for Liz's grading structure; her grades mirror her enthusiastic and encouraging written feedback. She is particularly generous with grades in Unit 1 in order to help students to "trust" that they won't be receiving "a disastrous grade as long as they're addressing some of the things that I tell them to." As her syllabus breakdown spells out, Unit 1 is also worth only 10 percent of the course grade—half as much as Units 2 through 4—to reduce early-semester anxiety and to provide students with a calibration period to see that the feedback on the drafts "eventually translated into an A– so I'm gonna kinda relax," Liz laughs. She then modulates the product grades somewhat for the following two assignments, allowing a wider range, but the final two units are "easier to get good grades on." In every unit, the process and product grades are weighted equally, with the process grade serving as the tiebreaker if necessary: a student who receives an A on process and an A– on product receives an A for the unit overall. The students' process grades are therefore cumulatively worth 40 percent of their semester grade, equal to the 40 percent devoted to the product grades on student papers (with the remaining 20 percent going to "writing community membership"). At the end of the semester, Liz tells me that the distribution of overall course grades in the class is consistent with previous cohorts: "more than half As, a little less than half Bs, and then a couple Cs and a D"—the last bestowed on a student who exceeded the five allowed absences and consistently failed to turn in required drafts.

Liz herself acknowledges that there are unresolved tensions in her grading philosophy, her enactment of that philosophy, and the students' grade-related goals and meaning making around the purpose of their effort—particularly at a selective college like Mayfield. "I feel like it might be a state school versus private school" thing, Liz says, but she finds Mayfield students "very, very sort of success focused" in terms of having already identified career goals and necessary steps to get there: "like, 'I wanna be a doctor, and here's what I have to do to get there.'" By contrast, she says, at "the state schools I've been to, both as a student and a teacher"—in addition to attending a state university for her MFA, Liz earned her undergraduate degree from the University of Michigan—"the students all kind of don't know what they're doing or why they're there. They're like, 'this is the thing you do after high school.'" That lack of purpose presents its own potential challenges, but conversely, Liz feels that Mayfield students can be "very focused on their grades . . . they're less focused on learning and more focused on like, 'what do you want me to do to get an A?'" She laughs, a little sardonically. "You know? Which is a little bit of like a high school mentality, I think." She continues:

> And I think actually the difference in my goals and their goals creates a lot of frustration for them. We're not communicating clearly with each other. Like when I give them comments on their initial drafts . . . they're like, "well what does this mean . . . like, would this be a B? Or would this be a C? How do I get to an A?" And I'm like, "What I want you to do is complicate this

argument" . . . You know, we're not talking in the same sort of framework. And so they feel—especially in the beginning before they see that, like, basically everyone gets Bs and As—a lot of anxiety that they're not understanding what they have to do to get what they want. And I can't . . . I can't really deal in that economy with what I want them to get from it.

Bestowing "encouraging" grades is therefore a way that Liz tries to foster students' authentic enjoyment of writing and motivate their continued practice of the skill, but it is also a concession to her students' more transactional "economy"; she theorizes that giving the students what they most want will free them up cognitively and emotionally to engage in what she wants for them.

Liz is aware, however, that she sometimes "struggle[s]" to strike the right balance with her "encouraging" grades: easing students' anxieties but also keeping them engaged in a process of effortful self-improvement. "Sometimes that'll give them the freedom to focus on what I want them to focus on, and sometimes it gives them the freedom to not revise that much 'cause they're like, 'Oh, this class is easy,'" Liz says. "I don't want them to stress out about their grades, but I don't want them to think it's not something that they need to try at, either." She knows that "doing" and "thinking" are not necessarily synonymous—"like someone could not write that much but could be thinking about it a lot," or vice versa—so assessing student effort based on production is not a "foolproof" method. "And there are some students who are, at this stage in their lives, better writers than other students," she adds, "so making a great essay isn't as much effort for them. And so, do you reward having a great product more than the effort that some other students put in to make a lesser product?" Liz is uncomfortable with how "murky" and "subjective" this question is, "so usually it just ends up that everyone gets pretty good grades," she laughs.

Without a clear alternative strategy, Liz opts to keep her generous approach to grading, prioritizing the potential positive emotional benefits for students who are willing to engage in the process and accepting the tradeoff that other students may disinvest. "For me at least," she tells the class on the last day of the semester, "I noticed a huge change in confidence in your writing . . . a lot of you realized that you ARE writing, you're good at it, you're finding your voice, you know what you're interested in and have something to say . . . that's a really important step." This uptick in confidence is precisely what Liz believes students—particularly weak or reluctant writers—need to motivate their continued effort and participation in a writing development process. Enacting a growth mindset, however, involves not just the willingness to exert effort toward improvement, but also persisting with that effort through setbacks and discouraging situations. Liz is aware that her "encouraging" approach to grading can create a tension over the former, but it also implicates the latter: if students consistently receive "pretty good grades" on their writing to boost their confidence, what opportunities exist for them to practice and make meaning of failure?

Practicing Failure

"Liz," Sara says, breaking the near-silence that has descended on the classroom during a peer review activity. "Did you grade our portfolios?"

Sitting at her desk, Liz smiles a little, as if she knows where this is going. She carried an extra tote bag into class today and stowed it under her desk alongside her purse, but it is clearly visible to any students who are paying attention—as Sara evidently is. Liz affirms that she has graded the Unit 1 portfolios but that she will hand them back at the end of class.

This news prompts a flurry of talk and activity, mostly from Sara's side of the classroom but rippling to other areas as well, as students want to know if they can get their assignments back now, and also how they did. "Yeah, Liz, did I fail?" Charlotte asks. Liz assures her that nobody failed, but Charlotte counters: "OK, how bad would getting a C be?"

"Well," says Liz, "A C is average . . ."

"Ugh," Charlotte says dismissively. "What was the lowest grade in this class?"

Liz pauses, and I'm not sure if her hesitation is from reluctance to share, trying to remember the grade range, or merely a flair for the dramatic. "No one got lower than a C," she finally says. This is apparently far from reassuring, as several students feverishly discuss the new information amongst themselves, and the contagion spreads to the back wall near me: Michael says something about a C+ and Dee moans, "I don't want a C." Liz overhears and intones dramatically, in a deep voice, "Everyone got a C. Heh, heh, heh. No, I'm just kidding," she says hastily, chuckling.

The students drop the subject as more of them finish reviewing their partner's draft and begin sharing their feedback. Thirteen minutes later, though, after the class has transitioned to a new writing task, they resume pestering Liz, with Leila wheedling, "Can you PLEASE give us our portfolios?"

Liz holds firm that she's giving them out at the end of class because "I don't want the distraction." She assures them, again, that "everyone did fine."

"What do you define as 'fine'?" Marcus asks.

"Yeah, that could mean a lot of different things," Leila agrees eagerly. "Every teacher has their own 'fine.'"

"That's so true," says Sara.

"Excuse me? When are we receiving our portfolios back?" Jackson—who has otherwise been quietly writing the whole time—asks with total innocence, perhaps believing this to be the first time the question has been posed today.

"Everyone's really, really excited to get them," Marcus deadpans, which makes Liz laugh.

"C'mon, Liz," Sara presses.

"You gotta focus," Liz protests mildly.

"I'm finished," Sara retorts triumphantly.

"My plan to not distract you with this is not working," Liz announces with a chuckle.

"Once you give it to us, we'll just look and put them away," Sara bargains unconvincingly.

Liz tries to ignore Sara by doing a time check on the rest of the class and giving them two more minutes to write.

This scene is a literal embodiment of many of the grading dilemmas Liz has articulated to me—several students are not focusing on or engaging deeply with the learning task at hand because they are too preoccupied with their grades—but it also raises a critical question for growth mindset development: How are students constructing meaning around the idea and experience of failure? The class collectively seems to agree that a C is equivalent to a failing grade, rejecting the notion that such a grade could be considered "average" or "fine." Charlotte seems to be angling for Liz to publicly repudiate the idea that she could have failed and asking for the information she needs to calibrate how she stacks up against her classmates once she does receive her grade. While Liz tells me that students are always anxious before receiving back their first grade of the semester, an only slightly more muted scene plays out a month later when the students learn that Liz has graded their Unit 2 essays and portfolios: though Liz again hands back papers at the end of class so that students "don't get distracted by what you got or why," the students continue to perform identities centered on grades through comments that are audible to me as well as their peers. "I don't like that minus sign," Michael says, while Dee asks Liz from across the room, "Is there anything higher than an A?" Through these classroom exchanges, the students enact the norm that an A is the only acceptable grade; all the remaining grades below that simply represent relative gradations of failure.

According to their expansive view of unacceptable grades, Liz's students do experience what they consider to be "failure" even within her generous grading policy; however, the critical issue for their growth mindset development is their understanding of what these "failing" essay grades reflect and how they can use the feedback to improve next time. This is an area that Liz self-identifies as a pedagogical challenge for her; she freely concedes that "there isn't as much transparency in the grading process as I think [students] would like and as I would like." She grades essays holistically and does not give students a rubric to translate these letter grades into a broader framework of writing strengths and weaknesses. "When I first started teaching" at the state university, she explains, "I would be super, like, mathematical and hair-splitting about all of these categories and spend forever figuring out grades for everything. And then, when I stopped doing that and was just sort of like, 'ehhh, that's an A-' or, 'that's like a B+' or whatever, I found that those results were exactly the same as if I spent hours and hours toiling over it." She recognizes, though, that the rationale behind the grades "would be clearer" to students if she had some kind of rubric or framework, but "I really struggle with trying to fit everyone's effort into the same . . . 'map,' I guess."

Liz actually gives her students a framework for their writing early in the semester, but she never explicitly returns to it or builds on it as the semester progresses. On the second day of class, after reviewing the syllabus, she draws a version of the rhetorical triangle on the board (figure 3.1).

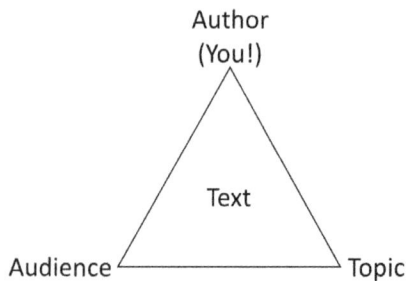

Figure 3.1. Rhetorical triangle in Liz's class. *Source*: Author provided.

She tells the students that the triangle "is a way of visualizing what's happening when you're writing a text." The three variables at the corners are "the things that define the text you're writing." For example, she explains, marking up the chalk triangle with notes as she talks, an email (text) to a professor (audience) asking for an extension (topic), "will look different than an email you're writing to your mom about how to do laundry. The choices you make depend on the audience and the topic." Liz sets the chalk down. "This exercise was basically to show you that you're already doing this," she explains. "Part of the point of this class is raising your awareness of what you're already doing and giving you more tools to do some really exciting things." However, this is the first and last time the triangle appears in class; although Liz talks throughout the semester about the importance of audience particularly, she never explicitly connects these comments back to the triangle. Nor does she use the triangle as an organizing framework for students' writing exercises or the feedback she provides on student work: she generally makes specific recommendations within each individual student's draft, rather than mapping students' work onto generalized terms and principles that can be carried across students and across assignments. For example, she underlines a sentence in one student's research paper draft and writes next to it, *Move to beginning + let this idea drive rest of essay* but does not reference the importance of making the topic clear to the audience early on, or use a more generalized term like "thesis," which would allow her to build on this writing principle in other assignments.

Given that Liz has a framework—albeit an underutilized one—I wonder if her self-identified "struggle" in this area stems more from a perception that imposing a common "map" onto her diverse students feels like an assertion of authority that conflicts with her other pedagogical commitments to encouraging individual expression, validating personal experiences, and challenging the notion of capital-T Truth—all of which she values as ways to help students enjoy and invest in the writing process. She also tells me that she has conflicted feelings about "White English, newscaster English" being held up as the gold standard in academic settings and valued above colloquial language and dialects. "To give one of those more value than the other, to train [students] to speak and write in one over the other, like I have a real problem with that," she says. These beliefs drive both her design of the analytical essay on James Baldwin's and Richard Rodriguez's views on this topic as well as her commitment to letting students "focus on what you're most interested in" from those readings. If she is truly trying to convey to students that "it's time to start thinking that what you think matters because it does," she wants to validate not only <u>what</u> they say, but <u>how</u> they choose to say it.

Ironically, though, the absence of a common understanding of what constitutes good writing ends up elevating Liz as the main arbiter of quality—the very didacticism that she philosophically rejects. On the last day of the semester, Ben tells Liz that when she gives them "specific things to look for in each other's papers, that's really helpful. But," he asks, "how do we do that moving forward?"

Liz replies, "Actually, if you think about it, I kind of tell you the same thing a lot of the time." She points out that her comments often relate to wanting to know more, wanting more specific examples, or identifying repetition. "Keep my voice in your head forever," she jokes. "Liz would want to know more here; Liz would want me to give more background here." She hints at common themes in her feedback that would comprise a "map" for revision, but she has not codified her own understanding into a shared vocabulary of effective writing that students can carry onward from her class.

Without generalizable principles or strategies for improvement, some students seem to persist in valuing an absence of mistakes in their writing, rather than viewing writing as a craft that can continually develop and improve. For example, while many students' final reflections identify a new appreciation for peer review as an important takeaway from the class, a few students convey the idea that peer review is about *minimiz[ing] any mistakes that you may not recognize . . . in grammar and sentence formulation* and that peer comments being *less everytime* signifies improvement. When Liz tells the students to review their partner's Baldwin/Rodriguez essay to make recommendations in three out of the six "polishing categories" she has written on the board,[4] some do not—or cannot—comply with the directive:

> Liz stresses that the students must pick three categories where the author can improve, even if they think the essay is already really good. After a few minutes of work time, Charlotte turns toward her partner, Sara, and they have a brief discussion. Sara turns toward Liz's desk and says, audibly to me in the back of the class, "Liz, we were supposed to say which ones to WORK on?" Liz confirms the original instructions, and Sara replies that Charlotte "said I did an awesome job on all of them!" I miss Liz's immediate response to this because next to me, Rafael has turned to Ellie and is telling her, "It's good, it draws the reader in; your point is very clear throughout. It's very well written.

You use a lot of quotes. Maybe just talk about your personal experience more. That's the only thing I can think of." Ellie just smiles with a quick intake of breath to acknowledge the feedback, a kind of modest little laugh, but as far as I can tell she gives him no verbal response. "You're perfect," Rafael adds, and Ellie makes the little noise again.

There are undeniably benefits to this kind of peer affirmation and praise, but conveying the idea of perfection is exactly counter to what Liz herself wants students to be thinking about when writing. The ongoing challenge for her is to find a way to balance those affective, social benefits of peer praise with students' acceptance of and willingness to work through flaws in their work.

The balancing act is especially important and especially challenging for students like Liz's: struggling writers who need encouragement and positive feedback to counter their negative mindsets, but who also have very real weaknesses in their writing. Throughout the semester, I constantly wonder how Liz's students are squaring the fact that they "failed" the Mayfield placement exam but then ace the class intended to address their failure on the exam. Some students' final reflections suggest that they have not fully reconciled these contradictory facts, as they couch their growth statements in disclaimers:

> *Although at times I felt that I did not belong in that class because I think my writing is at a higher level than [this class], I am still grateful I had the opportunity of starting low to fill in the gaps of my writing.*
> *In all honesty, I know I didn't need the writing practice but it's never a bad thing to get better at a skill.*
> *Everyone is gifted with a different level of talent than others . . . . there were few students in my class that struggle with the earliest of English lessons, while others will be excelled much higher than me. Yes, we were all placed in the same English class with the same exam, but perhaps we all should have been split up into two distinct writing courses.*

Additionally, the reflections suggest that when some students experienced a sense of failure on a specific assignment—most often, the research paper—they attributed the source of their struggle to external factors, counter to a growth mindset: the research paper lacked the *more personal touch* of the other assignments that were more engaging, the student picked a bad topic, or the length requirement was unreasonable. One student wrote, *I could have done [the research paper] in three pages only. However, needing it to meet the length of a five-page research paper enforced me to talk about two arguments instead of one which made it seem like too much. I think I prefer the teacher evaluating the students' writing based on the quality instead of the quantity. That's why I did not do well in Unit III.*

I find the students' enduring defensiveness especially ironic when I obtain from the writing director a copy of the 2017 writing placement exam administered to this cohort of students. The prompt provided students with two short popular press articles about failure and supplied ten questions that students could use to guide their response, including: *According to these authors, why are human beings afraid to fail if failure is integral to learning?* and *What is the relationship between failure, risk, and reward?* Whatever the students may have written in response to these questions on the exam, it seems they may still be working through them even after a full semester of college writing instruction.

The exam essay questions are also salient to Liz's own mindsets toward teaching and her attempts to enact growth mindset-promotive practices in her classroom. Liz has not substantially revised her course since discovering that "the exact class" she taught at her state university "fit all the criteria"—which are few—at Mayfield. "I still find it interesting to just teach the same stuff, over and over," she tells me. "And I trust myself to do a better job teaching something I've taught a bunch of times." Otherwise, she says, "I miss things, and if I'm not confident and someone asks me a question, then I totally undermine myself and stumble and . . ." she trails off, shaking her head and chuckling at herself. "So yeah, having a lot of practice—I think it's good for my students for me to have a LOT of practice." In our last interview, she shares with me something else she has carried with her from her pedagogical training at the state university: a theory of student development that is also, indirectly, a theory about teaching.

> When they were training us, they were like, "the eighteen-year-old brain is still not fully formed," you know? There's a reason that [students] don't have super complex ideas yet. Some have more than others, but it's also like . . . they're just not totally done "cooking." *[laughs]* That's sort of to be expected. And they would show us essays by this [age] group of students [from] all

over the country and all over the world, and they all looked so similar. Like, it was just this age, you know? That's the way that humans are thinking at that time, typically. And that was actually really interesting, 'cause you're always like, "My students are still doing this, and it's because I'm not teaching them right. I'm not a good teacher—I'm, like, failing teaching." But then you see everyone's students in the entire world doing that same thing, and you're like, "Oh, it's not me. We're all doing our best, and this is just part of the process of, you know, [student] development."

In addition to presenting a kind of stage-based fixed perspective on students' writing ability, this theory also has a corollary: a fixed perspective on teacher impact. This corollary gives Liz reassurance that "it's not me," that she is not "failing teaching"—a career that she has come to "love so much," after initially being "terrified" at the prospect, "'cause I hate talking in front of people," she laughs.

"How much do you think of yourself as a writer versus a teacher now?" I ask her.

"That's a great question," she says. "I guess I think of myself . . . well, when people ask what I do, I tell them I'm a teacher . . . I really want to just teach forever."

Despite sometimes expressing fixed perspectives on her teaching ability and impact, Liz simultaneously holds a powerful growth orientation toward this work that she "love[s] so much." She is unquestionably committed to improving as an instructor; she sometimes pauses during our interviews when a question prompts her to reflect in a new way, saying this is "exactly" why she signed up for the study, and in our last interview, she tells me that she participated because she "just felt like it would be good for me to think about the same things you're thinking about and to feel sort of accountable, and to get better."

Liz's own growth mindset toward teaching is just as authentically fluid and variable as her students' growth mindsets toward writing. In a parallel process to what she wants her students to experience with writing, Liz has overcome her initial fear of teaching and negative mindsets about her teaching skills, achieving a level of enjoyment and a willingness to keep doing it "forever." However, these parallel processes also illustrate parallel challenges in growth mindset development: even espoused growth mindsets can shift from moment to moment, sometimes making it difficult for educators and students alike to take risks that expose them to failure, to accept and embrace that failure as an opportunity to learn new strategies, and to continue engaging in the work even when it does not come easily.

Reflections on Promoting a Growth Mindset

Lay understandings of growth mindset often position it in a dichotomy with fixed mindset, but the two are probably better represented as ends of a continuum, with most educators' beliefs and classroom practices falling somewhere between the two extremes (Sun, 2018b). Liz's portrait illustrates this fluidity, as well as the need for synergy and consistency in growth mindset–supportive practices—within a given classroom and between an individual classroom and the institution as a whole—to provide an optimal environment of psychological affordances for students' growth mindsets to flourish.

A recognition of intelligence and skills as malleable lies at the heart of growth mindset. Liz explicitly articulates this concept to her students on the very first day of class when she tells them that "writing is very responsive to practice. The more you practice, the better you get." She does more than just pay lip service to this theory; one of her core underlying course design principles is to "defend time in class" for students to engage in that "brute force practice." Her allocation of class time conveys the value and importance of the activity. Consistent with research on the context sensitivity and domain specificity of growth mindset (Buehl et al., 2002; Yeager & Dweck, 2012), as well as the big-fish-little-pond effect (Marsh & Hau, 2003), Liz is aware that Mayfield students in general may experience a major adjustment to new academic and social challenges at college after feeling like they "kn[ew] everything" in their local high schools and that her students in particular may feel particularly insecure after their writing placement test. A similar awareness of the vulnerability of growth mindset during school transitions drives efforts to implement growth mindset interventions for first-year college students; without being specifically trained in growth mindset intervention, Liz intuitively tries to leverage the "brute force practice" time in class to support students in making the adjustment to college work without feeling stigmatized for experiencing difficulty with the transition.

Additionally, Liz's grading and feedback practices reflect her understanding of growth mindset's role in the writing process. Because her immediate goal is always to get students to write more, as the prerequisite for their improvement, her assessment seeks to encourage student production in a strategy that resembles labor-based grading approaches (Cowan, 2020; Farber, 1990; J. A. Smith, 1999), though she ultimately has to compromise on her ideals and adopt a more hybrid approach of equally weighted "product" and "process" grades (Elbow, 1997). She avoids being "controlling" in her feedback (Reeve & Jang, 2006): her comments are unfailingly positive and often ask students to elaborate or write more on a promising thread, rather than focusing on "corrections." Likewise, she deliberately tries to be "encouraging" to help students "feel good" about their writing and want to "write more next time." Liz intends for these grading policies to counter students' negative incoming mindsets; even students who view themselves as "bad writers" will likely earn positive feedback and a good semester grade if they invest the effort to follow the process, perhaps altering their self-concept and implicit theories about their own writing ability. Liz's desire to evoke positive feelings and stronger identification as writers may reflect her strong prioritization of the "affective dimension" of writing and writing transfer (Nowacek, 2011); she views this as a necessary precondition to students wanting to write and being willing to engage thoughtfully in writing in other contexts or in the future.

A recurring tension in Liz's practice, however, is the extent to which her definition of "brute force practice" resembles repetitive execution—doing things "over and over again"—versus "deliberate practice" (Ericcson et al., 1993), "different kinds of practice" (Yancey, 2016c), or what Wiersema and colleagues (2015) distinguish as "mindful effort" instead of merely "time spent." Liz wrestles with the subjectivity of trying to assess the quality of individual effort, so she defaults to a policy of rewarding evidence of time spent: "If you do everything, you get an A on the process grade." This could actually undermine a growth mindset message for some students in that it externalizes effort by defining it primarily as mechanical repetition rather than an internal process of deep cognitive engagement and, ultimately, mastery of writing as a craft (Downs, 2016). In other words, when students expect to be rewarded for "time spent," they may focus more on providing superficial evidence of effort, rather than engaging deeply in the learning process and deploying the strategy use and knowledge necessary to grow as writers (Flower et al., 1986).

Liz is not naïve about her grading policy; she knows that for some students, her "generous" grades convey a message that "this class is easy" and may lead them to reduce their effort—the opposite effect that she wants. Her dilemma is that she does not know how to counter the problematic interpretation while preserving a system that she believes helps "free" other students to focus on their writing by removing the pressure of grades, so she sticks with what seems like the less damaging option. This labor-based approach option may also present an option for Liz to counteract the discomfort she feels over the association between assessment and "White language supremacy" (Inoue, 2019) in the writing classroom, such as through "giving value" to "White English, newscaster English" over students' home dialects.

Importantly, "mindful effort" or "deliberate practice" also requires the experience of failure in order to develop strategies to target the areas most in need of improvement. I wonder whether Liz's commitment to "encouraging" and helping students "feel good" about their writing impedes her willingness to give more critical feedback and expose weaknesses in students' writing. The well-intentioned desire to protect students from negative feelings of failure is reflective of a more fixed-mindset instructional approach (Sun, 2018a) because it suggests that failure could psychologically cripple students and is something to be avoided, whereas a growth mindset reframes failure as an inevitable part of learning (Haimovitz & Dweck, 2016). Liz tends to deliver affirming feedback that, consistent with her philosophy, may help students "feel good" and more positive about their prospects for success but may not help them identify concrete areas for growth; her advice to Vera in office hours to focus on what she "liked" about Baldwin's essay and "leave out" anything she did not understand was a particularly striking example.

Though done in a spirit of generosity and forbearance, Liz's acceptance of students' limitations and her attribution of their underdeveloped writing to a universal developmental spectrum suggest the pervasive influence of fixed theories of intelligence/ability on how she views her students' mindsets toward writing, their actual writing skills, and her own potential for impact as an educator. It prioritizes the preservation of students' self-esteem over the productive discomfort that is necessary for the learning and growth that will ultimately foster a deeper and more meaningful confidence as writers (Schunk et al., 2014). Students can and do rise to the challenges of their instructors, and tools like "wise feedback" (Yeager, Purdie-Vaughns, et al., 2014)—in which teachers explicitly mark critical feedback as a sign of their confidence that students can meet high expectations—can help instructors manage students' feedback-related emotions while reinforcing a high standard for quality work.

In fact, although Liz seems to view grade-based affirmation as necessary for students to "like" writing, her curriculum and instructional design already contain ample opportunities for students to enjoy writing even if the task is challenging, does not receive a high grade, or goes entirely unrecognized or unrewarded. She has thoughtfully designed creative, open-ended assignments that students can personalize and use to cultivate their authorial voice; these should motivate students to exert effort and want to improve, even in the face of critical feedback. With peer review, independent work time in class, and mandatory one-on-one writing conferences in office hours, she has numerous structures in place to deliver impactful critical feedback to students in formative learning situations before they receive a summative grade. She also introduces students to the rhetorical triangle, a framework that could help them contextualize the feedback they receive and provide a visual heuristic for their ongoing writing improvement.

The design and intent underlying curriculum and pedagogy, however, are distinct from the details of enactment and implementation (Sun, 2018b). In many cases, such as with the rhetorical triangle, Liz does not take full advantage of these opportunities that she herself has structured into her class that could help her push students harder, help them self-assess their progress, and thus scaffold their motivation. Similar to Zachary, Liz seems to prefer taking a fairly nondirective approach, instead relying on somewhat wishful thinking that she can set the conditions for students to adopt her desired way of thinking, and they will hopefully come to endorse it through a process of osmosis (Shepherd et al., 2021). However, we see that while some students seem to engage in the spirit of Liz's course design and acquire a sense of personal responsibility for their writing growth by the end of the semester ("You are the only one who can improve your writing skills by practicing more and more throughout your life"), others still seem to view academic writing as a one-on-one negotiation to please an outside evaluator and are unable to fully own their failures, attributing them to external rather than internal causes ("I prefer the teacher evaluating . . . quality instead of quantity. That's why I did not do well").

As we saw in the high school portraits, greater transparency with students could potentially help Liz try to preempt students' misperceptions, clarify the purpose of activities, and reframe classroom events as opportunities for growth. Providing students with clearer rationales for not only evaluative but also routine instructional practices can help students interpret their classroom experiences in a more motivationally supportive light (Jang, 2008). For example, Inman and Powell (2018) advocate for explicit conversations between instructors and students about the role of—and desire for—grades and feedback in college writing classrooms. Liz strives to reassure students from the first day of class that their grades will be "fine," but she seems reluctant to engage students when they initiate the topic in anticipation of receiving their first major grade and instead tries to redirect or ignore them. This could be a reason why the students become habituated to stirring up drama on the days their portfolios are being returned (though they do become somewhat more restrained in their ostentation as the semester goes on).

Likewise, receiving grades may be more suspenseful when the students are unclear on the criteria by which they are being evaluated. Transparency is an underlying objective for the use of assessment rubrics (Panadero & Jonsson, 2013; Wollenschläger et al., 2016), which Liz abandoned as too time-consuming given that results "were exactly the same" as her holistic assessment of "ehh, that's an A– . . . that's like a B+." From a growth mindset perspective, however, the final grade is less salient than the student's *interpretation* of what the grade signifies, which rubric criteria would clarify.

Transparency is also key to "threshold concepts" (Meyer & Land, 2006), ideas that help students see and understand in transformative ways both *what* and *how* people learn in a discipline. In the context of first-year composition, a critical role of threshold concepts is to complexify students' understanding of writing, such as by disrupting students' existing conceptualizations of writing and the writing process (Downs & Robertson, 2015), both major goals of Liz's class. Students' value mindsets (or lack thereof) could play a role in how students encounter and respond to threshold concepts, including whether they are able to "cross" the threshold and adopt the transformative new way of seeing (Adler-Kassner & Wardle, 2016, p. ix). If students view the course through the narrowest of utilitarian lenses—something they must pass in order to get on with what they "actually" came to college to do ("I wanna be a doctor, and here's what I have to do to get there")—they may push back against the more integrative approach to writing that composition threshold concepts reflect.

Conversely, understanding threshold concepts can help students reframe writing as a situated, social, and rhetorical act (Roozen et al., 2016), giving it relevance outside the confines of the writing classroom. Making disciplinary threshold concepts explicit versus implicit to students is part of the goal of "nam[ing] what we know and how we can use what we know in the service of writing" (Yancey, 2016a, p. xix). However, similar to Zachary's indirect approach, Liz leaves much of her own understanding of threshold concepts implicit to students, perhaps precipitating Ben's striking question on the last day of class that laid bare that he lacked the disciplinary grounding in composition to know how to transfer an improvement process for writing to another context without Liz's direct aid. Liz's targeted feedback on concerns in each specific assignment, rather than larger-scale concerns (Wingard & Geosits, 2014), may have occluded Ben and other students' recognition and uptake of key threshold concepts.

Liz could also aid students' transfer while simultaneously supporting growth mindset by more fully embracing reflection as a component of writer development—itself a threshold concept—to greater effect (Yancey, 2016b). Liz already incorporates student reflection into her curriculum; indeed, she assigned reflections far more often than any of my other participants, and her portrait is richly imbued with student perspectives because these frequent reflections supplied a wealth of student data that she was able to share with me. Reflection is a key medium through which students can process the role of failure in their development as writers, another threshold concept in composition studies (Brooke & Carr, 2016) that closely aligns with growth mindset work in the motivation scholarship. Reflection also cultivates the metacognitive skills that are critical for writing transfer (Beaufort, 2016; Nowacek, 2011) and value mindsets, as discussed above. Recall Zachary's guided metacognitive reflection with his class about the "road trip" metaphor for the writing process. Zachary's limitation was in not consistently utilizing "metacognitive reflection, self-reflection kind of stuff" with his older students and on motivation-related topics; Liz has committed to the frequency and routine of reflection but without the scaffolding that Zachary provided at least intermittently. Her reflection prompts tended to be fairly open-ended, leaving open the possibility of students writing what they think Liz wants to hear (Pruchnic et al., 2021), rather than engaging in the critical reflection necessary for growth (Taczak, 2016).

For all of these strategies, the nuances of implementation matter, and the inevitable adjustments and tinkering that will be required to finetune that implementation themselves require a growth mindset in the instructor— something that Liz is somewhat inconsistent in articulating. For example, though she muses to me that it "might be a really good idea" to change up her use of reflection by integrating it more throughout the writing process, she also articulates reluctance to modify her course because "I trust myself to do a better job teaching something I've taught a bunch of times" lest she "undermine" herself by faltering in front of students. In fact, Liz is the only one out of my four participants who has never made substantial changes to her curriculum or teaching routines. Her hesitancy may reflect more of a fixed mindset toward teaching (in that she is disinclined to take risks because of the possibility of failure) and may implicate her efforts to instill a growth mindset in students, as suggested by recent findings on the impact of instructor mindsets on the efficacy of growth mindset classroom interventions (Yeager et al., 2022). After all, if an instructor is unwilling to fail in the classroom, can she successfully create an environment where students feel safe doing so?

Yet consistent with research on the fluidity of mindsets, Liz clearly does not hold an exclusively fixed mindset toward teaching, and the precarity of her position at Mayfield may play a strong role in her reluctance to take on curricular revisions. Liz actively wants to learn and improve as a writing instructor, missing the professional community she had as a graduate student, but she is thwarted by her own and the other instructors' adjunct status to the point where she views participating in my research study as essentially a professional development opportunity (a phenomenon discussed further from a methodological standpoint in appendix B). In many ways, Liz's mixed mindsets are authentic to what her own students carry into the classroom, and she is as willing a student as any teacher could hope for. Though she demonstrates some beliefs aligned with a fixed perspective, she is also eager to grow. What she needs is a professional learning environment that provides the affordances for her to capitalize on her adaptive mindsets and progress in her mastery of teaching—which would then enable her to create an analogous environment for her first-year writing students.

There is a deep irony in the Mayfield writing department essentially performing a growth mindset intervention on students through its writing placement exam prompt—*Why are human beings afraid to fail if failure is integral to learning?*—but neither taking that approach with its own instructors nor equipping them to be able to continue cultivating adaptive mindsets in students. Even simply sharing students' placement exam essays with instructors as an artifact to be revisited in class is the lowest-hanging fruit that would provide instructors with rich material and model to students a growth-oriented vision of writing as integrated with thinking (Bazerman & Tinberg, 2016; Graham et al., 2018) rather than merely a means of assessment.

I say this not to denigrate Mayfield specifically but to draw a structural contrast between its not-atypical approach to writing instruction and the concentration of professional growth resources surrounding Diane and Zachary at their high schools. It is impossible to overlook the strong sense of belonging that both Diane and Zachary felt at their schools and how both of them perceived themselves as recipients of significant investment from the school leadership (Diane "learning how to teach all over again," Zachary being entrusted with the upper school restructure). These perceptions seem pivotal to their sense of competence as teachers and their ability to embrace and enact a growth mindset toward teaching. All three cases present the importance of a parallel process of mindset support for educators that demonstrates the extent of the motivational ecosystem surrounding students; it implicates the educators' mindsets, motivation, and past experiences as well as the students'. We will continue to see this pattern play out in the final portrait.

Chapter 4

Mastering the Game

Sustaining Competence Mindsets through New Challenges in College Learning and Teaching

Overview: "I can succeed at this"

Many people think of motivation as the desire or drive to do something, but students' beliefs about their own competence and capability to succeed at academic tasks are also a key component of motivation. Indeed, there is evidence that an affirmative answer to the baseline question, "Can I do this?" is central to student motivation, rather than being something that primarily develops after students are motivated to engage in the task. The competence mindset "I can succeed at this" is therefore a key motivational belief that drives engagement and learning.

There are many closely related concepts in motivation theory that underlie the competence mindset, but one of the most commonly studied is self-efficacy (Bandura, 1997). Self-efficacy is different from self-esteem, which is a more general feeling of worth we hold about ourselves. By contrast, self-efficacy refers to "people's judgments of their capabilities to organize and execute courses of action required to attain designated types of performances" (Bandura, 1986, p. 391) and relates to specific academic tasks or subject areas (Butz & Usher, 2015). For example, someone can have high self-efficacy in math and low self-efficacy in writing or varying self-efficacy toward different tasks in the same class. Students' self-efficacy shifts based on how they are processing the information they receive from the learning environment at any given moment. Specifically, the features of a learning environment that foster self-efficacy can be categorized into four sources: mastery experiences, vicarious experiences, social persuasion, and emotional state (Bandura, 1997).

Mastery experiences occur when an individual successfully completes a task and interprets that success as a reflection of their competence (as opposed to something like luck or the task being easy). Importantly, it is the interpretation of the success experience that is critical to students' competence mindsets, more so than the success itself; research demonstrates that self-beliefs and judgments about ability influence students' academic choices and behaviors independent of their actual competence levels (Schunk & Pajares, 2005). Vicarious experiences occur when a student observes someone else successfully completing a task, boosting the student's confidence in their own ability to complete a similar task. This tends to have the strongest effect on competence mindsets when the student can identify with the vicarious model, seeing something of themselves reflected in the success exemplar. Social persuasion includes the explicit and implicit messages that students receive about their competence from others in the learning environment, such as the teacher or peers. Explicit persuasion could include things like the teacher expressing confidence in students' abilities. Implicit persuasion could include things like being part of a peer group that devalues academic success, making a student reluctant to try to succeed and therefore making it difficult for that student to have mastery experiences and near-peer vicarious experiences to boost their competence mindset. Finally, students interpret their own emotional states as signs of success potential. Feeling calm can enhance a competence mindset, whereas anxiety or stress can hinder it both because the student interprets the emotion as a sign of incompetence and because the emotion clouds the student's self-assessment of ability in the moment.

Self-efficacy or other competence-related beliefs appear in nearly every contemporary theory of motivation; thus, the competence mindset intersects with the other three motivational mindsets in critical ways. First, a sense of belonging can strongly influence the sources of self-efficacy a student perceives in a given learning context. Feeling a sense of connectedness and affiliation with peers can increase opportunities for—and the effectiveness of—vicarious experiences, and warm classroom relationships provide positive social persuasion and reduce stress and negative emotional experiences. We saw these mechanisms at work in Diane's portrait as she sought to combat her AP students' self-doubts through verbal "cheerleading" and collaborative learning activities so that "as a group we can all get this." Meanwhile, the prominent displays of achievement culture at the school as a whole seemed aimed at energizing vicarious feelings of success potential in Riverside students as their classmates' achievements and college acceptances were publicly advertised.

Perceived competence also intersects with the value mindset in expectancy-value theory, discussed in chapter 2 for its differentiation between types of value (utility, attainment, intrinsic). Broadly, people want to feel competent about the things that they value and, conversely, will tend to value tasks that they feel competent in. This relationship between the mindsets was evident in Zachary's portrait as he tried to hook students with a class about superheroes and use their interest to develop their competence mindsets, while at the same time recognizing that feeling competent with an "academic lens" can help students "value knowledge and information."

Finally, because the competence mindset reflects an individual's belief in their ability to "attain designated types of performances," it also implicates the individual's personal understanding of what success means and whether and how it can be achieved, connecting it to growth mindset. Chapter 3 discussed the distinction between mastery and performance goals from achievement goal theory (Ames, 1992) and their relation to growth mindset; these goals are also relevant in considerations of the competence mindset. Specifically, students' competence mindsets can relate not only to what types of goals students endorse, but also the impact of those goals on their academic performance and well-being. For example, a stronger sense of competence is often associated with mastery goals, whereas lower competence is often associated with performance goals (Chatzisarantis et al., 2016; Coutinho & Neuman, 2008; Dweck et al., 2014), especially a subtype of performance goals called performance-avoidance goals, in which students strive to avoid looking less capable than others. When performance-oriented students do not believe they can succeed, they resort to ego-preserving behaviors, such as opting for easier tasks or doing just enough to avoid drawing negative attention, rather than strategies focused on mastery. By contrast, mastery goals and growth mindset seem to buffer the potential negative effects of low competence beliefs. Liz was aware of this in her consideration of the transition from high school to college-level work, and especially the "embarrassment" some of her students experienced when they placed into first-year writing. She hoped that her strategies to promote growth mindset would temper the effects of their temporarily shaken confidence and eventually restore their competence mindsets as they wrote more and improved.

However, there are also mixed findings related to performance goals and achievement, particularly for students with higher levels of perceived competence who are less at risk for the negative psychological effects of a focus on performance. These findings may be especially salient for the students in the selective colleges profiled in this book, who may be experiencing a temporary disruption to their self-concepts in the transition from high school to college but who still have a long track record of academic success to sustain their competence mindsets. Some research has found that performance-approach goals, in which students strive to outperform their peers to *demonstrate* competence—regardless of whether or not they actually *develop* greater competence—are associated with value mindsets, effort, and achievement (Midgley et al., 2001; Senko et al., 2013). Consider the public posturing of Liz's students to call attention to their position within the class grade hierarchy; this competitive attitude may well have spurred some of them to put in the effort necessary for a good grade. However, other studies have linked both types of performance goals (approach and avoidance) to maladaptive behaviors like avoidance of help seeking and test anxiety (C. Huang, 2011; Senko et al., 2011). Recent work on multiple-goal endorsement suggests that performance goals may be associated with more positive outcomes when students have strong competence mindsets and simultaneously endorse mastery goals (Wormington & Linnenbrink-Garcia, 2017), as the mastery goals provide an alternative, internalized rationale for persistence even when students do not perform at their desired levels.

Instructional practices that support students' competence mindsets therefore often overlap with practices that support growth mindset and mastery goals. Reflecting the four sources of self-efficacy, educators can support students' competence mindsets by setting an appropriate level of academic challenge and providing the necessary learning scaffolds to help students meet those expectations (E. W. Gordon & Bridglall, 2007; Green, 2002) and giving students opportunities to master increasingly difficult tasks to support perceived mastery experiences (Bandura, 1997; Butz & Usher, 2015). As with growth mindset and mastery goals, teacher language, feedback, and assessment practices play a key role in conveying messages to students about the role of effort, improvement, and assessment in academic success and individual competence (S. C. Gordon et al., 2007; Kaplan et al., 2002). Clearly articulated learning goals and feedback on progress toward those goals through interim checks on skill or content mastery can help make success pathways transparent to students (Marzano, 2000; Panadero & Jonsson, 2013; Wollenschläger et al., 2016). Leveraging the influence of social persuasion and vicarious experience, teachers can also promote students' competence mindsets by verbally expressing confidence in students and providing success exemplars with whom students can identify (Ahn et al., 2017; Bandura, 1997; Green, 2002), and by promoting peer collaboration and mutual encouragement rather than practices that foster social comparison and competition (S. C. Gordon et al., 2007; Maehr & Midgley, 1991; Roseth et al., 2008). Together, these classroom practices convey important messages to students about whether to define success self-referentially (i.e., developing greater competence) or comparatively (i.e., demonstrating competence by outperforming others) and whether students can achieve their definition of success. They also emphasize clarity and transparency, aligning them with the idea of making explicit the often-implicit threshold concepts of writing discussed in chapter 3.

Though he is not specifically trained in rhetoric or composition and does not use the term "threshold concepts," Colin Zimmerman clearly embraces a similar notion through his use of a game metaphor to try to make the hidden "rules" of academic writing transparent to students in a manner that they can learn to master and apply to future writing. His portrait presents a striking contrast to Liz's even as the two instructors are also remarkably similar in their struggles over grades and their perceptions of the inadequacies of high school writing instruction contributing to students' difficult transition to college writing. The question asked on the last day of class by Liz's student Ben, "How do we [know what to look for in our writing] moving forward?" can almost be seen as the driving question behind Colin's instructional approach. His portrait reveals a thoughtful and intentional educator who focuses his students on skill mastery as the definition of success and strives to provide them with a "game manual" and numerous practice opportunities to build that mastery and support their competence mindsets. However, like Liz's, his portrait also reveals the extent of the motivational ecosystem as we learn that combatting students' preconceptions about what "game(s)" they are playing and what "winning" means may require a deeper understanding of the tenacity of performance-oriented beliefs about success in both students and educators.

Mastering the Game

UNDERSTANDING THE RULES

"Awkward grammar appals a craftsman. A Dada bard as daft as Tzara damns stagnant art and scrawls an alpha (a slapdash arc and a backward zag) that

mars all stanzas and jams all ballads (what a scandal) . . ." Katarina stumbles occasionally as she reads aloud from the PDF displayed on her MacBook screen. Her instructor, Colin Zimmerman, has given the class a scanned excerpt from the book *Eunoia*[1] as "an example of the kind of game we could play today," and Katarina volunteered to read the first section aloud—a choice she may be regretting now as she struggles through the tongue-twisting words that sound almost like a different language.

The room where Colin convenes his section of English 101, Abbott University's first-year writing course, is on the first floor of a building that feels like a converted residence. A door on one wall leads to a front porch; the opposite wall features an inactive fireplace where some of the students pile their belongings because of the limited space around the large seminar-style table that Colin has the students create by pushing four smaller tables together in the center of the room. The sixteen students who sit around this table seem to me a fair cross-section of Abbott, other than international students being slightly underrepresented; English 101 is mandatory for all first-year students except those with exempting scores on the AP, International Bac-calaureate (IB), or British A-Level exams deemed to assess analogous skills,[2] but English-language learners are placed in a different track. Among the roughly thirteen hundred students in a first-year cohort at Abbott, around 12 percent are international students, while 22 percent are domestic student of color and 13 percent are Pell Grant recipients.

Colin, a tall and lanky White man in his thirties who is teaching this course for the fifth straight year, sometimes pulls up a seat with the students around the table, but at the moment he is standing at the lec-tern where his laptop is connected to the classroom audiovisual system so that the enormous flat-screen monitor on the wall behind him mirrors his computer display. Dressed in his usual teaching attire of an untucked plaid button-down and slacks, he leans slightly forward on one hand as his eyes scan his laptop screen to follow along with Katarina. At the seminar table, the other students do the same, but nobody is reacting much to the gib-berish she is gamely continuing to recite except for Kyle, who breaks into a slow smile about halfway through.

"WHAT?!" Katarina gasps when she finally reaches the end of the page, which seems to break the ice for the other students to make similar noises of amusement and consternation.

"There's an *A* in every word!" Kyle bursts out triumphantly. With a hint of playfulness creeping into his typically quiet, even speaking style, Colin adds that not only does every word contain an *A*, "*A* is the ONLY vowel used in the whole piece." This pronouncement sparks a flurry of new noises and side conversations as the students scurry to verify it for themselves; Margaret cackles loudly in delight, apologizes for the outburst, but continues to grin at her screen.

Kyle volunteers to finish reading the A chapter, and another student reads a bit of the next, which follows the same rules but with the letter E. Colin then directs the students to the author's note at the end, which explains that, inspired by a French *avant-garde coterie renowned for its literary experimentation with extreme formalistic constraints*, the author intended his text to make *a Sisyphean spectacle of its labour, wilfully crippling its language in order to show that, even under such improbable conditions of duress, language can still express an uncanny, if not sublime, thought.*

"Even when you impose strict rules," Colin translates to the class, "you can get something interesting out of it." Sometimes rules have the benefit of getting us to "think creatively" and push our arguments in ways we might not otherwise think of. "Rules don't have to be limiting," he says. "They can be enabling."

The enabling power of rules forms the organizing principle of Colin's class. In our very first interview, he tells me that his approach to teaching draws on Ludwig Wittgenstein's theory of language wherein "learning a language involves . . ." He pauses briefly, and then he continues with what I assume is a vast oversimplification for my benefit: "learning to play a game, basically." Colin is about to complete his doctorate in English at Abbott, with a focus on modernism and language philosophy, and he connects Wittgenstein's "language game" to the goal of a first-year writing course. "So much of what people in their freshman year of college are doing," he says, "is coming into college and figuring out, 'What is this all about? How is this different from what's come before? What are the things that I need to do to succeed in this new culture, in this new discourse?'" Recognizing the relationship between success beliefs and feelings of belonging, he wants his students to "start to be aware that there's a conversation happening, and have some ideas about how they can engage with it and respond to it in a meaningful and appropriate way." Learning this new academic discourse is like learning any language—which is to say, like learning a game. "I think that when I'm teaching, a lot of what I'm doing is just showing how I play games," Colin says, helping his students to "see some of the moves that I make in those games . . . and then giv[ing] them a space and opportunity to try it themselves." Ultimately, he hopes his students gain enough mastery that they "feel like they have a place in this discourse community."

Experiencing mastery is a critical component of the competence mindset, and for Colin, mastering a complex game involves recognizing not only the existence but also the purpose of the game's rules. "When you're young and you learn to play a game," he says, "you learn the rules and you follow them." But as an older student of the game, "you have to start to understand why the rules exist the way they do . . . In basketball, it's to produce competition or difficulty that's just manageable enough. The free-throw line is fifteen feet from the hoop; it's not thirty feet from the hoop. There are particular reasons why things are the way they are." For Colin, understanding the underlying purpose of a game's parameters is critical to being able to play the game well. "I feel like high school writing is sort of like learning some rules but not always having a good handle on why the rules exist that way," he says. To develop as effective writers in college, students need to learn that the rules exist "to facilitate communication, to help deepen your thoughts, and to help improve or sustain or further some line of research or inquiry for discussion." Novice writers see rules as arbitrary limitations to follow blindly, but expert writers can recognize the opportunities that rules enable.

In the context of academic discourse, though, Colin recognizes that understanding these rules is challenging because "academia is particularly opaque about its own expectations." A major component of Colin's role as a first-year writing instructor is therefore to make those rules and expectations more transparent to his students—to provide a kind of game manual—so that students know what they are striving to master. "Belonging in the academic community means that you just learn to play a particular kind of game," he says. Colin illustrates this for students on the first day of the semester by having the class play the party game Apples to Apples, in which players creatively justify bizarre pairings of words to win points from a judge. "I make it pretty explicit on the first day that what we do at college and what we do in this class in particular is a lot like playing the game of Apples to Apples," Colin says. "I talk about how there are rules and expectations, how there are ways that you can win."

Apples to Apples is also meant to show students that they "have an intuitive sense already of how to make an argument," affirming their baseline competence before Colin sets out to teach them the "rules" of academic argument that will help them "win" more often or more convincingly. In a class that otherwise features few absolutes and little rote learning, Colin clearly designates each set of writing rules as foundational principles, writing them on the board and explicitly telling students to internalize them. In just the third class session, he begins asking students to recall from memory the four parts of an argument they learned in the previous class, groaning softly in mock horror when students need to refer to their notes. Later in the semester, when Colin teaches students four principles of clarity and cohesion adapted from Joseph Williams's work,[3] he again explicitly states his expectation that students learn the new set of rules and seizes the opportunity to check students' mastery of the previous set:

> "I would like you to memorize these four things," he tells the class. "I've asked you to memorize one other thing in this class, the components of an argument. Can anyone remember them?" Several students offer attempts, and eventually, all four components are named as Colin scribes them on the board: *1) context; 2) problem/question/disruption; 3) stakes/significance; 4) thesis/solution.* ("Whew!" someone says. "That took effort.") Colin shifts back to the four principles of clarity and cohesion written in a parallel list on the board and repeats them, and now several students start copying them down, though they had not been taking notes before. When one student re-enters from having gone to the bathroom, he surveys his classmates writing, figures out what's going on, and also starts copying from the board.

Despite his frequent memorization directives, Colin never formally tests the students on the writing frameworks he gives them; the collective recitations are the main accountability check. Beyond simply being able to parrot them back to him, though, Colin's students need to understand and master the rules, which Colin works toward by integrating them into multiple facets of students' coursework. Reinforcing the central metaphor of the course, he has populated his syllabus with readings about "rules or games or learning how to do specific behaviors," or readings in which the authors are playing stylistic or rhetorical "games," and he asks students to make the author's game transparent by identifying the four components of an argument or evaluating the thesis using the criteria they've memorized. Students also perform these tasks with each other's work in peer review and are consistently asked to apply the frameworks in their own writing—whether in the opening essay in which they use *reasons and observations from your own educational experience* to justify whether Carol Dweck, John Taylor Gatto, Paulo Freire, or Annette Lareau *offers the best solution for improving education*; in a Letter to the Editor responding to a course reading; in a free-choice MLA-formatted research paper; or in the *translat[ion]* of that research paper into *public writing . . . to appeal to nonexperts who need to learn what you know.* One student's in-class reflection at the end of the semester acknowledges the role of these multiple opportunities in furthering a sense of mastery as both a consumer and producer of writing: *After reading articles and writing responses then writing and peer editing, I learned how to spot good writing which also helped me write better.* Other students likewise use their reflections to show Colin that they have indeed internalized the "rules," especially around argumentation (emphasis added):

> *The most useful lesson we had was one of the first lessons talking about the parts of an Argument.* **Stakes, Problems,** *Scope,* **context** *evidence. Will never forget.*
>
> *The most important thing I learned in this class was how to really set up my introduction with the* **problem, stakes,** *and* **thesis.** *I think this was really helpful for me in forming an argument for the papers. I also learned the thesis should not just state what you are going to talk about, but also contain a greater* **significance.**
>
> *Learned about how to structure an argument in a non-5 paragraph simple essay. This means* **C[ontext]-P[roblem]-S[takes]-T[hesis],** *anticipating counterarguments, anticipating readers' questions.*

In a direct contrast to the natural "opaqueness" of academia, Colin's game metaphor provides him with a metavocabulary to talk to his students in an accessible way about how he is trying to develop their mastery and foster their belief that they can succeed "in this new culture" and "feel like they have a place in this discourse community." Critically, though, Colin's vision of college as a "discourse community" requires not just teaching students to master the discourse through the "rules" and frameworks of writing. Like the three other educators in this study, he recognizes the intersection of the competence mindset with a feeling of belonging to a community that nurtures and affirms students' success potential, providing students with the social motivation to keep playing the game.

ASSEMBLING THE PLAYERS

Having finished discussing *Eunoia* with the students, Colin explains the game he has devised for them: each student will invent two rules to constrain their writing and compose a short piece using those rules; they will then divide into groups, share their work, and elect one representative to compete against the other groups. The students settle into nearly silent individual work time, with only minimal conferring and reacting ("This is gonna be hard," Katarina says to no one in particular), but the noise level spikes when Colin directs them to form groups. He has stated that the winning composition will exempt the nominating group members from their next homework response paper—a prize that prompted a brief fizz of excitement—but it does not seem to me that the students are thinking of that now as they turn to their groupmates. "I really liked mine," I hear from a few voices. Kyle's explanation of his piece catches the ear of Tony, who is in a different group, but the two young men swap laptops to read each other's work anyway. Kyle bursts into a full-throated belly laugh when he finishes. "Tony and I aren't talented writers," he says as he hands back the laptop, "so we wanted to make them funny." Tony nods in agreement as he passes his device over to Margaret, who has also asked to read it. At the other end of the table, Ariana is realizing she missed the opportunity to invent "a rule where you had to swear every other word!" Lena points at her, nodding and laughing in agreement.

Colin, who circulated briefly during individual writing time but otherwise has stayed largely out of the process, reconvenes the full class and asks each group to read out the piece they have nominated for the class competition. He notes that the author of the piece does not have to be the one to read it, although all four authors choose to. Ariana goes first:

> *A nonstop array of gold, on blue, on green, an ocean to be cleaned. A nonexistent boat of future, on wood, on planks, a flank to be thanked. A nonrecurring dream of West, on pillows, on hay, a pray gone astray. A nonsignificant head of curls, on beauty, on grace, a place to be erased. A nonobservant strip of shore, on red, on yellow, a dead to be unsaid. A nonacceptable voyage of money, on bursar, on cash, a precursor of crashed.*

"Soooo good!" Margaret says, making muted little golf claps in appreciation. Ariana smiles modestly. Colin later tells me that "when we do these writing activities" in class, he finds Ariana's "poetry" consistently "really good . . . really impressive. It's really creative; it's sort of serious, and interesting—and I would vote for it every time," he chuckles.

Edwin is the reluctant nominee for the next group. "I didn't have anything better," he warns before he reads: *"Sipping on the red cup, scooping the ball up, throat burns from the liquid. Feeling the senses lifted, bend the arm up, loosen the muscle rigid. The projectile landed, hitting the target death cup, opponent's face livid. Crowd builds, watch me pull my pants up, Watch me do my dance, yup."* The class howls with delight, Margaret freely clapping with her whole hands this time. "Is this about beer pong?" Colin asks, arching an eyebrow. "Water pong," Edwin replies innocently, which generates more laughter from the class.

"I like it," Colin says, in a measured tone that conveys bemused tolerance more than whole-hearted admiration. "Very strong entries this year."

After Katarina reads her quite lengthy composition, which Colin praises as "very good, very vivid" but she twice laments is "corny compared to the others," it's Tony's turn. Margaret is squirming with anticipation. Glimpsing the opening line, Colin jokes, "Is this personally insulting to me? Because otherwise I'll just let you vote without having you read." Tony grins slyly but commences reading without comment:

> *I went to English class today*
> *A game is what we got to play*
> *The game is kind of cool*
> *But I'd rather just hit my juul*
> *Drugs are bad is what critics say*
> *But it just makes a better day*
> *This game we play is kind of fun*
> *I hope we're close to being done*
> *Im hungry so I want some food*
> *Maybe that will better my mood*
> *I took my good friend out to eat*
> *But supposedly she hates meat*
> *Practice today is gonna suck*
> *Hopefully I get out with some luck*

"I LOVE it," Katarina gushes when he finishes, applauding along with Margaret.

"I'm unfamiliar with 'juul,'" Colin says, which prompts snorts of amusement but no explanation forthcoming from the students. "Is this something for the young people these days?"[4]

"I thought you were young," Ariana says. "Aren't you like in your 20's?"

"Nooo," Colin says slowly, shaking his head wryly but good-naturedly before turning away to set up the chalkboard for the class vote.

Although Colin is not as far removed from his 20's as his response to Ariana would suggest, I can see that he feels a generational gap with his students. He often speaks to me about them with the same blend of amusement and mystification that he adopts toward them in class; his tone sometimes evokes a field biologist encountering a group of fascinating but perplexing creatures. I can understand why: the students embody contradictions befitting their literal and figurative transitional stage. They summarize Plato from memory, rail against Marxism, and overall demonstrate what Colin calls "impressive" intellectual insight one minute and then lapse into endearing—or frustrating—childishness the next. They laugh uproariously at thinly veiled references to drugs and alcohol, but some of them also make charmingly quaint efforts to sanitize their more colorful language in front of Colin and me ("er, I mean 'fudge,'" Margaret self-censors on one occasion). A few are in the habit of propping a foot on the seminar table and tilting their chair onto the two back legs at a precarious angle that I recognize as a favored position from my own childhood. One student regales Colin with a dramatic story before class about being device-less that day after upending a bottle of iced tea all over her laptop in her dorm room the previous evening. "Sometimes it feels like they're still in high school," Colin sighs during one of our interviews.

"They WERE in high school three months ago," I reply.

"Yeah, that's true," he says reflexively. Then he pauses to truly consider my comment and laughs, reiterating his response with merriment this time. "That's true. They talk about things like senioritis and AP classes like they were VERY important."

Colin recognizes first-year classes—especially writing classes—as critical spaces for students' concurrent academic and social transition to college, a perspective seemingly shared by Abbott's placement policy, which renders the course effectively a shared experience for the majority of incoming students; they are all in it together. Within his class, Colin seeks to build community from day one of the semester, again by leveraging games. Apples to Apples is actually the second game Colin's students play in class; the first is a name game where each member of the class must remember and recite everyone else's name in order. Colin himself cheats a bit in this game by practicing beforehand with the photos in the online class roster, but his own grasp of student names and faces is only partly the goal: he also wants to be sure that students know each other's names as soon as possible, to set the foundation for their collaborative work. "In the class, I try to have them work in groups a lot," Colin says, "and when they do peer reviews, they really need to know who another person is, or they may end up giving some really scathing critique, which isn't helpful for anyone." Knowing names is the necessary first step to "feel[ing] comfortable" with each other as "human beings" and eventually coming to "respect each other." Colin acknowledges that Abbott's placement policy facilitates his work in this domain: the fact that most Abbott first-years take the course but international students with extra language needs are filtered into a separate class means that "there are no nonnative speakers in the class; there's nobody who has a serious learning disability; there's nobody with an age difference—it's a pretty homogenous group," he says. However, Colin does not assume that "homogeneity" automatically translates into feelings of comfort and mutual respect; he continues to enforce community building throughout the semester by mixing up how he groups students for collaborative work: he alternates between assigning partners, letting students choose, or counting off to randomize groupings.

Indeed, this establishment of a trusting classroom community is so important to Colin that he requests that I not begin observing until he has had a chance to play these introductory games and ask the students about their comfort level in participating in the study. Thus, I do not witness the first-day games, but Colin's care with names and community building is still evident to me in my first observation. Though it is only the third session of the semester—and there are actually four new students that day who have just added the class—the students' energetic preclass chatter is audible from the hall as I approach the classroom. Students refer to each other by name frequently during class discussions and more informal moments. The large central table helps to bring classmates literally closer together, but the students also change seats constantly of their own accord. While friendships do form over the course of the semester, the students seem to hold no strong attachments to particular seats or neighbors and instead will claim whatever empty seat is available as they filter in, seemingly content to sit next to different people every day.

Interestingly, while the room set-up seems conducive to the students befriending each other, Colin feels that it sometimes leaves him the odd man out. Though he spends a good amount of time sitting with the students around the table, he also often needs to stand to control the laptop or write on the chalkboard, bringing him outside of the circle and making eye contact with every student difficult. "It's like this weird sort of tight molecular structure that I'm talking at," he says, gesturing with his hands to demonstrate the words emanating from his mouth toward the seminar table. "It's hard to feel like it's a cohesive group that I'm included in." This distance is relational as well as physical; despite Colin emphasizing names from day one and telling students to call him by his first name, it is seven weeks into the semester before I hear a student do so. In total, I only hear two students use his name; the others seem to take great pains to avoid hailing him verbally, contorting their bodies in their seats to make eye contact from across the room or waiting until he is near enough for them to simply launch into their question without preamble. Even in conversations amongst themselves before Colin arrives, students simply use the pronoun "he" in a tacit communal understanding of the antecedent.

When I share this observation with Colin in our last interview, he attributes his decision to be on a first-name basis with students in part to his desire not to claim an honorific he has not yet earned ("I don't have a PhD. I'm not 'Professor Zimmerman.' I'm not 'Dr. Zimmerman'"), but also to his intentional acculturating of students to college norms. "I take it seriously that 'collegiality' is related to 'college,'" he says. "Like there's a sense of being a peer and sort of rising to the level of the people who are your seniors," in contrast to high school, which Colin says he "hated . . . I want to make sure that the experience of college is NOT like high school." In his view, once students reach college, they become cohabiters of an academic community with their instructors and should begin learning how to interact accordingly.

However, Colin is not surprised by my observations of some students' seeming discomfort with the new dynamic; he recognizes that relationships with college instructors can be "confusing" and "fraught" for students—and instructors as well—because the college culture is simultaneously "collegial" and hierarchical. Colin wants students to address him as a "peer" but still respect and defer to his "senior[ity]" and expertise. "A lot of times [students] want to argue with me, and they want to push me on things, and I'm like, 'No. You're wrong. Like, you can call me Colin, but I'm still your teacher—and I'm still gonna grade your paper,'" he chuckles. Colin acknowledges that being on a first-name basis with an instructor is new to many of his students and may "contribute to a general confusion about their role in the class and my authority. But at the same time," he says, "I don't feel like I should have to reinforce my authority constantly" by demanding that students use a title to address him. His authority should be tacitly understood, no matter how students address him; they have to learn to accept that duality.

Yet this tension around negotiating authority is also salient to the development of students' competence mindsets because authority—like the judge in Apples to Apples—often determines what success looks like and whether students have achieved it. But while the authority in Apples to Apples rotates so that *everyone gets a chance to be the judge*,[5] Colin is always the ultimate judge of his students' formal writing in this class, even as he tries to coach students' mastery of the rules in order to build their capacity to self-assess independently of him. Like Diane, Colin has to enact his classroom authority through multiple roles: he is both coach and referee for the larger "game" of academic communication that his students are learning, and he is also a gamemaker in his own right. He designs the classroom-level "game" that plays an important role in the messages students receive about their own success potential "in this new discourse."

Leveling Up

At the beginning of her TED talk "The Power of Yet," psychologist Carol Dweck introduces the audience to "a high school in Chicago where students had to pass a certain number of courses to graduate, and if they didn't pass a course, they got the grade 'Not Yet,'" she says, drawing out the two words for emphasis. "And I thought that was fantastic! Because if you get a failing grade, you think, I'm nothing, I'm nowhere. But if you get the grade 'Not Yet,' you understand that you're on a learning curve." Dweck traces an arc through the air with her right hand. "It gives you a path into the future."

Colin assigns Dweck's TED talk to his students—it is, in fact, the first "text" in his syllabus—and it is fitting that they discuss her growth mindset theory on the same day that Colin introduces the four components of an argument. In addition to making the rules of the game transparent to students, Colin recognizes that students need to perceive and embrace the challenge of writing in order to understand how and why mastering the rules will help them succeed; competence and growth mindset have complementary and mutually reinforcing dimensions. The realization that "writing is hard, and it takes time" is something Colin "didn't encounter as a writer until I was well into grad school," and he wants his students to understand it much earlier in their academic careers. "Good writing is revised writing. It's writing that's been seen by other people, almost always. Unless you're like a brilliant, amazing wunderkind or something," he chuckles. "To make good writing, you have to try and try and try." Thus, from the beginning of the semester, Colin seeks to blend the development of students' competence mindsets with the development of growth mindsets and motivation that will sustain them through the inevitable challenges of college-level writing.

Colin views these challenges as inevitable not only because of the inherent difficulty of the skill but also because "I have rarely met high school students who were well-prepared for college writing," he tells me. "Some students are, but it's very few. Like one student per semester MIGHT be already there. The rest have very little awareness of the kind of depth of thinking and complexity and just the general expectations of the kind of communication that is necessary for college." Likewise, "they're terrible readers. They don't know how to read. I mean that in a sort of literal sense," he chuckles. "They don't think while they read, they just like look at every word and pronounce it; I think that's how they've learned to read. But the readings that we look at in college are more difficult and require a lot more thinking." At the same time, he readily compliments Abbott students as "very conscientious, very quick, and very good at picking up new things. They have a lot of confidence and a lot of potential." Abbott students have also successfully negotiated an undergraduate admissions process that rates among the most competitive in the country: the acceptance rate is 16 percent and average math and verbal SAT scores for incoming students are in the 700s. Yet Colin maintains that even most of these students' skills are "not yet" adequate for the increased difficulty level of college.

Unlike the Chicago high school praised by Dweck, though, Colin has to operate within a traditional grading scheme; although Abbott undergraduates have pass/fail grading options, they must take first-year writing for a letter grade. Accordingly, the writing program communicates the idea of "not yet" through two interrelated policies: a two-semester writing requirement for most students[6] and some pointed advice to instructors to be stingy with their grades. The very first reference to letter grades in the writing program's instructor handbook is a reminder about the departmental policy that an A grade signals mastery and should be given sparingly:

> *Whatever strategy you choose, remember that an A or A– in English 101 exempts the student from English 102. In recent years, our colleagues have reported many students in their classes who did not take English 102 but should have. Moreover, a poll in [the student newspaper] a few years ago named English 101 as an easy course to get an A in. We may be giving too many high grades. Please think*

> *twice before giving an A or A– in English 101, remembering that*
> *only exceptional students should be exempted from the two semesters*
> *of First-Year Writing instruction specified in the Abbott requirement.*

Colin tells me he hasn't looked at the handbook in years, but his description of his grading philosophy strongly parallels the departmental criteria; his own assessment of students' incoming skill levels and needs seems aligned with the institution's, and he does not seem conflicted in enacting a grading policy that demands excellence. He "tr[ies] to lower [students'] expectations on the grades" when he reviews the syllabus on the first day and is "pretty harsh" on grades at the beginning of the semester. By the end of the semester, he tells me that typically "maybe like 10 percent, roughly, would get an A, like the top one or two" students in each section, calling it his "personal philosophy" that students "have to really be ready to take on all kinds of papers" for their other college classes to receive an A from him. "Most people I think will get like a B or a B+, and generally they're OK with that?" Colin chuckles a little, as if conceding some uncertainty over this point. He adds, though, that he believes a first-year writing class is "the place" to adjust students' expectations about grades in college. "I think they're sort of ready for a new challenge. And they understand on some level that their college work is going to be tougher."

Critically, Colin supplements his exacting final evaluation standards with some flexibility in grades that allows him to communicate improvement to students. His "harsh" early-semester grades function partly as a signal to students that they have leveled up in academic difficulty, but also as a low baseline that gives Colin room to create an upward grade trajectory for each student over the course of the semester. While he thinks students' writing genuinely does improve, he "also sort of 'let[s]' them get better" by occasionally "let[ting] things slide" in later papers that he might have critiqued more heavily early on. "I don't know if that's bad," he says, "but it seems to me like it's more important to help boost their confidence as they go than it is to have absolutely objective grading policy. I don't even know what that would be." He also allows students the option to revise one paper after receiving their grade so that they can see the direct translation of their additional targeted effort into an improved grade. Thus, while the vast majority of students will not earn As as their overall course grade, Colin exercises discretion with specific assignment grades to try to reward student effort and improvement.

Colin also communicates messages to students about effort and process engagement through what he does <u>not</u> grade. Leading up to the final graded paper for each unit, Colin grades almost none of the smaller individual assignments, which include reading responses, occasional reading quizzes, preparatory notes for class discussions, the discussions themselves, paper drafts, and peer review exercises (other than two more formal peer response papers that he does grade). Instead, he factors their completion and general quality into the three categories of his semester grade breakdown that are not the final paper grades. He hopes this approach helps to show students that "the point is not always to get a grade from me, but to have them go through the effort" of working through authentic interim steps in the long and rigorous process of writing well. While he gives "fairly copious amounts of feedback" on students' graded essays to help them understand what they can do to improve, he has increasingly scaled back his commentary on the smaller homework assignments that students post to the class website, realizing that the website—a minimalist Google+ page that Colin set up himself—provides its own kind of accountability because postings are public to all invited members. "That's a change for me," he laughs. "I used to think that I had to judge everything, all the time." As a more experienced teacher now, Colin recognizes that he has influence not only through what he does but also what he does not do; removing himself from the equation as an evaluator can shift students' focus from trying to please him for a grade to doing the actual work necessary to improve.

This shift in thinking is important not only for fostering students' growth mindset in Colin's particular class but also because it is authentic to the "game" of advanced academic writing, where students have to increasingly exercise their own authorial judgment and not rely on the verdict of an external authority. As a doctoral candidate, Colin can model the self-directed, effortful advanced writing process by being transparent to students "about my own experience of writing, which is that it's painful and awful," he laughs to me in an interview. I see him do this in class through spontaneous responses and anecdotes, such as when he opens class one day by inviting students to reflect briefly on their experiences writing the Letter to the Editor assignment that they have just turned in:

> Quinn raises her hand and says she struggled to find her argument: she was trying to apply the idea of "stupid games" described in a course reading to an analysis of Pokémon Go, but ultimately she "had to rewrite [the assignment] three times."
> "Oh NO!" Colin says in his gently theatrical manner. "That sounds like MY writing process!" Several students laugh at this, and Colin elaborates by estimating that he re-wrote the

first chapter of his dissertation three times, "and it was like thirty-five pages."

I hear "woah"s and other shocked reactions around the table. Milking the response a bit, Colin spells out the arithmetic for them: three full-blown rewrites adds up to "writing one hundred pages and only getting thirty good ones out of it." ("GEEZ," someone mutters.) Colin explains, though, that the process of rewriting ultimately makes any piece better.

In this and similar exchanges, Colin affirms the importance of effort by showing students that even their teacher, the authoritative expert who evaluates them, has to work hard at his craft. Success and expertise do not mean that the work gets easier—if anything, it gets harder and requires more effort.

The codevelopment of growth and competence mindsets is therefore critical for students as they advance in their academic careers, starting with their current transition to the rigorous and elite academic space of Abbott University. When Colin talks to me about lowering his students' expectations about grades, he explains:

> I don't know if I say this to them, but because it's such a highly selective pool, to be the student who really shines, you have to work really hard and sort of be exceptional. So, being in this place, you're going to succeed, that's fine, and I still have to make some distinctions between the people who are doing an exceptional job and the people who are doing a good job. I don't want to have to make those distinctions, but I mean, some people put in a lot more time on their papers than others.

Colin voices some passing discomfort at essentially having to rank students through grades, but this is assuaged by his belief that exceptional effort leads to an exceptional product and should be rewarded accordingly, especially among such a "highly selective" group.

However, the selectivity of the group poses its own challenges in enacting Colin's approach to the competence and growth mindsets. For Colin, the highly selective educational context seems to lower the stakes of grading; because his students are invariably "going to succeed . . . being in this place," he is simply demarcating relative degrees of success within a fairly narrow range. But Colin admits through his disclaimer ("I don't know if I say this to them") that he is not sure how transparent he is to students about his philosophy, opening up the possibility of alternative understandings on the students' part. At a highly selective private undergraduate institution, attempts to recalibrate students' expectations and definitions of success, failure, and effort can run up against a substantial barrier: the possibility that the students themselves are playing quite a different game from the one their instructor has designed.

How to Win

On my way to Colin's classroom, I pass a few of his students sitting in a nearby lounge area, all silent and staring at their laptop screens; the final drafts of their second papers are due today and I suspect there is some last-minute work happening. When I reach the classroom, Erika and Quinn are the only people inside. Quinn is regaling Erika with a description of a Teaching Associate for one of her other classes who is the "harshest grader I've ever had." Knitting her brows together, Quinn deepens her voice to play-act the TA lecturing her class that the grades indicate that their work does not meet the quality standard for <u>graduate</u> students. "Well, no fucking kidding!" she exclaims in her own voice—though she whispers the curse word, the only indication that she is aware of my presence. She estimates that she's slept seven or eight hours total over the past two nights: "I'm drowning."

"That's the word," Erika agrees, along with "defeated." Quinn proposes "drained." As the room starts filling up shortly before noon, they invite their classmates to join the game: "We're brainstorming words that start with a D that describe our mental state," Quinn says, since "we're all getting D's on this essay" that is due for Colin today. "Dead," someone offers. "Dumb." "Doomed."

As far as I know, nobody in the class ever received a D on any essay; the grading scheme in Colin's syllabus, which is adapted from the sample in the department handbook, only goes down to a C-, and Colin tells me the average grade on each essay "is probably a B." But this preclass exchange is not novel to me; in similar situations, the students have also articulated unrest over the syllabus criteria that begin with Cs as the baseline, "satisfactory" grade. "We're all getting Cs," one student announces before class on the day their first papers are due. "Did you see what it said for B/B–?" another asks, alluding perhaps to the syllabus's framing of B papers as "exceed[ing] expectations" (As are reserved for "exceptional" work).

While the Abbott writing program handbook gives instructors plenty of guidance on how to make sure that only "exceptional" students earn A's and tells instructors that *the idea that a B is a 'bad' grade must be shed*, it does not provide any concrete guidance on how to alter students' meaning making around grades. In fact, it seems to take some pride in Abbott students' achievement orientations, acknowledging that *most of our students are used to receiving A's and A-s in high school. They would not be at Abbott if that were not the case!* The department suggests that seeing Bs as "bad" grades is a delusion that "must be shed"—but it is a delusion that has been reinforced by Abbott's own highly selective admissions process; the students would not even be at Abbott if they had been content with mostly Bs in high school.

Nor does the institutional reinforcement end at the admissions process; both Colin and the university continue to leverage the extrinsically motivating power of grades and achievement culture for their students while simultaneously articulating a desire for students to be less fixated on grades. In one interview when Colin initiates a conversation about pass/fail grading policies, and I tell him about the mandatory pass/fail first-semester policy at my alma mater, Swarthmore College, he initially exclaims that he "would have loved that!" before backtracking to admit that he "never would have opted for that" as an undergraduate student himself. Though Colin did not attend a college as selective as Abbott, instead splitting his undergraduate years between the University of Denver and the state university where Liz earned her MFA, he empathizes with the "pressure to get high grades all the time" that he believes his students have internalized. Yet in his teaching, Colin takes advantage of this very same internalized pressure; in concluding his comment justifying the distinctions he makes between the "exceptional" and the good, Colin observes that at Abbott, "if [students] want higher grades, they'll work for them . . . like they'll try to earn them."

The paradox in Colin's approach reflects the balancing act that the Abbott writing program asks its instructors to perform, essentially dangling the prospect of an A as an eternal carrot for their achievement-oriented students:

> *It does not beat our students down to create grading standards that reward hard work yet still insure that all but a few of them will go on to English 102. It does, however, beat students down—make them feel their efforts are pointless—if you announce that no one, or only a few people, can or will receive an A or A– in your English 101 class.* **Please do not do that.** *Explain your grading policies and standards but do <u>not</u> announce that there will be no or few A's.*

That, understandably, makes students frustrated and hostile, which *of course does not contribute to their ability to learn.* (Emphasis in original)

The writing program encourages Colin and the other instructors to leverage grades as an extrinsic reward for "hard work," but with a ceiling; the next page of the handbook directs instructors to *be sure that you do not* *allow* class participation to count for more than 10 percent of the semester grade, which could *trap you in giving too many A or A– final grades.* Colin weights participation at 5 percent, although his largely completion-based grades in other categories give him some flexibility to reward student effort and engagement in other ways; students' paper grades, however, still count for 75 percent of their overall course grade. Colin is expected to engage essentially in a dual act of obfuscation: first, students should be "rewarded" for hard work with grades, but not the grade the department believes/knows they want; and second, the unattainability of that reward should never be made transparent because it will "understandably" upset them—suggesting that such a reaction would be justified.

Colin faces a steep challenge in enacting this departmental directive, especially because it drastically underestimates student resourcefulness and capacity for conspiratorial thinking. He never tells his students that there is a ceiling on their grades, but he does not need to. Either through word of mouth or from adding up the English 102 exemption policy—which is publicly stated—and the "lowered expectations" about grades, they already know. Katarina vents her frustration over the policy in another preclass conversation, telling a classmate, "You might deserve an A from all the work you do, but they don't want you to get an A because then you place out of English 102." The lack of transparency gives the students' knowledge an illicit tinge that seems to inflame their perception of injustice. On another occasion when I arrive before Colin does, the students who are present are uncharacteristically quiet as they review their homework reading for the scheduled reading quiz,[7] but they break the silence before long:

"Is it bad that I don't care what I get on this quiz?" Quinn asks.

"No," says Lena.

Rachel observes that Quinn won't even know what she gets "because he doesn't tell us."

"Or like that last one when he was like, 'it's just an exercise to make you think,' " says Lena in a mocking tone.

"I'm just always gonna get a bad grade in this class," Rachel sighs, "no matter what I do." Lucas and a couple others nod or otherwise agree with Rachel's assessment that Colin has "picked one person to give an A to" and that's it; Lucas, however, shrugs off the injustice, saying that he wanted to take English 102 anyway.

Though they never do so in Colin's sight and hearing, the students seem to me to be exhibiting the "frustrated" and "hostile" attitudes the Abbott writing department is seeking to avoid. I wonder, then, what impact the not-so-secret-after-all departmental policy is having on students' mindsets and attributions related to their own effort and success.

I pause here to acknowledge that there is a performative element to these student conversations occurring in Colin's absence. I do not think the students were performing for me, but I suspect they may have been performing for each other, with varying degrees of self-awareness. I recall the "misery poker" culture I perceived (and occasionally participated in) at Swarthmore—another highly selective college that, like Abbott, pools high achievers and explicitly tells them on the first day to adjust their expectations.[8] In these environments, there is cultural capital in academic martyrdom, as students broadcast their onerous workloads and brag about their all-nighters, seeking to one-up each other on sleep deprivation and stress levels:

> Rachel asks her classmates how many of them are taking the option to revise their first essay. Several students respond in the affirmative, with Kyle saying he already turned in his rewrite. Rachel recounts her experience of revising and seeing the essay get "longer and longer and longer" until she decided, "Fuck it" and "started over" from scratch.

> "You STARTED OVER?" Tony repeats in disbelief.

> "At 1:00 a.m.," she confirms, with a touch of pride.

> Ariana chimes in that her own long revision experience culminated in her declaring, "Fuck it, I give up" and deciding to turn in what she had.

For students, having their superlative efforts go unrewarded grade-wise ("I'm always gonna get a bad grade in this class, no matter what I do") potentially only adds to the narrative. Their outrage at being "played" by the institution feeds their own game of belonging: performing struggle is their way of performing membership in a rigorous and demanding academic community. There are multiple overlapping and embedded games occurring here—all of which instructors like Colin have to contend with as they try to build students' writing mastery.

These overlapping games being played can also lead to genuinely mixed messages being sent and received among the various players about what grades reflect and how students should interpret them. It seems to me that some of the students' frustration over the reading quizzes stems less from a competitive desire for a certain grade, but rather from a lack of specific feedback and transparency about the assessment criteria—the opposite of Colin's very explicit and recurring articulation of what he is looking for in their essays. When Rachel says "he doesn't tell us" how they do on the reading quizzes, she is not being hyperbolic. Earlier in the semester, Colin told the students one day that they all did "fine" on their first reading quizzes but then paused when the students asked if and when they would receive the quizzes back, as if he had not anticipated the question. He eventually answered that he "mostly just skims" them and doesn't write comments, but that the students were welcome to pick them up from his office, or else, "I can keep them as handwriting samples," he joked. To Colin, the quizzes truly are "just an exercise to make you think," a low-stakes check on whether students have understood key points from their homework readings. In fact, when I ask him in our first interview what strategies he uses to promote the mindset, "I can succeed at this," Colin names the fact that he gives the students "pretty easy" reading quiz questions. "I think?" he adds, acknowledging that he and the students might have different assessments of the level of difficulty. "They're all doing fine. Maybe I need to, like, put smiley faces on their papers and give them back or something," he says; because we are speaking by phone, I cannot see if he is rolling his eyes, but his tone certainly conveys that sentiment. "But yeah, I'm not sure if there's a whole lot built into the course that gives that sense of success. I don't know, maybe they should develop the mindset without getting rewards constantly." He pauses, repeating the mindset phrase softly to himself. "'I can succeed at this.' Does that require rewards?"

Turning my interview questions back around on me to tap into my pedagogical knowledge is a habit I will come to expect in my conversations with Colin. "I'm always curious what I'm doing wrong," he tells me on another occasion, "because I don't really have pedagogy training." He explains that Abbott is "not a really super prestigious research university, so the people who graduate often go into teaching jobs," rather than pure academic research, but also that he is "more interested in the teaching side" of higher education anyway. "I'm interested in making classrooms work," he says. "That's one of the things that really excites me about this kind of job . . . I see myself as a teacher as much as—or more than—a researcher."

Early in our research relationship, though, I am hesitant to say too much. "It might depend on how you define 'reward,'" I say.

"Mm," he muses. "Mmhmm." When he does not immediately offer further thoughts, we shift to another topic.

This is one example of students and an instructor viewing the feedback, evaluation, and "reward" structures of a class differently, potentially leading to mutual frustration. Colin sometimes seems mystified or slightly annoyed when students don't always understand or appreciate his aims; he describes to me in our last interview how long it took one student to let go of the anxiety over "getting it right," something Colin himself views as a holdover from more formulaic writing in high school and antithetical to the complexity and nuance of college-level writing. Yet it does not seem strange to me that the students, presented with a guiding metaphor of gameplay and mixed messages about success from multiple institutional actors, stubbornly cling to the idea of a master algorithm that will unlock the secret to victory. As Colin himself tells them on the first day of the semester, in the game of academic writing, "there are rules and expectations . . . There are ways that you can win."

The students are also being asked to trust that the new writing game they are learning from Colin is the real, true game that will set them up for success in the future, even as they are simultaneously told that the writing game they learned in high school—which, at the very least, did not impede their acceptance to Abbott—is flawed and obsolete. Although in interviews Colin describes the progression from high school to college as a shift in meta-awareness of the same game—following the rules as a young player, understanding the rules as an older player—in class he more often than not implies that the college game is completely different from the high school game. When working on thesis statements on two separate days, he mocks a formula that he calls "typical . . . I don't know why" of high school writing instruction, which is "to start with some comment about history," such as: "*Throughout the course of human history,*" he intones in a dramatic movie-trailer voice, drawing giggles from some of the students. "Or, *Since the dawn of time . . .*" When discussing the principles of clarity and cohesion, he tells the students that using many different synonyms is "a tendency that high school teachers promote . . . but in general it's not good for readers—at least not THIS reader," he says, indicating himself. Finally, in setting up the *Eunoia* activity, Colin tells the students that the theme of today's class is rules:

> "I'm sure you learned a lot of rules in high school," he says, "such as: every good essay has five paragraphs?"
>
> "Eww," someone says.
>
> "Three body paragraphs, and then an intro and a conclusion?" Colin teases, before continuing: "We've learned lots of new rules in this class." He asks the students to name some as he scrawls *Rules* across the chalk board as a heading for the brainstorm.
>
> "The five-paragraph essay is dead?" Rachel offers.
>
> Although this echoes something Colin himself wrote on the Unit 1 assignment sheet (*The five-paragraph essay is dead, dead, dead!*), I sense this is not quite what he was looking for in this context—he's again asking the students to recite some of the frameworks they've learned—but he also does not disagree with it, so he obligingly writes *5P* on the board and then emphatically draws a big *X* over it.

Later in this same class period is when Colin tells the students that "rules don't have to be limiting. They can be enabling." It seems, though, that he applies this principle only to certain kinds of rules—a distinction that the students must ultimately discern for themselves in a game that is constantly changing around them. As Colin's "stupid games" course reading points out: *Games tend to reflect the societies in which they are created and played. Monopoly, for instance, makes perfect sense as a product of the 1930s—it allowed anyone, in the middle of the Depression, to play at being a tycoon. Risk, released in the 1950, is a stunningly literal expression of cold-war realpolitik. Twister is the translation, onto a game board, of the mid-1960s sexual revolution.*[9] In other words, games are a product of our context and culture. But culture is like the water we swim in: it can be hard to see. "Having never taught high school," Colin tells me, "I never really know what students have learned. I don't know where they came from." Yet he also adamantly "want[s] to make sure that the experience of college is NOT like high school" and tells me he is trying as an educator to be less "heavily invested in a particular outcome" for his students. "Because it's more just about the process," he says. "It's about playing the game." I wonder, though, how far educators can go in developing their students' mastery of a game without a deeper understanding themselves of not only "the rules of the game" but the multiple, sometimes contradictory objectives and rules of the multiple games that students—and the educators themselves—are playing.

Reflections on Promoting a Competence Mindset

The key features of Colin's first-year writing class map nicely onto the sources of self-efficacy—mastery experiences, vicarious experiences, social persuasion, and emotional states—that have been shown to promote students' competence mindsets (Bandura, 1997; Usher & Pajares, 2008). The transparency in his approach to writing instruction and his explicit articulation of the game metaphor to students sets the foundation for their mastery experiences in the class. The "game" is an intriguing provocation that establishes writing as a complex and challenging task that all students can master—with practice and effort. The "rules of the game" allow Colin to make his expectations and criteria for quality writing clear and consistently infuse them into class activities. He periodically checks students' retention and understanding of the rules to monitor their progress, and he has students practice their skills multiple times and in multiple contexts so that they have numerous opportunities to build their mastery. These criteria also drive his comments on student work, ensuring that his feedback is informational rather than idiosyncratic.

This approach is also consistent with the notion of threshold concepts from composition studies; indeed, Colin's Wittgenstein-inspired game metaphor echoes discussions of threshold concepts in first-year writing as working toward students developing their own theories of writing as a way of "understand[ing] 'the game' of writing" (Downs & Robertson, 2015, p. 110). In contrast to Liz's emotion-centered approach, Colin makes the explicit articulation and even memorization of certain "game" features a centerpiece of his instruction. His approach is an impressively well-considered and well-developed framework for supporting students' writing development, especially considering how little training he has had in writing pedagogy.

Like the other three educators, Colin recognizes a reciprocity between students' belonging and competence mindsets and attends carefully to the social dimensions of the classroom to ensure that the peer community provides opportunities for vicarious learning and supportive social persuasion and reduces anxiety or negative emotions. Recognizing the first year of college as a vulnerable transition period for many students, he works from the first day of the semester to help students feel a sense of belonging in "this discourse community" to view each other as learning supports and near-peer success exemplars. The *Eunoia*-inspired writing game illustrates the power of the social learning environment; as far as I can see, the students all but forget about the extrinsic reward that Colin initially dangles in front of them and become much more engaged at the prospect of sharing their work with their peers and cheering each other on. Two of the nominated students downplay their writing competence in various ways (Edwin saying "I didn't have anything better," Tony nodding in agreement at Kyle's assessment that they both "aren't good writers"), and yet both receive enthusiastic social validation for their compositions—the class actually votes Edwin's ode to beer pong the overall winner. Although goal orientation literature generally advocates against competitive structures in a classroom, the *Eunoia* game is a playful riff on competition: it is unconnected to students' overall achievement in the class and actually seeks to reinforce a mastery approach by allowing students to generate and master their own criteria for excellence rather than perform to an external normative standard.

However, while the social relationships in classrooms can support an educator's emphasis on mastery goals, they can also contribute to an alternative set of social goals that may not align with the intended design. Similar to Liz, Colin clearly strives to emphasize mastery goals, in which students are motivated by the task to develop their skills and improve over past performance, versus achieving with little effort or outperforming peers (Kaplan et al., 2002; Urdan & Schoenfelder, 2006). He tries to coach students away from performance goal orientations by shifting students' focus away from grades as the external assignation of success that motivates them. When the students themselves try to raise the issue early in the semester by asking about their reading quizzes, he declines to comment specifically on students' performance other than to say that "everyone did fine." Many of the students' other assignments are likewise ungraded, at least in terms of the normative grade scale that students expect, with Colin relying on other sources of accountability (such as public posting of homework response papers) to motivate students, rather than merely the threat of a failing grade, which could reinforce performance-avoidance behaviors. Although he is ultimately required to give students letter grades, he still tries to use these in more of a mastery-approach focus on individual improvement by allowing everyone the option to revise one graded paper and "letting" each student's grades improve over the course of the semester to "build their confidence" even while most of them will not earn the mark of success they are hoping for.

Despite Colin's efforts, his students may be acting out "social status goals" (Patrick et al., 2002) in which the desire for status—as its own kind of competitive performance—potentially interferes with students' ability to focus on the mastery goals their instructor is emphasizing. As a counterpoint to Colin's planned writing games, we see his students literally inventing and playing their own alternative game ("words that begin with 'D' to describe our mental state") that hints at a metaphorical alternative game as well: a kind of achievement misery poker where the players try to one-up each other on having their superlative effort go unappreciated. In addition to fulfilling social goals, the students' game operates on an external locus of control that is also consistent with performance orientations (E. Jones, 2008); they frame their lower-than-desired paper grades as something that Colin bestows on them with ulterior motives, versus a reflection of the quality of their work and/or the effectiveness of their effort. When students view success as normative and externally defined, their competence mindset may look less like, "I can succeed at this," and more like, "I can't succeed at this . . . but it's not my fault."

In this respect, Colin encounters a similar challenge to what Liz experienced, even as both instructors seek to engage their students in a learning process focused on mastery and personal improvement rather than on As as the only acceptable grade *and* even though their approaches to this goal are nearly polar opposites. The contrast is neatly encapsulated by their essentially inverted course grade distributions: almost no one gets an A in Colin's class, whereas a majority of Liz's students do, partly because Colin weights paper grades more in his semester grade (75 percent versus 40 percent for Liz), and partly because he is a deliberately "harsh" grader on those essays, whereas Liz saw "encouragement" as a better motivator of sustained effort. I note that their distinct approaches may also align with the differences in the selection procedures for their courses; while Colin's course is a default for most Abbott freshmen, Liz's students place into her class due to poor performance on the summer writing assessment. As such, Liz may be keenly attuned to students' emotional state, whereas Colin focuses more on giving students a reality check about college-level writing. Yet, they both encounter challenges in weaning their students off a grade-focused mentality, which they likewise both attribute to the enduring competitive, grade-oriented effects of high school. In addition to their perceptions that high school provides inadequate writing preparation ("They aren't taught to trust themselves," "I have rarely met high school students who were well prepared for college writing"), Colin and Liz both saw themselves as needing to combat the "high school mentality" of working primarily for external validation and reward.

This dim view of high school is echoed elsewhere in composition research (Fanetti et al., 2010) and certainly was evident in the commodification of achievements seen at Riverside Academy in chapter 1; however, I argue that in Colin's case especially, the college is not neutral in students' manifest attitudes. Studies suggest that the overall mastery versus performance culture at a school may be more influential on students' perceptions than individual classroom dynamics, especially starting in secondary grades when students divide their time among many individual instructors and learning experiences within a school (Deemer, 2004). It is certainly plausible that Abbott's undergraduate selectivity and its specific school-wide and departmental policies around grading and course exemptions play an outsized role in framing students' beliefs about performance that Colin cannot fully overcome. These elements of institutional culture may also shape Colin's own belief system and his subsequent enactment of those beliefs to students, as when he describes to me the miserly distribution of As as his "personal policy"—when it also happens to be the writing department's policy. It is important to remember, however, that performance goals are not unequivocally negative. The fact that Colin seeks to shift students' thinking away from grades but still accepts grades as markers of quality and even actively leverages students' grade-based motivations ("If they want higher grades, they'll work for them") is not necessarily a paradox; it may reflect a hybrid emphasis on mastery and performance that is authentic to this particular institutional environment and the highly competent students it admits.

The question that remains, however, is whether there are untapped opportunities for Colin to *balance* mastery and performance goals more effectively for students, perhaps by clarifying the seemingly contradictory or mixed messages around individual growth versus standards-based performance and evaluation. This was a trend across all four educators, who each admitted to me at times that their pedagogical intent was probably not as clear to students as it could be. The trend is particularly evident in the college instructors' attempts to promote the growth and competence mindsets concurrently through feedback and grading practices, consistent with threshold concepts related to the importance of failure, revision, and assessment in writing (Adler-Kassner & Wardle, 2016). Though Colin has a much clearer framework for writing quality than does Liz, they share similar sentiments about possible miscommunications or misunderstandings with students, with Liz saying, "There isn't as much transparency in the grading process as I think [students] would like and as I would like" and Colin reflecting that he thinks about grades in ways that he did not always convey to students ("I don't know if I say this to them . . .").

In particular, Colin is far less transparent with students about smaller course assignments, such as the ungraded and unreturned reading quizzes, than he is with essays, which may have the opposite effect of what he intends. For Colin, it is entirely natural that he would not return the reading quizzes because his intention behind the assignment does not require them to be graded or commented on in any way. He has skimmed them and is generally satisfied with the students' demonstrated mastery of basic concepts from the readings; my sense is that if he saw any concerning patterns in a particular student's quizzes, he would approach that student individually. However, this mental calculus stays in Colin's head, never spoken aloud. I can see Colin's off-hand joke about keeping the papers as handwriting samples potentially further inflaming students' frustration and confusion over the purpose of the task. Meanwhile, Colin is frustrated by what he perceives as students' immature need for validation when he sarcastically suggests that he could "put smiley faces on their papers and give them back." The two sides' mutual misunderstanding could lead to students perceiving the reading quizzes not as a check on mastery, as Colin intends, but rather a performance task where their performance level is concealed from them. Thus, Colin's nondiscussion of grades or performance in class—though intended to shift students' focus to mastery—might actually contribute to at least some students' continued obsession with grades because they do not receive explicit guidance in an alternative way to think. In this respect, Colin's and Liz's students seem not dissimilar in how they end up thinking about their grades, though the instructors' approaches are so different and Liz's students air their thoughts publicly to her while Colin's students keep their gripes (relatively) private.

Such a misalignment between the teacher's intent and students' inter-pretation would be consistent with other studies finding that students report significantly lower use of mastery-promoting instructional practices than do their teachers: Deemer and colleagues (2004) speculate that the variation may arise from teachers "not always enact[ing] their reported beliefs" about mastery (p. 84), but it is also possible that teachers do teach for mastery, but students fail to interpret the practices as such. Kaplan and colleagues (2002) note that classroom goal structures are "primarily . . . subjective" in that their influence on student motivation "depends more on how students *perceive* the various policies and practices . . . than on the objective reality of the policies or practices themselves" (p. 25, emphasis in original). Studies have also found that students in the same classroom perceive the same practices differently (Urdan et al., 1999) and that there is more variation in student perceptions *within* classrooms than between classrooms (Wolters, 2004).

While some scholars interpret these findings to mean that educators have limited influence on students' perceptions and mindsets, an alternative interpretation is that educators need more support in how to make mastery goals transparent in their classrooms and how to scaffold students' uptake of those mastery goals and positive competence mindset messages. In other words, paralleling Colin's approach to academic writing with students, educators could use a kind of game manual themselves to help them master the rules of the motivational teaching game. Although I must temper expectations by assuring readers that there is no magical cheat code for teaching just as there is none for academic writing, I nonetheless take up this challenge in the final chapter of this book by offering insights and takeaways from a synthesis of the four portraits.

Chapter 5

Illuminating the Invisible

The preceding chapters illustrated how four educators sought to promote motivational mindsets in their classrooms. Each chapter profiled one educator and a focal mindset—Diane and belonging, Zachary and the value mindset, Liz and the growth mindset, and Colin and the competence mindset—and discussed how the educators' practices might promote, or thwart, students' development of the focal mindset. I also highlighted key intersections between the mindsets as the chapters progressed, some of which I revisit in this chapter. My goal has been to provide readers with insights into the challenges and complexity of navigating the motivational ecosystem in secondary and postsecondary classrooms, hopefully evoking recognition, empathy, and self-reflection. In this chapter, I aim to scaffold readers' meaning-making process by offering synthesized findings related to classroom implications, secondary and postsecondary sector differences, and educators' motivational mindsets.

In each of these sections, I first foreground recommendations and action steps that are within educators' control. The portraits of Diane, Zachary, Liz, and Colin speak to the immense potential of individual educators to intuitively develop strategies that, in many cases, align with themes in extant motivation theory and research. Their practical expertise gained through experience (Richardson, 1996; Shulman, 1986) and their reflectiveness as educators (Hillocks, 1995; Schön, 1983) supply them with many already-effective tools and skills for developing new tools through fairly minimal nudges or suggested modifications.

That said, I cannot in good conscience conclude this book by suggesting that the mechanisms for improving student motivation lie solely within classroom educators' hands. We can appreciate their professional knowledge and agency within the classroom without simultaneously expecting them to solve an impossible puzzle single-handedly. Therefore, following the educator implications in each section, I step back to acknowledge influences at the "outer" levels of the motivational ecosystem that implicate educators' optimal enactment of these recommendations. The guiding question across these sections is: How can we best support classroom educators as they practice implementing the recommendations outlined above?

Classroom Implications for Supporting Mindsets: Recommendations for Educators

I began this book with the vignette of my former student Damian and the questions that plagued my mind and drove me to a career in research. While I cannot answer all of these questions for Damian specifically, each of the four classrooms profiled here offers different affordances and challenges for student motivation. With a projection of Damian as my metaphorical avatar, I identify the strategies that would likely have strengthened his motivational mindsets in each classroom as well as the practices that might have undermined his motivation. These strategies fall under three general categories that I have formulated as takeaway recommendations for fellow educators: (1) cultivate validating and growth-promoting relationships, (2) incorporate transparency and scaffolding for motivational development on par with academic skill development, and (3) prioritize informational feedback on strategic effort over esteem-building "rewards." The complexity of the portraits affirms the need for educators to tailor strategies to their specific teaching contexts, so these recommendation categories are deliberately broad—principles, rather than prescriptions—to allow educators to consider how they would enact them in light of the results from the focal educators.

Throughout this section, I intentionally view Diane, Zachary, Liz, and Colin through their shared identity as classroom educators, independent of sector affiliation, because foregrounding similarities over difference is so rarely done in college transition literature and because the recommendations are relevant across sector lines. I discuss differences and opportunities for synergy between the secondary and postsecondary sectors in the following section.

CULTIVATE VALIDATING AND GROWTH-PROMOTING RELATIONSHIPS

I start with belonging in part because, as the first focal mindset, it received less cross-case comparison in the chapter 1 commentary, but also because belonging is foundational to the recommendations that follow. All four educators seemed to be aware of the importance of belonging; they all devoted considerable thought and effort to building positive relationships with students and were aware of the role that belonging could play in mitigating negative competence mindsets. The educators were responsive, personable, and supportive toward their students—relational features that Damian and many other students also seem to value in teachers (Cornelius-White, 2007). They communicated both implicitly and explicitly that they were there to help students learn; no one would be written off or expelled from the classroom, even if they repeatedly failed (Janie, in Diane's case), didn't comply with class activities (Alicia, in Zachary's case), or interrupted tasks to push their own agenda (Liz's students). Though it may seem obvious, the importance of the relationship between an educator and each student in the class cannot be understated as a critical foundation for belonging and school engagement (Quin, 2017).

The educators also helped students build positive relationships with each other through group work and interactive learning tasks, a dimension of belonging that may have been underdeveloped in Damian's experience. Damian had positive relationships with at least some of his teachers, but peer relationships and belonging are also important for supplying the vicarious experiences, social persuasion, and positive psychological classroom climate that can bolster students' self-efficacy and competence mindsets (Bandura, 1997). Diane and Colin were particularly invested in the idea of the overall classroom community, not just the dyadic teacher-student relationship, helping students strengthen their competence mindsets as well as their actual competence. As an extension of the overall school culture in Diane's case and of Colin's personal theory of writing, both educators engaged in intentional peer community building that might ostensibly seem silly (decade dress-up, *Eunoia* writing game) but that ultimately made the more academic collaborations (activism projects, peer review) possible.

Importantly, all the educators aimed to convey both "room for authenticity" and "value for authenticity" (Jansen et al., 2014) in their relationships with students, though they also encountered tensions and challenges with this goal at times. Demonstrating an acceptance of students' interests and experiences in the academic space of the classroom, they all tried to incorporate some degree of student choice in their coursework—most often through students choosing their own paper topics—in an attempt to make the work relevant and personally valuable to students, linking supports for the belonging and value mindsets. Diane asked students to focus on a "national issue [that] affects or will affect you or your family" for their research papers, while Zachary asked his American Literature students to "writ[e] about their place in American literature and American history" and aimed overall for his students to let their interests drive their academic experience. Likewise, the first essay in both Liz's and Colin's classes allowed students to use their own personal experience as evidence. Liz and Zachary both articulated to me the explicit belief that fostering perceived value and relevance in the classroom could stimulate students' growth mindsets by motivating their efforts to improve.

While all four educators conveyed positive intentions in welcoming students' authentic selves, this was also an area of potential growth. The two White women, Diane and Liz, were explicitly (to me) reflective of their racialized authority positions within the institution and/or academy at large, discussing their unease with promulgating White middle-class norms that may be inconsistent with or repressive of students' cultural identities. However, neither had fully settled on a coherent and consistent strategy for enacting this consciousness in their interactions with students or for inviting the students themselves into the conversation. Out of the four, Diane's classroom hosted the most explicit conversations about the impacts of inequity and injustice on students, but her school also imposed the most restrictions and control over students in the name of achievement, and Diane herself sometimes conveyed dichotomous messages about college versus "real life" and issues that mattered to students. Colin was accepting of (though somewhat bemused by) the selves that the Abbott students brought to class and encouraged them to develop their individual voices as writers, but he did not necessarily communicate much overt interest in students' goals or passions. Zachary was able to articulate an integrated vision of academic skills enriching students' existing interests and natural curiosity, rather than being an add-on, but he did not always engage the students themselves in making these connections more explicitly.

I confess that this is something I also could have worked on more in my approach to Damian. Though I genuinely cared about him, most of my concerns about him revolved around his academic success; I viewed him as underachieving and wished he would get his act together to go to college because I could see that he had the potential to be successful there. I did not necessarily consider what college would help him do or how it could align with his own goals for himself. I recall that hallway conversation and our endless conversations about behavior and grades, but I don't recall exchanges where I did more questioning and listening in the interest of truly understanding Damian rather than constantly viewing him through the lens of underachievement and missed potential. In short, I spent a lot of time agonizing over why he didn't fit the mold, but I never really questioned the mold itself.

Merging the findings from these cases with my own reflections on Damian, I see developing a more complex and nuanced understanding of culturally validating relationships as an implication and recommendation for educators. Developing intentional strategies to cultivate relationships that promote students' sense of belonging with their teacher and peers remains a critical foundation, but educators can also consider what implicit and explicit messages they are sending about students' belonging in the discipline and about the discipline's stance of cultural inclusivity toward students that could impact the intersection between belonging and the competence, growth, and value mindsets. Do students know that their struggles and areas for growth do not signal a lack of "fitness" for the work? Do they understand how the skills in this class can help serve their goals or those of their community, rather than only the goals of the academy or hegemonic societal expectations? Part of this work is in educators developing and endorsing these understandings themselves so that they are likelier to convey consistently aligned implicit messages to students, but the other part involves attending to the frequency and nature of their explicit messages on these topics. I address the importance of this transparency and explicit structures in the following sections.

INCORPORATE TRANSPARENCY AND SCAFFOLDING FOR MOTIVATIONAL (AS WELL AS SKILL) DEVELOPMENT

I have already noted on numerous occasions in the preceding chapters that the educators often provided me with an extensive rationale for their pedagogical choices, but evidence from students—in the form of questions in class (Zachary, Liz), written reflections (Liz), and pre- or in-class venting sessions (Colin and Diane, respectively)—suggests that these carefully considered rationales did not always reach the intended targets, thus limiting their desired impact on students' motivational mindsets. This finding is consistent with multiple motivation studies documenting discrepancies between teacher and student perceptions of class (e.g., Bardach et al., 2019). Such divergences are not solely due to the possibility that teachers are positively biased toward their own instruction; research has also found inconsistencies between third-party observer ratings and student perceptions of motivational affordances in classrooms (e.g., Liu et al., 2023).

In other words, even beyond the many instances when an educator thinks they have done or expressed something that they have not, the fact that they said something aloud or facilitated an activity in the classroom does not ensure that students 1) noticed and internalized its occurrence, and 2) interpreted it in the desired way. Thus, educator transparency about their motivational rationales (explicitly saying what they're thinking) is necessary but insufficient for student uptake without intentional scaffolding. This is the case for learning goals and academic skill development as well (e.g., Wollenschläger et al., 2016), something that Liz in particular was still working on, but Colin's and Zachary's cases suggest that educators may be more familiar and comfortable with these practices in a disciplinary context compared to the domain of motivation.

Colin was explicit about his framework for evaluating student writing ("I would like you to memorize these four things"), and he incorporated numerous scaffolds for students to practice these skills, as well as checks for their recognition and understanding of his expectations ("I've asked you to memorize one other thing in this class, the components of an argument. Can anyone remember them?"). Without naming threshold concepts, he recognized the importance of "naming what we know" (Adler-Kassner & Wardle, 2016) for supporting students' entry into "this new culture . . . this new discourse." Zachary similarly leveraged frameworks like the road-trip metaphor to try to provide students with a schema for their ongoing negotiations with the writing process. However, both educators expressed hesitation at using similar strategies to influence students' motivation, with Zachary worrying that this would be equivalent to "telling" students why something is important and Colin musing that "maybe [students] should develop the [competence] mindset without getting rewards constantly."

Beyond the potential direct impact on students' motivation, incorporating scaffolding tasks like reflective writing or discussions affords the added benefit of providing educators with valuable student perception data, a key source of evidence in determining whether pedagogical intentions have been taken up by the target audience. As my hallway conversation with Damian showed, rich insights into how students think about their own motivation can emerge when they have space and circumstance to reflect on and try to express how the "invisible forces" are at work inside of them. Developmentally, high school and college students are well positioned to engage in this metacognitive self-examination (Nakkula & Toshalis, 2006; Piaget, 1972); Damian clearly could not only handle the conversation but probably also welcomed it as an opportunity to figure out more about himself and the contradictions within his identity. In turn, I learned more about how he viewed his own behavior and the attempted influences on his motivation.

However, writing studies literature reminds educators that all reflection is not made equal, nor does it automatically result in writing growth (Pruchnic et al., 2021; Yancey, 2016b); the same cautions hold true when applying the strategy to motivation. Reexamining my memory of the conversation with Damian, I notice missed opportunities to ask Damian more guided questions to coach his self-reflection in this moment. I am quick to offer an interpretation of his participation-trophy critique (*I reply that some people believe that we're raising generations of people who never develop self-reliance because they are dependent on praise for everything they do*), eager to play the sage with worldly wisdom and insights to offer the novice, rather than using the opportunity to help Damian make his own meaning of his observation and connect it to his school experiences. This moment, as with so many of my most memorable exchanges with Damian, also happened one-on-one outside of class time and because he was in trouble with a teacher. I wonder how he might have benefited from having this kind of thinking integrated more meaningfully into his classes.

Diane and Liz both tried to facilitate students' metacognitive meaning making in promising ways, though they both could go further to strengthen and extend that scaffolding. Diane's note-taking packet for the activism expedition included reflective questions that could have helped students process the guest speakers and prepared them (and teachers) for a critical dialogue around the perceived conditions and benefits of Riverside community membership—if that had been identified as an appropriate focus of their "activism." The newness of the expedition and sprawling focus on "national issues" as opposed to localized topics made it difficult for Diane to build in some of those linkages more deliberately, and the reflective questions instead seemed to be treated more as an accountability check that students had paid attention during the session rather than an opportunity to spark discussion.

As noted in chapter 3, Liz incorporated the most reflection into her class of any participant and therefore had a strong foundation already in place for metacognitive work. With students' meaning making around grades and failure being a particularly salient concern in her class, however, the students might have benefited from more structured reflective opportunities that specifically targeted those areas to prompt students to go beyond relatively superficial "narratives of personal progress" (Lindenman et al., 2018). Additionally, neither Liz nor Zachary engaged students in revising essays after receiving a grade, which would present another metacognitive reflective opportunity—one that Colin and Diane could also incorporate into their existing revision policies by having students write metacognitive "process memos" (Parrott & Cherry, 2015), or a similar type of assignment. In many cases, minor modifications to the educators' existing assignments would optimize them as metacognitive scaffolds for students' mindset development.

PRIORITIZE INFORMATIONAL FEEDBACK ON STRATEGIC EFFORT OVER ESTEEM-BUILDING "REWARDS"

A final key takeaway from across the focal classrooms is the role of informational feedback in supporting student motivation, and specifically distinguishing feedback from rewards. At first glance, Damian's critique of participation-trophy culture seems like the cautionary tale affirming Colin's hesitation to give students too many "rewards" to boost their confidence, but the educator portraits illuminate the need for a more nuanced understanding of rewards. In particular, the cases align with motivation research that demonstrates that receiving feedback on one's performance on a challenging task is a more meaningful and motivationally supportive "reward" than receiving a material token for merely completing a task regardless of quality (Wentzel, 2021).

Reward culture was prominently on display at Riverside Academy, Diane's school, in a way that felt familiar to me as a teacher and likely would have resonated with Damian, too. Though our school's systems were not as comprehensive as Riverside's, we too publicized college acceptances and honor roll and experimented with attendance awards in the hopes of incentivizing students' performance; none of this made any impression at all on Damian. Insights from research on autonomous motivation can help us to understand why. Studies suggest that providing students with material rewards for behaviors they should be doing anyway, such as paying students to attend school, can paradoxically cause them to devalue those behaviors as well as enact them less often and less automatically because they come to expect the reward each time (Deci et al., 1999; Robinson et al., 2021). An intuition about this behavioral pattern was likely at the foundation of Colin's concern about giving students "rewards constantly," though he was unaware of the specific motivation research on the issue.

Riverside's school policies also illustrate the importance of considering what implicit messages are conveyed through the nature of the reward. Many of the rewards for earning Scholar status with a high habit of work GPA were presented as privileges but could also just as easily be viewed as negative reinforcement in classic behaviorist terms: the removal of something unpleasant to reinforce the desired behaviors. For example, Scholars were relieved from uniform requirements and restrictive bathroom policies, practices that the expedition speaker explicitly called out as racist forms of bodily control of poor youth of color. Thus, these special privileges hinted at the underlying injustice of the status quo policies such that the "reward" was to receive a reprieve and actually be treated like a competent, autonomous adult. I saw a lot of Damian in Diane's seniors who seemed thoroughly unmoved by this system of rewards and punishments.

The Riverside Scholar system was a schoolwide policy that Diane did not control, but it illustrates the need for educators to think carefully about the rewards they do control in their own classrooms and the messages that these rewards convey. For example, Liz was aware of her authority to create her own grading system and have her grades serve the purpose she intended: to boost students' confidence and self-esteem as writers. Self-esteem can be an important factor in student motivation, as low self-esteem can contribute to anxiety and other negative emotions that impede motivation and performance. However, esteem-preserving strategies, which often occur in the moment, can also counteract the development of more flexible and robust patterns of academic motivation for the future. For example, a student reassuring herself that she is still smart and only did poorly on a research paper because the instructor did not "evaluate the students' writing based on the quality instead of the quantity," as one of Liz's students wrote, may preserve her self-esteem in the moment but does not develop a resilient mindset schema that will help her the next time she earns a lower-than-expected grade on a writing assignment.

It may help educators like Liz to know that motivation research generally suggests that self-esteem stems from competence mindsets, not the other way around (Schunk et al., 2014). Thus, rather than tending to students' self-esteem as the primary mechanism for fostering motivation for writing, Liz could promote a more enduring and well-founded self-esteem by employing the strategies of providing challenging work with informational feedback that are recommended in the motivation theories and empirical work underlying the competence mindset. Importantly, her grades themselves do not necessarily need to change to accomplish this goal. Rather, it is the students' *interpretation* of the grades that shifts, in keeping with research on effective rewards as providing students with informational feedback about the nature and sources of their successful performance (Wentzel, 2021). An A can still feel like a reward, but the motivational implications of that reward are different if students understand what the A represents in terms of their mastery of desired skills versus if they see it as the equivalent of a gold star that the teacher arbitrarily bestows or not—a viewpoint observed among both Liz's and Colin's students.

The fact that Colin's students hold some similar attitudes to Liz's toward grades is not insignificant given the large difference in where the two instructors' grading systems fall on the informational feedback versus esteem-building continuum. Colin developed an impressively coherent and cohesive approach to assessing his students' writing that provided students with a clear framework for interpreting their feedback, as evidenced by multiple students reciting the criteria on their final reflections. As with the transparency and scaffolding theme, his main opportunity for growth may be in more consistently thinking through other areas in the class where students need that same clarity—and taking seriously the informational feedback *he* receives from them about when their needs aren't being met, rather than dismissing it as an immature need for "smiley faces."

In making this recommendation, I explicitly defend Colin's decision not to grade and return every little assignment (similar to Liz's portfolio approach) since it is simply not feasible for educators to provide feedback on everything a student does. However, in alignment with the transparency recommendation, educators can take care to ensure that information about which tasks receives grades/feedback and which do not is communicated to students to avoid confusion or resentment building over opaque practices. In Colin's case specifically, he could perhaps provide brief feedback on and return the first reading quiz and use that opportunity in class to clarify that in the future, students can assume that subsequent reading quizzes have been deemed satisfactory in line with the feedback on this one and that he will reach out to individual students if he sees anything problematic.

Educators could also lean on a classroom affordance that was evident in Colin's portrait as well as Zachary's: the intangible social rewards that students can reap from an activity that can motivate their engagement without the external manipulation of an offered tangible reward. Think of the excitement of Zachary's student Eric who got to talk about comic books *in school* with his equally enthused English teacher, or the students who didn't love comic books but could rely on Zachary to ask questions that invited their lived experience into the classroom and to accept whatever offbeat questions they proffered. Colin's one uncharacteristic dabble in a cheap reward—a homework pass for the winning team of the *Eunoia*-inspired writing game—briefly excited the students but then proved entirely unnecessary as social interaction and validation became the reward (it was also unclear to me whether any students ever remembered or redeemed the officially stated prize). Cultivating this kind of classroom community, where relationships both supply their own source of value and help students appreciate the value of the offered curriculum, brings my three main cross-case findings/recommendations full-circle.

Before I transition to discuss the outer ecological levels needed to support this work, it is important to note that the practices described in the recommendations above may not yield directly observable outcomes during a student's tenure in the class. Motivation research identifies fluctuations in students' motivation over the course of the school year (Turner et al., 2013) and composition studies likewise note the long and nonlinear process of writer development (Shaughnessy, 1975; Sternglass, 1997). The invisibility and ineffability of student motivation can make efforts to support it feel like a leap of faith at times. Still, educators can and should engage in motivationally supportive practices and collect what evidence of student outcomes they can, while they can—just with the recognition that they may not be present to see their efforts come to fruition. As I noted after the vignette of Damian in this book's introduction, I witnessed marginal improvements from him in the years that followed, but like Diane, I sent him off into the great postsecondary unknown with the hope that some lasting good had been done, then I turned my attention to figuring out more about motivationally supportive teaching. Even with all I have learned since then, however, I must still make peace each year with never truly knowing in what ways I have tipped the balance on my students' motivation. I draw on my own growth, competence, and value mindsets to motivate the work of trying to improve year over year. I expand on this theme in the final section of this chapter but wish to note here that while the classroom practices within our own sphere of influence may sometimes feel insufficient to tackle an ephemeral phenomenon, they are absolutely essential, and our willingness to continue honing our craft as educators is the lifeline of each student's motivational ecosystem.

Classroom Strategies: Outer Influences and Implications

Research suggests that pre-service writing educators frequently rely on their personal ideas about writing and anecdotal experiences and observations when thinking about writing instruction, rarely drawing on research-based knowledge of students and student writing—which would include knowledge about student motivation and the role of motivation in writing (Zuidema & Fredricksen, 2016). This pattern was born out with the experienced educators profiled here. While my participants' strategies were often consistent with theory and comprised valuable holistic awareness of how mindsets intersect in students' classroom experience, there were also variations, inconsistencies, and misconceptions in some of their understandings that can only be addressed by directly engaging educators with theoretical and empirical work on the relevant constructs. There is a limit, in other words, to what even experienced and reflective educators can intuit or learn through classroom experience. Preservice and in-service educators alike would benefit from targeted learning experiences about motivational mindsets, including appropriate scaffolding and practice to help them implement mindset-supportive practices.

Introducing these kinds of learning experiences would fulfill calls for more robust applied psychology and human development work in both K–12 teacher education (Battle & Looney, 2014; Leibbrand & Watson, 2010; Pianta et al., 2010) and faculty development in higher education (Destin, 2018). In keeping with arguments for better integration of "foundational" and "methods" courses in K–12 teacher education (Grossman et al., 2009), part of any clinical experience could pair explicit instruction in the theories underlying the motivational mindsets with identification of mindset manifestations in live classroom settings and hands-on practice with mindset-supportive instructional moves. For in-service K–12 teachers, professional learning designed and delivered by instructional coaches, department chairs, and faculty developers could address the growth edges identified above. Diane's portrait shows the power of intentionally designed professional development experiences for educators who want to learn and improve. (Her school's next level of work might be to use that existing structure to facilitate critical conversations on race and culture.) An initiative to create professional learning experiences focused on motivationally supportive instruction is underway at the middle-school science level (Marchand et al., 2022); similar approaches could be built out for different levels and disciplines.

Studies of educator uptake of professional development suggest that, beyond simply being taught new practices, educators need support to integrate the new practices with their existing frameworks of understanding that stem from their teaching experience and current school contexts (Garner & Kaplan, 2019; Lillge, 2019). Without this integration and accommodation, educators are unlikely to endorse or implement new practices in effective ways (Joram et al., 2020). I maintain that giving educators suitably complex depictions of classrooms is essential to their buy-in toward new approaches and their ability to reconcile new practices with their existing educator identities; it is what I have aimed to do with these portraits. Proponents of case-based professional development make similar arguments about the value of narrative for introducing theoretical principles in the context of authentic problems of practice, facilitating educator understanding and uptake (Darling-Hammond & Hammerness, 2002; Gravett et al., 2017; Heitzmann, 2008; Merseth, 1991; Moje & Wade, 1997). Instructional developers could therefore consider the use of cases and other rich learning materials that promote educator identification by depicting teaching practices in complex classroom settings.

As a transition to the next section on sector differences, I acknowledge that these kinds of professional training and ongoing learning experiences may look different for college instructors compared to their K–12 counterparts. Given the absence of formalized or systematic training in pedagogy at many institutions of higher education, college instructors may need more comprehensive foundational work in which to contextualize their learning about mindsets. The recent proliferation of university teaching and learning centers and increased public and political scrutiny of college student outcomes have brought greater attention to student-centered teaching in higher education (Menges & Weimer, 1996; Weimer, 2012) and could help drive institutional commitments to this foundational work. Additionally, many colleges and universities are far better positioned than K–12 schools to tap into existing institutional resources—in the form of resident psychology and education scholars—for relevant content for these professional learning opportunities. Thus, the exact format of these trainings would vary depending on institutional context both within and across sectors, but new or refined understandings of mindsets would be valuable learning for educators at all levels.

Sector Differences in Mindset Understandings and Prioritization: Recommendations for Educators

Having taken a sector-agnostic approach in the previous section's recommendations about motivationally supportive classroom strategies, I now examine the two pairs of educators by their sector membership to contextualize my recommendations within a discussion of students' experience transitioning from high school to college. As with the previous section, I start at the classroom level within the educator's control, discussing insights from the portraits about what a student might experience moving from either of the two high schools, Riverside Academy or Oak Bridge School, to either of the two colleges, Mayfield or Abbott University. I then examine the sector-specific educator beliefs that might contribute—positively or negatively—to that student's motivational landscape. I then, again, move outward into the educators' ecosystems to explore the structures and constraints that could support or thwart educators' abilities to foster student motivation across the college transition.

MINDSET IMPLICATIONS IN THE STUDENT TRANSITION EXPERIENCE

While both Mayfield and Abbott were quite selective, making this perhaps not a "typical" pathway for graduates of Riverside or OBS, it is also not an implausible one: recall that Diane's student Talia was accepted to Mayfield and that one of Zachary's former students attended Middlebury, which is similar to Abbott in its selectivity. This speculative exercise may reflect a fairly narrow sliver of student trajectories but still an important one to examine, especially given the imperative perceived by many urban teachers like Diane to "have a bigger chunk of high-reaching kids" getting into and attending "better" colleges than the local public universities. In many ways, such a trajectory represents an ideal scenario for high schools like Riverside and OBS: their most motivated students moving on to selective and generally well-resourced private colleges. What do the portraits reveal about the classroom motivational landscape they might encounter on both sides of this transition?

First, the previous section's description of all the educators' strengths at building relationships with students and attending to their perceptions of belonging, both in class itself and within the discipline of writing, should assuage the high school teachers' fears about what awaits the graduates of their small high schools. I do not mean to downplay the very real possibility that students might struggle academically, but at least in the motivational arena of belonging, the college instructors were mindful of first-year students' potential anxieties and prepared to give them a warm welcome. Liz had students interview each other on the first day of class and built in plenty of in-class writing time as an intentional support for students who could be struggling with time management. Colin's use of Apples to Apples on the first day and other games throughout the semester invited students in and made the metaphorical "game" of academic writing seem more accessible.

Both instructors encouraged peer collaboration and scaffolded assignments with drafts, peer review, office hours consultations, and a revision opportunity in Colin's case. These two first-year writing classes, at least, seemed to recreate some of the small high school experience with regards to belonging and academically supportive classroom relationships.

However, the high school teachers' prioritization of students' value mindsets, as discussed in chapter 2 and the interlude between chapters 2 and 3, may have been warranted given that explicitly conveying and scaffolding perceived value was not a major focus of either of the college instructors, beyond allowing choice opportunities in assignments. This pattern might reflect both colleges' approach to first-year writing as a stand-alone course not taught by departmental faculty and not embedded in a particular discipline (Harris, 2006), but even within the topic of writing itself, references to value in both classrooms were largely implicit. Both Liz and Colin identified the improvement or effectiveness of writing as an outcome of certain strategies, but there was little, if any, discussion devoted to how the general goal of becoming a better writer translated into concrete goals for specific students. I was surprised, for example, at how little I could gather from my classroom observations about what other courses the college students were currently taking; there were no explicit conversations about writing assignments that students were completing in other classes or about differences in writing across different disciplines.

Lest I seem overly critical of the college instructors, I remind readers that promoting value mindsets in the high school classrooms was an inconsistent and occasionally fraught endeavor, despite the depth of both teachers' thinking about the mindset. Zachary's lack of scaffolding for value made it uncertain whether students were appreciating their coursework in the way he intended. Diane attempted to give students work with "lifetime value" in her expedition curriculum, but her default rationale for more traditional curriculum was "it's gonna help you in college," which may be only marginally better than no rationale at all, especially for students who lack personal investment in attending college. We might envision the motivational struggles of a student moving from a high school English classroom that "brainwashed" them to think about their schoolwork almost exclusively in college preparatory terms to a college writing classroom where their supposedly college-preparatory skills do not seem to measure up and where there is no explicitly articulated rationale or application for the new writing-related tasks they are being set. Developing the skills to articulate sources of value and scaffold students' value mindsets (Brophy, 2008), such as through the strategies discussed in Zachary's case in chapter 2 and the recommendations above, may therefore be an especially important consideration for educators working at the college transition.

Finally, as noted in chapters 3 and 4, the two college instructors were highly attentive to students' growth and competence mindsets in ways that should support first-year students' motivation if supplemented with the greater transparency, scaffolding, and informational feedback strategies outlined in the prior recommendation section. This mindset work builds on a high school foundation, with Diane's growth mindset talk and revision policies and Zachary's commitment to giving every student an "entry point" into the lesson. Support for these mindsets is critical both before and after the college transition and for every level of student skill. The interlude between chapters 2 and 3 identified the high school and college educators' differing perceptions of their students as, respectively, underserved and high achievers, in line with the selectivity of their schools, but there was variation within those designations as well, especially among the college students. Liz's students, in particular, had earned admission into a selective school but then confronted the stigma of "failing" their placement exam and therefore needing the extra class. She herself noted that graduates of the surrounding public school district—which included OBS—often placed into the class. Thus, the high school and college students could share more similarities than might be readily apparent, necessitating similar attention to their motivational mindsets from educators on both sides of the transition.

CROSS-SECTOR EDUCATOR ASSUMPTIONS AND BELIEFS

Although their students may have been more similar than different from a motivational perspective, both pairs of educators articulated assumptions about those in the other sector that suggested they perceived entirely different paradigms for teaching at the secondary and postsecondary levels. These perceptions played at least a small role in how they conducted their classes. Yet, as with the students, the supposedly stark differences were not necessarily reflected in my data, a finding that is in line with surveys identifying greater convergence between high school and college writing expectations than the general rhetoric might suggest (Addison & McGee, 2010; Patterson & Duer, 2006). Keith Hjortshoj (2009) discusses the "mythical high school" and "mythical college" phenomenon in the domain of writing specifically, in which writing instructors on both sides of the college transition lack specific information about what their counterparts are doing and therefore can tend to overly extrapolate from their own personal experience and piecemeal or anecdotal student data. In the following section, I discuss my observations of this phenomenon within my data and its implications for student motivation.

Before doing so, however, I pause to acknowledge that readers may object to what they see as an attempt to generalize about all high schools or all colleges from two classrooms apiece and a glossing over of the fact that my four participants opted into a research study and therefore may not be "typical" educators. These are valid concerns, especially given my critique of educators using anecdotal data to draw conclusions. However, my intention here is not for educators to walk away feeling like they now know what happens in all high school English classrooms or all first-year writing classrooms; to do so would be impossible for any study. Rather, my larger point is that even if Diane and Zachary or Liz and Colin are the exceptions rather than the rule, what can these exceptions tell us about the repercussions of relying on a "mythical high school" or "mythical college"? How can educators seek to disrupt their reflexive thinking, and what kinds of supports would foster authentic, myth-busting cross-sector educator dialogue and collaboration?

Contrary to Diane's fears, both Liz and Colin proved to be worthy colleagues who were prepared to "pick up where she left off." As noted above, the college instructors were attuned to first-year college students' needs and took responsibility for their charges. In addition to hopefully providing some reassurance, I encourage high school teachers to reflect on the extent to which "mythical college" beliefs like these are expressed in class to students and whether they are promoting the motivational mindsets that will best help students in college. I know that I was guilty of similar messaging to my high school students, reasoning that this would give urgency to our work and prepare students for worst-case scenarios where they really were not receiving support from college instructors. Now, however, in line with the recommendations about transparency and scaffolding discussed in the previous section, I wonder whether a more productive approach would be to have explicit discussions with students about academic struggle as an inevitability in college and appropriate help-seeking strategies when it occurs. Rather than making students feel like they should have everything they need to be successful on the first day of college—perhaps leading to feelings of guilt and inadequacy when they fail to pull themselves up by their own bootstraps—this approach would leverage growth mindset and mastery goals in reminding students that success is neither linear nor innately preordained and that strategies and resources, rather than unfocused effort or sheer will, are their best tools.

Likewise, a corollary to the pervasive "it's gonna help you in college" utility rationale discussed above was an absence of clear messaging in both high school classrooms about what college learning was, or could be. In her interviews with me, Diane frequently juxtaposed college preparation and the "real world," a stance that seemed to treat the two goals as orthogonal, with college skills being abstracted from students' opinions about "life issues"— which Diane valued, just saw as incongruous and incompatible with her mandate of college preparation. To Diane, college involved "taking a piece of literature and [doing] New Criticism, sort of just sticking with the text and talking about the elements of literature . . . as opposed to more of a reader response, like what does this make you feel, how does this relate to your life?" The latter approach would be more to her preference, but she felt constrained by the college imperative. Yet Liz explicitly endorsed the idea of students drawing from their personal lives, using their writing as a way to announce, "This is my experience and this is valuable." Though less dogmatic than Liz about the issue in general, Colin also assigned a paper where students used their personal educational experience as evidence in responding to different authors' stances toward education. It is important to note that my focal classrooms were first-year writing classes, not English classes, but the writing course was the requirement at both Mayfield and Abbott, not an English literature class in which the "New Criticism" skills that Diane describes might directly apply.[1] Moreover, Diane's distinction between literary analysis and personal writing suggests a view of authorial voice as something exclusive to personal narrative rather than contributing to a rhetorical stance in college-level analytic writing (Acker & Halasek, 2008; Strachan, 2002).

My hope is that reading these cross-sector cases helps high school teachers like Diane feel empowered to teach more of what they feel in their gut to be important and valuable for all students, regardless of college intentions, and to understand that doing so can have motivational benefits for the students who do go on to college. Surveys of college faculty suggest that they care about students taking initiative, demonstrating creativity, and problem-solving in their writing rather than the following of procedures that is often emphasized in secondary education as a consequence of standardized testing and high-stakes accountability (Fanetti et al., 2010). Zachary's approach seemed more aligned with these patterns, but as noted in his case and the preceding sections of this chapter, he did not consistently or explicitly scaffold the students in both the understanding and skills to support his "You love Pokémon? You can write about Pokémon" philosophy.

A possible takeaway for both Zachary and Diane, as well as high school teachers like them, is to understand that their intuitive desire to teach for personal relevance can be built out into a deliberate instructional schema—rather than relying on idiosyncratic one-off "hits" like the *V for Vendetta* bumper sticker or the wandering uterus reference at Middlebury—that can support students' motivational mindsets entering college and still accomplish their goal of giving students college-ready academic skills. For example, Shay's spontaneous question in Zachary's class about whether people "dedicate their lives" to critical analysis could lead to a planned discussion about where students might encounter the critical lenses in different classes or departments in college and the real-world relevance of the kinds of questions that are central to those disciplines. Building in these connections in high school can help students see (and remind teachers) that a college education is a dynamic experience that students have the autonomy to manage for themselves and their own purposes, not just an abstract academic credential to earn before starting their "real lives."

While there were areas for growth in the high school teachers' approaches to college preparation, there were also numerous strengths that in many cases contradicted the college instructors' assumptions about what was happening in the "mythical high school." Despite admitting to me that they did not know much about high school English beyond their own personal experiences, both Liz and Colin articulated many opinions, to me and to their students, about the writing instruction their students had previously received. These included Liz's observation that high school students are trained to feel that "using 'I'" means they're "doing something wrong" because "they aren't taught that they are the expert or that they have valid ideas" and Colin's public indictment of five-paragraph essays, grandiose "hook" statements in introductions, and the use of many synonyms, all of which he attributed to "typical" high school writing instruction. Some of these perceptions received confirmatory evidence from current students, such as Liz's student Alexander telling her in office hours that he was taught not to use first-person in academic writing, but the others did not, at least not in my direct observation. Nor did I observe them in either of the high school classrooms: neither Diane nor Zachary assigned students a five-paragraph essay, outlawed the use of first person, or articulated prescriptions about essay openings or vocabulary. In fact, it was Liz who possibly reinforced one of Colin's pet peeves when she included "an opening that engages the readers" as one of the "polishing categories" that peer reviewers could look for in each other's papers.

Likewise, both Liz and Colin viewed students' obsession with grades as "a high school mentality" that they tried to acculturate students out of. Notwithstanding the students' very recent graduation from high school providing a logical reason for the continuation of their high school attitudes, this implicit critique of high school teachers feels a little overly simplistic to me. It is true that the outright grade-grubbing displayed by Liz's students and the misery poker of Colin's students may be an artifact of the competitive high school environments some students experienced (and that catapulted them into selective colleges to begin with, as the Abbott English Department's faculty handbook notes). However, as we saw in Diane's and Zachary's portraits, at other high schools grades have very different, and much higher, stakes for the teachers as much as the students. Grades are the currency with which these students can access opportunities that are only available to those who succeed academically; they are what students need to "get accepted to college . . . graduate, and take [their] rightful place on the throne of change," as the eighth-grade Riverside teacher said on the expedition kick-off day. When teachers view the alternative as students "becoming the next hashtag," pushing students to care about their grades takes on a different significance.

Moreover, the college instructors would be likelier to find their high school counterparts to be partners in commiseration over tensions caused by grading and assessment. Liz's portfolio approach, which she used to resolve her "struggle with trying to fit everyone's effort into the same 'map'" by allowing it to "just end up that everyone gets pretty good grades," shares some similarities with Diane and her twelfth-grade team's dilemma over habit of work grades, which are in many ways an assessment of effort operationalized through evidence like attendance and homework completion. I see the overlapping philosophies in the confirmatory question asked by Liz's student Derek on the first day of class: "So, if you complete all the steps, your process grade is fine?" He seemed to recognize the approach, as I imagine many other high school students would. Neither sector has satisfactorily cracked the code of how to decommodify grades; it does not seem to me a uniquely high school problem. I should also note that grades were in fact the least present in Zachary's class out of the four; there were very few references to grades in any of my observations, and I had to ask him about deadlines like when quarter and semester grades were due because

I could not tell from the regular proceedings of class. Thus, once again the perception of "mythical high school" practices did not align with the reality of my two focal high school classrooms.

Similar to my recommendation about high school teachers' messaging to their students about the nature of college, college instructors could consider the motivational implications for students of expressing their perceptions of the "mythical high school" in class in a negative or dismissive manner. These features of high school writing instruction may not have been experienced by all students, and even if students are familiar with the tropes, what is the motivational purpose of denigrating the instruction they have previously received? As noted in Colin's portrait in chapter 4, destabilizing students' confidence in what their high school teachers taught them has implications for college instructors as well because it throws into question who can be trusted as the "true" authority on matters of writing. Rather than viewing writing as a developmental and situational process, in which different features or skills might be emphasized in different contexts, the denigration of some writing instructors by others can lead students to view every class as a new game of sussing out what this particular instructor wants and trying to deliver that, as opposed to considering their ongoing development as writers. Colin himself took a more generous view of high school in an early interview with me when he observed, "When you're young and you learn to play a game, you learn the rules and you follow them . . . High school writing is sort of like learning some rules but not always having a good handle on why the rules exist that way." When he discussed this in class with students, however, the framework was no longer helping students to understand why they might have been taught to write with certain rules in high school and how slavish devotion to those rules may limit more sophisticated writing. Instead, the formulaic rules of high school writing were held up as a subject for mockery and then replaced with the new rules of college writing.

I do not mean to castigate my participants for their attitudes but merely to illustrate how easy it can be for even seasoned educators to fall back on simple heuristics; indeed, experience may make a teacher more prone to these kinds of pronouncements as they may feel they have seen it all. Yet student characteristics and their needs shift over time, making it important for educators to be aware of their assumptions about students' experiences in the other sector and to be willing to challenge these assumptions by directly asking current students about their experiences rather than automatically assimilating them into the existing schema. This practice is more challenging for high school teachers because the relevant student experiences they want to know about are in the future, but high schools might consider ways to invite in college students from the local community to speak to both students and teachers, such as during times when colleges are on break but high schools are not. However, these initiatives would likely best be accomplished through coordinated partnerships, as discussed below, rather than individual teachers.

College instructors are better positioned to tap their current students for information that could combat their "mythical high school" perceptions, but it is important to systematically collect data from all students, not just the ones who are most outspoken in class or feel the most strongly about their high school experiences. Such an activity does not need to be limited to providing information to the instructor; it affords the opportunity to invite students to reflect on their own high school learning experiences and the ways in which their learning in college may require different strategies. These kinds of learning strategy discussions can help bring the threshold concepts for postsecondary learning into the open and support students' belonging and competence motivational mindsets by making explicit that struggle or perceived incongruities between high school and college are not a sign of deficiencies in the student but rather features of different educational contexts that students can learn to navigate.

Approaches like these are admittedly limited due to possible constraints on what students are able to recognize and articulate to educators about their own learning experiences. Often, they have not been asked to think before in this metacognitive way, and they may need scaffolding to help them express their ideas, just as Zachary coached his student Jessica in applying a travel metaphor to her writing process. Beyond these classroom approaches, though, high school and college educators would benefit from a more systematic way of learning directly about their counterparts' work, unfiltered through student perception. Such cross-sector communication could not only promote new pedagogical insights but could also contribute to educators' greater appreciation for each other and the unique instructional challenges within each sector that could translate into different kinds of messages being communicated to students about what high school or college entails. I discuss possible starting points for these cross-sector partnerships in the following section.

Sector Differences: Outer Influences and Implications

All four of my participants would have benefited from cross-sector partnerships to learn directly from each other with the goal of clarifying educators' conceptions of their role in the P-16 pipeline and contextualizing their support for student mindsets within a reframed understanding of where their students are going (for high school teachers) or coming from (for college instructors; J. Jones, 2007). Such partnerships could promote greater alignment and a more generous and appreciative perspective on counterparts' efforts. Organizations like the National Writing Project that span both sectors can be instrumental in bringing writing instructors together (Cook & Caouette, 2013); similar initiatives have proven fruitful in math and science (Alford et al., 2014; Frost et al., 2012).

Independently of structural efforts to bring educators physically together, teacher educators and developers can also play a key role in bridging the secondary and postsecondary sectors by leveraging their pedagogical expertise to facilitate work on alignment issues in teaching and learning. The licensure process for public school K–12 teachers and norms of staff-wide, departmental, and/or grade-level professional development or collaborative learning are logical places to situate work on teaching for college readiness and success, including the role of motivational mindsets. In the postsecondary sector, analogous work examining secondary perspectives and academic preparation could at least start within first-year writing programs (Crank, 2012).

Guidance on how educators can gather data more systematically on students' prior learning experiences—so as not to rely so heavily on selective anecdotal evidence—would also be a welcome faculty development initiative. Mayfield included a questionnaire about students' prior literacy experiences in its writing placement test but then never shared it with instructors. Making that kind of institutional/departmental information available and/or supporting instructors in creating their own student learning inventories and analyzing the responses would be a quick way of introducing cross-sector perspectives without leaving the classroom.

Beyond these more immediate supports for educators, however, I feel obligated to acknowledge institutional policies and sector-specific issues that affect students' motivational ecosystem within each classroom and that lie outside the control of individual educators as well as instructional development initiatives. Though a detailed analysis of and proposed reforms to these forces are beyond the scope of a book focused on classroom environments, I would be remiss not to acknowledge that these outer ecological levels infiltrate the classroom and demand that we situate educators' practices within their complex, multilayered contexts. On the most basic level, it is important to reiterate that Riverside Academy and OBS are public schools that admit local students on a random lottery basis, whereas Mayfield and Abbott are highly selective private colleges. Their respective institutional statuses drive many of the educators' beliefs about their students, as discussed in the interlude between chapters 2 and 3.

Then, within that overall framework, broader debates in the K–12 sector about the achievement gap, urban education, and social justice are implicated in the very founding of small schools like Riverside and OBS and continue to influence the extent to which they are open to radical curricular changes or feel obliged to conform to the Advanced Placement system, for example. On the college side, institutional policies about the role of AP credit in exempting students from classes like Liz and Colin's reinforce the pressures on high schools, while decisions about the structure of first-year writing at each institution reflect larger debates about learning outcomes and educational quality in higher education. All of these ultimately trickle down into classrooms in some form with motivational implications for students, such as Colin's grading policy aligning with the college's desire to mandate two semesters of writing for most students.

Finally, as previewed in the interlude between chapters 2 and 3 as well as the previous recommendation section, sector-specific differences in the training and professional role of educators are highly salient to my findings. Diane and Zachary were both certified teachers and enjoyed supportive professional communities in their small schools; they knew their colleagues, had access to professional development, and felt empowered to raise questions about curriculum and even personal identity to their school leaders. As nonpermanent instructors, Colin and Liz had very few of those supports available even though they both actively wanted them. The director of writing at Mayfield went so far as to call it "unethical" to demand more time of her underpaid adjunct faculty. Thus, sector-specific professional contexts form a motivational ecosystem for educators that in turn influences the kind of motivational ecosystem they can provide for their students. This is the focus of my final set of findings on the role of educators' motivational mindsets for teaching.

Teaching Mindsets: Recommendations for Educators

The portraits reveal that the educators' own mindsets toward teaching—and the extent to which their institutional contexts did or did not provide ongoing support for positive teaching mindsets—implicated the educators' classroom practices related to student mindsets. Improving classroom motivational supports for students therefore demands attention to the larger motivational ecosystem at work within schools and sectors, including the intersection of an educator's ecosystem with that of their students.

In each portrait, the focal mindset that we saw the educator working to promote in students was also at play in a parallel process for the educator in relation to teaching. Diane's feelings of belonging as a teacher at Riverside were instrumental in her willingness to enact the institutional mission, even as it changed over the years. Zachary's curriculum restructuring also helped *him* feel a greater sense of relevance in his own teaching and built on his strengths and interests as a teacher, just as he hoped it would for students' mindsets toward school. From the first class of the semester, Liz drew a parallel between the growth mindset she wanted students to adopt toward writing and her own teaching, explaining that she "gets better every time" she teaches her class. As Colin sought to help students master the "rules of the game" to help their competence mindsets toward writing, he turned to me to help him feel more efficacious at a teaching game whose rules were not always transparent to him.

Beyond the focal mindset-educator pairings, however, all four educators revealed clues about their growth and competence mindsets related to teaching because I was constantly asking them to reflect on instructional design and enactment decisions, which inherently included their responses to nonideal student behavior or imperfect student work, challenges they perceived in achieving their pedagogical intent, and their ideas for future modifications. The growth and competence mindsets also align with constructs that are commonly studied in relation to pedagogical strategy adoption: locus of control and perceived teaching efficacy (Deemer, 2004; Henson, 2002; Lai, 2018; Midgley et al., 1995). Teachers are likelier to adopt new teaching strategies when they feel a foundational sense of competence in their own teaching, when they feel in control of their own effort, and when they feel that those efforts will lead to greater teaching skill.

All four educators demonstrated growth mindset through their belief that they could always improve as teachers and that strategic effort was the main mechanism for that improvement. For example, even after nearly two decades teaching in Connecticut, Diane had been willing to "learn to teach all over" again at Riverside, acquiring pedagogical strategies "I had never even heard of" and essentially learning "a new language." Despite the effort this required from her, she found working at Riverside more fulfilling than the years she had spent not being challenged in her previous school. Diane, Zachary, and Colin also enacted growth mindset through their willingness to take risks and experiment with their curriculum. During the semester of my data collection, they were all teaching at least one unit that they had never taught before that school year: Colin's opening unit on education was new, Zachary had created two entirely new courses, and Diane was teaching AP for the first time and had also cocreated the new activism expedition. In line with growth mindset principles, these educators embraced the intellectual challenge of designing new curricular units and willingly put forth the effort to become better teachers and achieve their goal of improving student learning.

Zachary, Liz, and Colin also explicitly used their participation in my study as an opportunity to learn and grow professionally. Zachary took my interview question to him about students' reading strategies—which I had asked genuinely in a spirit of inquiry, not as a veiled recommendation—and turned it around on his students, acknowledging that it was important information for him to have. Liz told me that she "would love to have more meetings with other teachers" to discuss and reflect on teaching and said that our interviews were in some way a substitute for that kind of collegial, professional learning community. Colin was especially interested in my feedback on his teaching; I frequently had to deflect his questions about how I thought class had gone or alternative approaches he could take. "What would *you* do?" he often asked me. (Appendix B expands on how I negotiated the research relationship with these three educators—including at the moment when they read their own portraits—and the implications for research as well as teacher development.)

Yet just as the educators' mindset work with their students was "messy," so too were the educators' own mindsets toward teaching: while all of them acted in ways that reflected positive mindsets toward their teaching ability, they also all contradicted or undermined those same mindsets at times, often by adopting an external locus of control toward a perceived constraint. Colin's game metaphor and his stance that "rules don't have to be limiting; they can be enabling" is an apt frame here, as are the tensions he experienced with getting his students on board with this philosophy. Like the Abbott students' external attributions of classroom or institutional structures that impeded their growth and competence mindsets ("I'm just always gonna get a bad grade in this class, no matter what I do"), the educators' perceptions of external limitations suggest that even experienced and reflective practitioners still struggle at times to maintain positive motivational mindsets in the face of institutional or systemic challenges.

For example, despite Diane's many enactments of growth mindset, her expansive pedagogical toolkit, and her philosophy of teaching as activism that she invoked during the expedition, she simultaneously perceived herself and her school as largely powerless within the overall educational system, viewing it as "not possible" for testing companies to lose legitimacy and seeing the source/direction of meaningful change as "having to start from the top down." Her perception of the inequitable system fed her acceptance of Riverside's increasing conformity and of certain constraints on what she as an educator could do. To her, achieving the desired student outcomes justified squelching her own innovation and creativity as an educator.

Meanwhile, Zachary identified time constraints—especially with the shift to the semester elective system that he himself precipitated—as an obstacle to incorporating more reflection in his class, telling me, "I only have this short amount of time to get through all this content, so I can't spend as much time doing self-reflective stuff." The use of "can't" is interesting coming from a teacher who had already implemented much more drastic changes to his curriculum in order to address a different perceived need: the need to "legitimize school" to students. Zachary does not actually have no time for more reflection and revision in his classes, but he would need to shift his external perception of "can't" to an internal locus of control that recognizes his ability to *make* time for those activities by reallocating it from his self-imposed imperative to "get through all this content."

Overall, though, both high school teachers expressed much stronger competence mindsets toward their teaching than did the college instructors, perhaps due to the sector differences in professional training and community discussed in the previous section. Even as they were asking for my insight or self-deprecatingly describing a lesson gone astray, it was clear that Diane and Zachary's growth and competence mindsets gave them resilience to talk freely about their mistakes and areas for improvement as an authentic part of the work, even for veteran educators. By contrast, even though each college instructor identified themselves foremost as a teacher rather than a writer (Liz) or researcher (Colin) and both were excited and energized by the work of teaching, they also seemed more inclined to interpret pedagogical challenges or mistakes as problematic. There seemed to be a heightened attention from the college instructors about their classroom performance reflecting something essential about themselves as educators.

For example, it struck me throughout data collection that when Colin invited my feedback, he often asked me what he was "doing wrong" pedagogically, using the very kind of language that he did not want students using about their writing. In our last interview, he asked me in a lighthearted tone but, I thought, only semijokingly, "Am I, like, failing Pedagogy 101?" Just as he described his students' experience with academic writing, he seemed to find some aspects of teaching "opaque" and mystifying. While he was more than willing to put in the effort to improve, he also at times resembled his students in searching for the "right" path or algorithm to "win" the puzzling and complex pedagogical game in which he found himself.

Meanwhile, Liz worried about making mistakes in front of students if she moved out of her comfort zone ("I would undermine myself and stumble"). In her two years at Mayfield prior to this study, she had never acted on her curiosity about the students' writing placement exam, and a key reason why she did not develop rubrics or frameworks for students' writing was because she found it challenging and difficult. Thus, although both she and Colin welcomed our interviews as opportunities to reflect on and consider new possibilities in their practice, they also often used fixed or defeatist language when describing their own teaching efficacy and potential impact.

My hope and recommendation for educators is that reading about the vulnerabilities that Diane, Zachary, Liz, and Colin so bravely laid bare in these portraits will spur greater self-reflection and self-awareness about their own teaching mindsets. Just as I advocated for inviting students into metacognitive conversations about their own learning and motivation, educators can practice turning the motivational mindset lens on themselves to monitor and assess when their mindsets are sustaining versus hindering their pedagogical and professional growth. However, they should not be asked or expected to undertake this self-examination and improvement work on their own. The parallels between the educators' "messy" growth and competence mindsets and what we saw from the students in the portraits also directs us to a parallel implication from the portraits and the final section of findings: the importance of providing educators with a motivationally supportive teaching context.

Teaching Mindsets: Outer Influences and Implications

Just as educators try to supply learning experiences to help students develop positive mindsets toward and skills in academic writing, the educators themselves need professional learning experiences to cultivate their positive teaching mindsets and the skill set to enact mindset-supportive instruction for their students. As with students and new academic content, imbuing educators' understandings of mindsets with a stronger theoretical base is a necessary but likely insufficient step to improving their support for student mindset development. Educators are unlikely to incorporate new conceptual knowledge into their teaching without direct scaffolding and support in the practical applications of that knowledge (De Hei et al., 2015; Fisher et al., 2013; Zuidema & Fredricksen, 2016), meaning hands-on practice with feedback so that educators can master the strategies and build a sense of teaching efficacy (Urdan & Schoenfelder, 2006). Teacher educators can embed this work as part of clinical preparation: models of clinical practice in K–12 teacher education such as "microteaching" (Allen & Eve, 1968) or "pedagogies of enactment" (Grossman et al., 2009) offer preservice teachers a lower-stakes context to practice mindset-supportive strategies in front of a peer audience and participate in reflective debriefing afterwards.

In higher education, finding the space and time for instructors to build this pedagogical mastery may require more of an institutional commitment to improving teaching and learning through faculty development. Liz's state university seemed to have made such a commitment to its undergraduate writing instructors, and Liz was still citing what she had learned from that training program years later. Such existing programs could be strengthened by looking to K–12 models of teacher education and incorporating similar kinds of microteaching or simulation experiences for novice instructors. Faculty development programming and initiatives in graduate student teaching certifications through university teaching and learning centers provide additional opportunities for instructors to accumulate mastery experiences and gain a stronger sense of teaching efficacy.

The absence of more formal structures in higher education for practicing instruction with peers and mentors illuminates another key implication for building educator efficacy. In addition to mastery experiences, vicarious learning and social persuasion from peers are key contributors to self-efficacy (Bandura, 1997). The focal educators in my study expressed this connection through their merging of students' belonging and competence mindsets, and the same relationship held for the educators' own teaching efficacy. Working in small high schools, Diane and Zachary experienced both a culture and the accompanying institutional structures—professional development, department and grade-level meetings—to promote collaborative professional learning. Their frequent use of the pronoun "we" signaled both their feelings of belonging at their schools and the fact that they felt part of a teaching collective; they experienced social persuasion and support in their teaching, which in turn helped their growth and competence mindsets.

By contrast, both colleges in my study had made a commitment to first-year writing as a valuable class for their incoming students—indeed, the portraits show the richness of writing class as an environment for mindset development—yet paradoxically, neither institution seemed to invest much in the training and ongoing development of its writing instructors. Neither college's writing department had a particularly strong professional culture or structures in place to help instructors feel a sense of belonging, learn from colleagues, and build their own efficacy. Liz wanted to collaborate with other instructors at Mayfield but received no institutional support in making those connections and likely felt ill-equipped to reach out on her own in a place where "no one knows my face." The fact that both Liz and Colin identified strongly as teachers and wanted to improve as writing instructors, despite their lack of institutional status and power, is a remarkable testament to their value mindsets toward their work and an asset that their departments would be remiss not to prioritize and nurture.

As a baseline, something as simple as an administrative email soliciting instructors interested in a light-touch, opt-in peer observation program could be a starting point for higher education departments that lack the norms around and structures for professional collaboration more commonly found in K–12 schools. All four of my participants volunteered for my study through a very similar process, and all four spent as much time—or more—with me over the course of a semester as they might have devoted to professional development, with a token honorarium the only tangible incentive. Especially for the college instructors who were otherwise quite isolated, the desire to reflect with someone else about their work, to grow professionally, to contribute to knowledge in the field, to feel more confident, and to be demonstrably better at their jobs were their main rationales for participating. These are powerful motivations that—fittingly—map onto the very mindsets they strived to cultivate in students.

Conclusion

With the goal of translating mindset and other psychological research into classroom practice, the authors of the UCCSR framework advocate for developing "instructional practices that could be readily employed by teachers in a variety of school settings" (Farrington et al., 2012, p. 37). But my portraits show that educators' understandings and enactments of positive mindset development are complex, deeply contextualized, and influenced by the educators' own mindsets. Meaningfully changing teachers' practices in ways that promote students' positive motivational mindsets will therefore require an ecological approach that includes attention to the "outer" levels of influence, including specific considerations of secondary and postsecondary education characteristics and constraints, in addition to classroom-level pedagogical recommendations.

As an educator, I have always been highly critical of my own practice because, at the end of the day, I want to know that I have done my best for students like Damian, and I know that my "best" is an elusive goal; there is always room to improve. I bring this critical perspective to my work as a teacher-researcher as well. But I am also a staunch defender of educators because I know there is also goodness to be found in every classroom, a goodness that is complex and by no means synonymous with perfection. Like asset-based approaches to students, supporting educators' growth and improvement (as a mechanism for supporting students' growth and improvement) must begin with an assumption of that goodness and a willingness to explore its complexity. Rather than merely seeking to evaluate and correct classroom educators, we must take a broader perspective on their existing strengths, their situated experience, and the mechanisms through which they can grow and develop.

I have identified several potential areas of growth for the four focal educators in this book to strengthen their instructional supports for motivational mindsets. But my findings also point to the need to develop educators' understandings of mindsets (to help them recognize *how* strategies like increased transparency, scaffolding, and informational feedback would aid in student mindset development) and their own mindsets toward teaching—specifically, their growth and competence mindsets. Finally, the goal of better supporting students' positive mindsets as a protective factor in the college transition requires greater efforts to facilitate cross-sector communication, as academic alignment initiatives have argued.

The risk of a case study approach is an outsized emphasis on the profiled individuals; readers may think I am holding up these four educators either as paragons of effective teaching or as archetypes that are somehow representative of a highly diverse group of professionals. This is not my intention. Rather, my hope is that the nuance and texture of the portraits enable readers to see the full complexity of these educators' approach to teaching, with the *complexity* being the point of resonance with others, rather than necessarily specific similarities of experience.

Indeed, what I discovered through the process of writing about them is that all four of these educators were both exceptional *and* typical. They were exceptional in their willingness to open their classrooms to an outside researcher for a semester, to share their teaching, their thinking, and their imperfections. They were exceptional in their ability to reflect on their flaws as well as their successes, all in the interest of contributing to a broader conversation about good teaching and student support across the college transition. Yet in many ways, these educators were also typical, and their very ordinariness is heartening. They were not products of specialized training. They had not won any awards or even been particularly recognized or acclaimed within their own schools. They arrived at their current positions through multiple pathways and life experiences.

There are educators like Diane, Zachary, Liz, and Colin in secondary and postsecondary institutions across the country, already using some strategies to support students' positive mindset development and eager to do more—if they knew what else to do or how to do it. Just as their students need them, they need *us*—researchers, teacher educators, faculty developers, program directors, school administrators—to commit to understanding them, their diverse teaching contexts, and their authentic problems of practice, in order to develop *their* mindsets and teaching efficacy to their fullest potential.

Appendixes

Appendix A

WEAVING THE TAPESTRY: RESEARCH METHODOLOGY

The aesthetic qualities of portraits can mask the methodological rigor underlying the work. In these appendixes, I seek to make transparent the portraiture process and its affordances as a translational research method that can speak simultaneously to scholarly and practitioner audiences. Appendix A expands on the overview of the portrait development process described in the introduction, unpacking the portraiture methodology, as well as my specific methods for this study, in greater detail. Appendix B describes a rarely discussed step in the research process—sharing findings with participants—in the context of this study.

PORTRAITURE

Pioneered by sociologist Sara Lawrence-Lightfoot, portraiture is a phenomenological qualitative research method that seeks to "blur the boundaries of aesthetics and empiricism in an effort to capture the complexity, dynamics, and subtlety of human experience and organizational life" (Lawrence-Lightfoot & Davis, 1997, p. xv). The core underlying principles of portraiture—an assumption of goodness, the recognition of goodness as complex, and the self-aware dialogue between portraitist and participants throughout the research process—were particularly resonant for my goal of crafting a translational work of classroom-based research.

The Search for (Complex) Goodness

In contrast to classroom-based studies that begin with an a priori assumption of what is good and then rate instruction against that standard, often through self-report surveys or deductive observational methods, portraiture allows for more expansive and alternative conceptualizations of good instructional practice and illuminates an educator's own understandings of goodness that drive their pedagogical choices. The complex manifestation of educators' understandings and enactments in classrooms means that exploring the *why* of teaching, rather than only the *what*, is critical for promoting instructional change and improvement. By taking a "generous *and* critical stance" toward participants' expertise and understandings (Lawrence-Lightfoot & Davis, 1997, p. 143, emphasis in original), portraiture also refutes the assumed deficit in educator knowledge conveyed in much psychological research. As a portraitist, I begin from an assumption that educators are knowledgeable and that researchers can learn from educators' expertise.

Portraiture's five "essential features"—context, voice, relationship, emergent themes, and aesthetic whole—allow for the depiction of goodness that is highly complex. I present a brief overview of these five components here and expand on them in later sections of this appendix where relevant. Portraiture defines **context** as the intersecting "physical, geographic, temporal, historical, cultural, aesthetic" settings of participants' experience that provide the researcher with "a rich resource for examining and interpreting behavior, thought, and feeling" (Lawrence-Lightfoot & Davis, 1997, p. 41); such contextualized analysis is especially salient for studying instruction, which is highly influenced by individual educator and school characteristics (S. M. Johnson et al., 2012). The portraitist also engages in multiple intentional uses of **voice**—her own, and in conversation with participants—that in turn invite the reader's internal voice as part of the collective, "generous *and* critical" interpretation of complex data to yield **emergent themes**. This intersection of voices requires the establishment of "productive and benign **relationships**" between researcher and participants (Lawrence-Lightfoot & Davis, 1997, p. 135), rooted in the search for goodness discussed above, as well as the development of empathetic regard, reciprocity, and boundaries. Finally, a key distinction between portraiture and other qualitative approaches is its concern with the **aesthetic whole**, a tapestry that is "both authentic and evocative, coded and colorful" (Lawrence-Lightfoot & Davis, 1997, p. 243)—its richness mirroring the complexity of the phenomenon it is depicting—and that can speak to multiple audiences.

The Portraitist

Portraiture also acknowledges and accepts that in the process of weaving this complex tapestry, "the voice of the researcher is everywhere" (Lawrence-Lightfoot & Davis, 1997, p. 85). This book's preface makes clear the personal experience and inspiration underlying my inquiry. Having occupied the roles of English teacher and mentor teacher at the secondary level, faculty developer at both the K–12 and postsecondary level, and currently a faculty member at a liberal arts college, I cannot ignore the professional expertise I bring to my scholarly work. Rather than silencing that voice, portraiture provides the researcher with a framework for establishing an authorial voice that is omnipresent but restrained in the final portrait. In a study that I have grounded in recognizing and valuing educators' understandings, it is fitting that I recognize and value my own: I do not see teachers and teaching in the way that many motivation researchers do, and that is an asset to this work—provided I utilize appropriate tools and strategies to temper my voice appropriately. I describe those strategies later in this appendix, in the discussion of authenticity.

PARTICIPANT SELECTION

My sampling procedure employed the principles of literal and theoretical replication in a multiple-case study design (Yin, 2009). I selected two high school participants and two college participants to prevent a single educator being cast as a representative case for each sector (Yin, 2009) and to allow for triangulation of findings within as well as across sector. It is important to note here that rather than seeking to demonstrate the "prevalence of phenomena" (Yin, 2009, p. 56), I employed portraiture's stance toward generalization, in which even a single case—including its particular idiosyncrasies—can yield "resonant universal themes," evoking "identification" through the specificity and subtlety of description (Lawrence-Lightfoot & Davis, 1997, p. 14). Thus, I sought to illuminate specific features of participants' practice that would inform our broader understanding of how to promote positive motivational mindset development in classrooms, while simultaneously acknowledging the uniqueness of each individual educator.

I recruited participants first by sampling schools that I theorized would be promising places to find educators interested in motivation research. I identified my two focal high schools through "purposeful selection" (Maxwell, 2005) of traditional public or public charter high schools that expressed—through a mission statement, curriculum reform, instructional improvement plan, or programming like advisories—an interest in social-emotional development, college readiness, or student engagement. I theorized that faculty at schools with some form of articulated institutional commitment to these domains of student development would be familiar both with concepts analogous to academic mindsets and some classroom strategies to promote them.

I sampled public schools in an effort to portray school experiences that would be accessible to any student in a given community, but I looked for similar types of districts in the same state so that the two schools would be situated in similar demographic and policy contexts. I prioritized small schools (around one hundred students per grade), hypothesizing that smaller schools would feature more cohesive faculty culture and investment in holistic student support. At each school, I contacted the principal to request permission to recruit among their twelfth-grade English teachers and to obtain permission to conduct my study on site if a teacher agreed to participate. Table A.1 provides details about the two focal high schools, Riverside Academy and Oak Bridge School.

I identified my two focal colleges through a similar process of purposeful selection. I searched for colleges that had a first-year writing program specifically, rather than first-year seminars, which tend to be more interdisciplinary. I also looked for colleges that were similar enough to each other for me to be able to draw some cross-case comparisons within sector. Because the administrative and governance structure of colleges differs from high schools, I contacted either the English Department chair or the faculty director of first-year writing to request permission to recruit among their writing instructors; this faculty member then assisted me in making any additional contacts with central administration that were necessary to secure permission for the study. Table A.2 summarizes institutional information for the two focal colleges, Mayfield University and Abbott University.

In both sectors, I sought educators with at least three years of teaching experience prior to the data collection year, theorizing that this was the baseline level of experience to have sufficient comfort in the classroom to be willing to host an observer, be able to identify specific pedagogical strategies and engage in reflective commentary through interviews, and generally feel able to manage participation in a study. After securing permission from the relevant administrator at each school, I sent an email to eligible educators that provided a brief overview of my study and invited them to contact me if they were interested in learning more. I spoke with each interested

Table A.1. Demographic Data on Focal High Schools, Compared to District and State Data

	Oak Bridge School	Oak Bridge District	Riverside Academy	Riverside District	State public schools
Total enrollment	275 (grades 7–12)	25,000	700 (grades 6–12)	25,000	
% of enrollment					
Male	55	51	52	52	51
Female	45	49	48	48	49
African American	10	15	25	20	9
Asian	20	7	1	2	7
Hispanic	54	42	47	65	19
Native American	<1	<1	<1	<1	<1
White	12	31	25	12	61
Native Hawaiian/ Pacific Islander	<1	<1	<1	<1	<1
Multirace, Non-Hispanic	3	4	<1	1	3
First language not English	69	54	12	27	20
English language learner*	26	34	2	16	10
Students with disabilities	11	19	16	21	17
Economically disadvantaged**	57	57	48	74	30
Passed Spring 2016 grade 10 English state exam	95	82	92	77	91
Passed Spring 2016 grade 10 math state exam	84	60	68	43	78
Passed Spring 2016 grade 10 science state exam	79	51	69	30	73

Note: All data are from the 2016–17 school year. Numbers are approximated to mask school identity.
*Defined as unable to perform ordinary class work in English.
**Defined as participating in one or more state food assistance programs, foster care, or Medicaid.
Source: State Department of Education.

Table A.2. Demographic Data on Focal Colleges

	Mayfield University		Abbott University	
	n	%	n	%
Total enrollment, degree-seeking students	3,200		11,000	
Degree-seeking undergraduates (day college)	2,200		5,000	
Men		39		45
Women		61		55
International		14		12
Domestic students of color		22		22
Average retention rate		89		97
Four-year graduation rate		77		87
Receive financial assistance		89		50
Pell Grant recipients*		22		13
First-year undergraduates	540		1300	
Admissions rate		55		16
Live in campus housing		96		70
First-year average high school GPA	3.65		*Not available*	
First-year average critical reading/math SAT scores	600/610**		700/710	
Undergraduate tuition***	$44,000		$50,000	
Undergraduate room and board	$8,000–$11,000		$13,000	

Note: All data are from the 2016–17 school year unless otherwise noted. Numbers are approximated to mask school identity

*From *Forbes* (2017), using 2015–16 school year information

**Mayfield University has a SAT/ACT-optional admissions policy

***Tuition and fees are for the 2017–18 school year

Source: Mayfield University and Abbott University websites, unless otherwise noted.

educator either in person or by phone to discuss further details of the study and eventually obtained their official consent to participate. In each sector, I accepted the first participant who agreed to the study and then took the next interested educator whose institutional context sufficiently "matched" the first participant's, thus completing my sample. Each participant received a fifty-dollar gift card as a token of appreciation at the conclusion of data collection.

DATA COLLECTION

Individual Interviews

With each educator, I began with a baseline one-hour interview, modeled on Seidman's (2006) phenomenological interviewing strategy, to explore each participant's understandings of motivational mindset development and their instructional enactments of those understandings (see table A.3). These prompts included showing each participant the four mindset statements and explicitly asking them about pedagogical practices they used to support the mindsets.

I then conducted follow-up interviews approximately once per month. These interviews followed a responsive interviewing structure (Rubin & Rubin, 2012), with main questions related to observed classroom events, document features, and emergent themes pertaining to motivational mindsets; and "second questions" (Kvale & Brinkmann, 2009) to acquire the necessary level of detail about how the educator understood these incidents, documents, or approaches to be supporting mindset development. I also interviewed the director of writing at Mayfield once for thirty minutes to obtain additional information about how their first-year writing program was set up.

I conducted interviews with the high school teachers on site during the teachers' free periods, whereas the college instructors' part-time status and lack of physical presence on campus meant that I had to arrange separate meetings for those interviews. Thus, I ended up interviewing the high school teachers five times, but generally for about forty-five to fifty minutes at a time (the typical duration of a school period, minus transition time), and the college instructor four times for about an hour each time. Because of scheduling difficulties, I had to conduct Colin's first interview by phone, but all other interviews were in person. I audio-recorded and transcribed all interviews.

Table A.3. Initial Phenomenological Interview Protocol

1. Please tell me a little about what you teach and how you came to be teaching here.

2. As a twelfth-grade English teacher/first-year college writing instructor, what goals do you have for your students?

3. What do you think your students need in order to be successful beyond your class?

4. I'm interested in the beliefs, attitudes, and self-perceptions that students have about themselves and their learning. Can you tell me what this description makes you think about in regards to your own students?

5. The student beliefs that I'm interested in are commonly referred to as "mindsets." I have sticky notes here that articulate four such mindsets: 1) "I belong in this academic community"; 2) "My ability and competence grow with my effort"; 3) "I can succeed at this"; 4) "This work has value for me". I want to invite you to reflect on these four student mindsets and what you do in your classroom that promotes them. Then, create a concept map or visual representation of how students develop these mindsets in your classroom. You can either feel free to think and diagram individually first, and then I'll ask you to explain your thinking after, or we can talk as you diagram. I'm most interested in your thinking around these mindsets, not the map itself.

6. Talk to me about what you've done here / what you're doing.
   Possible follow-up prompt / prompts while participant creates the concept map:
   a. How do you try to promote these mindsets in students?
   b. How do you communicate these mindsets to your students?
   c. How do you think about these mindsets during your planning for the course?
   d. . . . at the beginning of the year?
   e. . . . on a weekly/daily basis?
   f. Do the different mindsets manifest in different classroom or instructional features?
   g. Do the mindsets have equal importance to you? Why or why not?
   h. Do you collect information or feedback about these mindsets from students?
   i. Would you add anything to these mindsets?

7. Where and how did you develop your ideas about how to support these mindsets in students?

8. How does your school context influence your approach to supporting mindsets?

9. What are some challenges you've encountered in trying to promote these mindsets?

10. What would help you be more effective at promoting these mindsets in your students?

Source: Author provided.

Nonparticipant Observations

I worked with each participant to identify a cohort of students whom I would observe and a procedure for explaining the study to that cohort and securing student and/or parent permission according to the school's requirements. I then established an observation schedule with each focal participant. The distance between the high schools and Riverside's rotating schedule led to an original plan to observe each teacher twice a week. However, I was quickly reminded of how irregular a high school schedule can be, especially in a New England "spring" semester stretching from January to June: snow days early in the semester, special school and grade-level events later in the semester, school vacations, and my own availability reduced the number of observations I was able to achieve at each site. In the end, I observed Zachary seventeen times over the course of the semester and Diane, nineteen times.

Colin and Liz's class schedules—and the far fewer disruptions to class time in higher education—were much more conducive to my observing both on a regular basis.[1] I was able to observe all twenty-three of Liz's whole-class sessions, plus two class meetings that were converted into individual office-hour meetings with students (there were two additional conference days that I did not attend), for twenty-five total observations. Colin asked me not to attend the first two classes while he was settling in with students, but subsequently I observed all twenty-one of his remaining class sessions. In total, I spent close to one hundred hours observing classroom instruction.

During each observation, I sought to capture as much low-inference "thin description" as possible (Lawrence-Lightfoot & Davis, 1997), documenting patterns of interaction between educator and students; choice of instructional language, particularly in feedback and praise of students; and other classroom dynamics that conveyed support for students' positive mindset development, as established in my anticipatory framework drawn from relevant motivation literature (see table A.4).

Course Documents

Finally, I asked the participants to share with me as many relevant course documents and materials as possible. As a baseline, all participants shared their course syllabus and any handouts or assignment sheets distributed to students during classes I observed or that were relevant to the students' ongoing work. I also arranged a system with each educator to obtain student work. Because Diane, Zachary, and Liz primarily collected student work in

Table A.4. Preliminary Etic Codes Derived from the Literature

Mindset	Etic codes for interviews, observations, and document analysis

"I belong in this academic community" *(Belonging mindset)*	• Teacher involvement and immediacy with students
	  —Verbally or physically acknowledging students
	  —Demonstrating personal knowledge of students
	  —Use of (correctly pronounced) student names
	• Expectations of and opportunities for student participation
	• Representation of different demographic groups in the classroom and curriculum
	• Statements of inclusiveness and diversity

"This work has value for me" *(Value mindset)*	• Explanations of relevance/applicability of learning • Use of real-world examples and connections • Support for students' individual goals, aspirations, and interests • Opportunities for student choice, self-direction, and reflection
"My ability and competence grow with my effort" *(Growth mindset)*	• Teacher verbal and nonverbal recognition and affirmation of student progress, improvement, strategy, focus, persistence, etc. • Teacher language around effort, ability, potential for growth, and the value of challenge/struggle • Time for students to practice independently • Assessment that includes effort and improvement/progress • Feedback on student work that encourages continued effort
"I can succeed at this" *(Competence mindset)*	• Teacher uses strategies to check for student understanding • Multiple opportunities for students to demonstrate mastery (e.g., revising work) • Success exemplars with whom students can identify • Peer groups and class community encourage individual striving for success • Praise and affirmation of student competence

Source: Author provided.

hard copy and because the high volume of student work in English classes made it impossible to copy everything while not disrupting the educators' feedback and grading flow, I generally asked them to select a representative range of student work to pass on to me after they had written feedback on or graded the work. Occasionally at the high schools, I was able to remain in the classroom after my observation and quickly photograph student work. Colin's students submitted their work on a Google+ class website, and Liz's students submitted their final assignment to her via email, which facilitated my access to them.

Similar to the class observations, I was interested in how these documents reflected instructional practices consistent with those recommended in the motivation literature (see table A.4). For example, I looked at how the participants communicated expectations and provided feedback, whether and how participants broke down large or complex assignments and constructed assignments that accommodated student choice and interests, as well as evidence of students' responses to instruction and, of course, their motivational mindsets.

DATA ANALYSIS

In portraiture, as in many qualitative research methods, the process of collecting, organizing, and analyzing the varied data sources occurs in "iterative cycles" (Miles & Huberman, 1994). I began with the anticipatory framework of the motivation literature, which provided me with an etic framework (see table A.4) that guided my eyes and ears during observations, document analysis, and interviews. Throughout my data collection process, I wrote impressionistic records (Lawrence-Lightfoot & Davis, 1997), similar to field notes and interpretive memos used in other qualitative research (Emerson et al., 2011). These impressionistic records included initial interpretations, questions, and preliminary hypotheses about the educators' understandings and enactments of positive mindset development according to my etic framework, informing subsequent data collection and analysis. For example, my reflections in early impressionistic records noted the use of numerical grades in Diane's class that I did not fully understand and the near-total absence of classroom talk related to grades in Zachary's class. As the motivation literature identifies grading structures as relevant to students' growth and competence mindsets, I developed a follow-up interview protocol focused on eliciting the participant's philosophy and approach to grading to ensure I had that data on this topic for both high school teachers and the next semester with the college instructors.

However, at the same time that I was maintaining my etic framework to ensure comprehensive data collection, I also had to be open to the unique nuances and character of each participant's classroom and instructional practice. I hand coded observation notes, interview transcripts, and course documents for each participant to explore new "theoretical possibilities . . . in the data"

(Charmaz, 2006, p. 47). I then used portraiture's analytic techniques of listening for repetitive refrains, resonant metaphors, and cultural and institutional rituals (Lawrence-Lightfoot & Davis, 1997), ultimately developing a set of "focused codes" (Charmaz, 2006) that characterized each participant's practice. For example, Colin explicitly used a metaphor of games in his course design, but there were other resonant metaphors in his data that he was less consciously aware of, such as his frequent use of performance metaphors to describe teaching (e.g., "Every class is sort of a wild improv routine;" "I feel like I'm on stage"). Though these exact metaphors did not ultimately appear in his final portrait, they provided me with critical insight into how he understood the work of teaching and his own role as a teacher and contrasted with the kinds of metaphors that his counterpart, Liz, used to describe teaching. I continued documenting my emergent thinking about these codes, triangulated them across the different data sources and across participants, and began to identify emergent themes and patterns through the contrasting data, ultimately finalizing a set of ten to twelve codes for each participant that described the key characteristics of their teaching (see table A.5).

At this point, I returned to my original anticipatory framework and mapped my etic codes onto the emic codes to create a visual matrix of thematic convergence and divergence across individual participants (see table A.5). This visual helped me begin to "weave the tapestry" (Lawrence-Lightfoot & Davis, 1997), not only of each individual participant's portrait, but of all four portraits in conversation, collectively addressing my overarching research questions for the study. I used the matrix, informed by the impressionistic records and memos I had written throughout the process, to prioritize which themes felt most resonant for each participant, which felt well-supported with multiple data sources, which ones would "hang together" (Willig, 2008) best in an individual narrative, and which would complement the narratives of the other participants. It was at this stage that I decided to focus each participant's portrait on a focal mindset.

AUTHENTICITY

Portraiture operates with "authenticity" as the standard for validity, seeking to achieve "resonance" with three audiences: the participants, other readers, the portraitist herself. To achieve a "credible and believable" portrait for these three audiences (Lawrence-Lightfoot & Davis, 1997, p. 260), I employed multiple strategies, consistent with other approaches to validity threats in qualitative research (Willig, 2008), during both data collection and analysis.

Table A.5. Emic-Etic Code Matrix

Mindset	Etic codes
[B]elonging *"I belong in this academic community"*	• Teacher (***involvement***) with students — Verbally or physically acknowledging — Demonstrating personal knowledge of — Use of (correctly pronounced) names • Expectations of and opportunities for student (***participation—current / future / past***) • (***Representation***) of different demographic groups in the classroom and curriculum • Statements of (***inclusion***) and diversity
[V]alue *"This work has value for me"*	• Explanations of (***relevance***) / applicability of learning • Use of real-world examples and (***connections***) • Support for students' individual (***goals***) / aspirations, and (***interests***) • Opportunities for student (***choice***) / self-direction and (***reflection***)
[G]rowth strategy, *"My ability and competence grow with my effort"*	• Teacher verbal / nonverbal (***recognition***) and affirmation of progress, improvement, focus, persistence, etc. • Teacher (***talk***) around effort, ability, potential for growth, and the value of challenge / struggle • Time for students to (***practice***) independently • (***Assessment***) includes effort / improvement • (***Encouraging***) continued effort through feedback

continued on next page

Table A.5. Continued.

[C]ompetence
"I can succeed at this"

- Teacher uses strategies to check for (**monitoring**) student understanding
- Multiple opportunities for students to demonstrate (**mastery**) (e.g., revising work)
- (**Vicarious**) success exemplars with whom students can identify
- Peer groups and class community provides social (**persuasion**) for individual striving for success
- (**Praise**) / affirmation of student competence

Diane

1. "How we do school"
   [B-participation (current)]
   [V-reflection] [G-assessment]
   [C-persuasion] [C-mastery]
   [C-vicarious]
   a. "Brainwashing"
      [B-participation (future)]
   b. Broken windows
      [B-involvement (anti)]
      [B-participation (current)]
   c. "Hand-holding"
      [B-involvement] [C-mastery (anti)]
2. Competition & conformity / "playing by those rules"
   [B-participation (future)]

Zachary

1. Validating student experience / ideas / interest
   [V-interest] [V-choice]
   [B-involvement]
   [B-participation (future)]
2. "Little things to latch onto" / concrete things / "natural interest"
   [V-interest] [V-relevance]
   [V-connections]
   [B-participation (future)]
3. "Fun & inspiring"
   [B-involvement] [V-interest]
4. Say anything
   [B-participation (current)]

Liz

1. Lowering anxieties / positive affect
   [B-involvement] [C-praise]
   [G-recognition]
2. "Brute force practice"
   [G-practice] [G-talk]
3. "Encouraging" grades
   a. product
      [C-praise] [C-persuasion]
   b. process
      [G-assessment]
      [G-recognition]
      [G-practice] [C-mastery]
4. Validating student experience / interest
   [V-interest] [V-choice]

Colin

1. Rules / framework / "objective" quality standards
   [C-mastery] [C-monitoring]
   a. HS games / rules
      [B-participation (past)]
   b. "Writing is hard, and it takes time" / personal experience
      [C-vicarious] [G-talk]
   c. High grading standard
      [G-encouraging]
2. Instructor expertise / authority (shaping TSR)
   [C-monitoring] [B-involvement]
3. Categorization of students / "temperament & training"
   [B-involvement] [G-recognition]

3. Operation Graduation
[B-involvement] [V-relevance]
4. "Our kids do / don't..." / expectations
[B-involvement (anti)]
[B-inclusion (anti)]
[G-recognition (anti)]
[C-mastery (anti)]
[C-praise (anti)]
5. "Old hippies" / activism
[V-relevance] [V-connections]
[B-participation (future)]
6. Thinking routines / protocols
[C-monitoring] [C-mastery]
7. Breaking down tasks
[C-monitoring] [C-mastery]
8. College
[V-relevance] [V-goals]

[V-interest] [V-connections]
5. "Lenience" / flexibility
[B-involvement] [C-monitoring]
6. College
[V-relevance] [V-goals]
7. Lifetime value
[V-relevance] [V-connections]
[V-interests]
8. Sharing personal experience / personality
[B-involvement]
9. Circulating / support / undivided attention
[B-involvement] [C-monitoring]
[C-praise] [C-persuasion]
10. Modeling and metacognitive strategies
[C-mastery] [C-monitoring]
[S-vicarious] [G-recognition]

[B-involvement]
[B-participation (future)]
[B-participation (past)]
5. "Everything is complying" / allowing natural development
[B-involvement]
[C-monitoring (anti)]
[G-practice]
6. Writing community membership
[B-participation (current) (future)] [C-persuasion]
[V-relevance]
7. Reflection
[V-reflection]
8. Peer review
[B-participation (current)]
[V-choice] [C-persuasion]

[C-praise]
4. Student independence / responsibility / trust
[V-choice] [G-practice]
5. Prizes / rewards / "sugar" / ROI
[B-involvement] [C-praise]
[C-persuasion] [V-relevance]
[V-interests]
6. Extensive feedback
[G-encouraging]
7. Being known as human beings
[B-involvement]
8. Cold-calling
[B-participation (current)]
9. Circulating / support
[B-involvement] [C-monitoring]
[C-praise]

continued on next page

Table A.5. Continued.

Diane	**Zachary**	**Liz**	**Colin**
9. "Lifetime value" [V-relevance] [V-connections]	[G-talk] [G-practice]	[G-practice]	10. Peer review [B-participation (current)] [V-choice] [C-persuasion] [G-practice]
10. Modeling [C-monitoring] [C-vicarious]	11. Writing rubric [C-mastery]	9. Giving positive feedback [B-involvement] [E-praise] [C-persuasion] [G-recognition] [G-assessment] [G-encouraging]	
	12. Group work [B-participation (current)] [V-choice) persuasion] [G-practice]	10. Considering audience [V-connections] [V-relevance] [V-choice] [V-interests] [B-participation (future)]	

Source: Author provided.

My semester-long involvement with research participants through observations and periodic interviews provided a check on validity threats by affording me ongoing opportunities for "respondent validation" (Maxwell, 2010). The interviews were both a data source in and of themselves and a setting for hypothesis checking of my emerging interpretations of the participants' understandings and attempted enactments of motivationally supportive practices. For example, in at least one interview with each participant, I shared an excerpt of observation field notes or a classroom artifact that I had written about independently in my impressionistic records or thematic memos and explicitly asked the participant for his or her interpretation. In some cases, the participants' interpretations were consistent with my own, but in other cases they provided an important counterpoint that gave me new insight into their thinking or illuminated an important tension through our contrasting views. I also sent the participants near-final drafts of their respective portraits to review. Appendix B discusses this process in more detail.

The immersive data collection process also supported my accumulation of "rich data" that allowed for triangulation across multiple data sources; these are additional strategies to address threats to validity (Maxwell, 2010) and achieve portrait authenticity for all readers. In my portraits, I balance the "thin" description of specific observational details with the "thoughtful, discerning interpretation" that constitutes "thick" description (Lawrence-Lightfoot & Davis, 1997, p. 91), seeking to equip the reader with sufficient data to evaluate whether the narrative themes of the final portraits feel earned and resonant. I also wanted my portraits and their phenomenological approach to resonate within the landscape of motivation research, which is grounded in more positivist traditions of inquiry. As such, I sought to address construct validity, a common challenge in case study research (Yin, 2009), by utilizing the analytic methods described above to connect my emic codes and emergent themes back to the etic anticipatory framework drawn from the motivation literature.

Throughout this process, portraiture's emphasis on balancing multiple intersecting voices has guided my work on achieving resonance for myself with these portraits while also observing restraint to allow other voices, perspectives, and interpretations to stand alongside mine. I employed "disciplined skepticism" toward my own interpretations by writing reflective memos in which I identified the biases and "personal predisposition[s]" (Lawrence-Lightfoot & Davis, 1997, p. 13) that could be informing my emerging analyses and forced myself to articulate counterinterpretations and alternative hypotheses (Maxwell, 2010). I also shared excerpts of data, emerging findings, and portrait drafts with an interpretive community of colleagues who assisted me in the process of "listening for gaps, inconsistencies, and associations" in the raw data as well as in my understanding of those data (Luttrell, 2000, p. 517). Their insights as fellow researchers but also as a general audience were invaluable to me in crafting final portraits in which I hope the rich, varied, and detailed description supports my interpretations but also invites readers to contemplate and evaluate both the portrait and the portraitist for themselves.

Appendix B

AFTER-WORDS: NEGOTIATING PARTICIPANT AND PORTRAITIST RESPONSE IN THE STUDY "AFTERMATH"[2]

Sara Lawrence-Lightfoot frequently uses anecdotes of being sketched or painted to illustrate one of the key goals of portraiture: to "make the subjects feel 'seen' in a way they have never felt seen before" (Lawrence-Lightfoot, 1983, p. 5). Portraiture culminates in the unveiling of the portrait to the participant, extending the methodological process into what many other researchers might consider the "aftermath of their work" (Lawrence-Lightfoot, 1983, p. 377). Yet this moment has received little attention in portraits themselves or in methodological writings. Lawrence-Lightfoot gives participant responses perhaps their most extensive treatment in *The Good High School* (1983), which she bookends with stories of portrait confrontation. She begins the book by describing the "odd sensation" she felt on confronting a portrait of herself that the painting "did not look like me, and yet it captured my essence" (p. 4), then she concludes with an afterword describing her participants' responses to the portraits of their schools. In a survey of other published portraiture studies, I found only one other example of participant responses included alongside the portraits: a study of science educators (Quigley et al., 2015) where, again, the responses appear briefly near the end of the article.

I believe multiple factors contribute to the opaqueness surrounding participant response and the ensuing choices made by researchers in the "aftermath" of portraiture studies. First, overlapping and potentially conflicting rationales exist for sharing portraits with participants, each of which positions the portraitist in a different stance of power and authority in relation to the participant. These shifting stances create uncertainty as to how the portraitist can or should respond to the participant's response; in turn, this uncertainty may make portraitists reluctant to expose their process at this stage, resulting in a dearth of models and guidance for both conducting and recording such interactions.

In this appendix, I attempt to catalyze a clarifying conversation among portraitists and other qualitative researchers about the role of participant response and strategies for negotiating and documenting that researcher-participant interaction. I begin by outlining what I see as the main rationales for soliciting participant response in portraiture before exploring the challenges and tensions that emerge through the intersection of those rationales. In an effort to model greater transparency in the methodological literature, I then present three cases of my own experience negotiating participants' responses to their portraits, inviting readers' perspectives on the choices I made as portraitist. I conclude by identifying three commitments that could help me and others more intentionally incorporate participant response into our work, treating it as an integral dimension of qualitative research.

Why Seek Participant Response?

The notion of seeking participant response is not unique to portraiture. I describe three prevailing rationales—methodological, ethical, and interventionist—for participant response in qualitative inquiry more broadly and discuss portraiture's stance within each rationale. It is important to note that these are not discrete categories; a study that employs participant response procedures likely does so for multiple, overlapping reasons, and it is this overlap that often produces the most potent tensions. However, it is useful to articulate and attend to each rationale in turn to make transparent the paradigms underlying the solicitation of participant response and to lay the groundwork for identifying the conflicts and paradoxes that infuse the portraitist-participant negotiation of this response.

Methodological Rationale

Historically, the methodological rationale for incorporating participant response in qualitative social science research was for the validation of data, interpretations, and conclusions (Colaizzi, 1978; Lincoln & Guba, 1985). Though debates continue over the proper terminology for such a process, the consistent thread is that systematic "member checking" strengthens the credibility (Lincoln & Guba, 1985) or legitimacy (Onwuegbuzie & Leech,

2007) of the study by providing participants an opportunity to address and correct potential misrepresentations and misinterpretations of their data (Maxwell, 2005). Under this methodological rationale, participant response functions largely as an analog to internal validity checks in quantitative analyses; it is meant to help ensure the accuracy of the data and emerging analyses and to fortify the rigor and quality of the study (Morse et al., 2002; Willig, 2013).

However, in addition to disputes over how participants' subjectivity complicates their ability to verify interpretations about themselves (Bradbury-Jones et al., 2010; Goldblatt et al., 2011) and whether participant validation renders study findings any more robust (Varpio et al., 2017), qualitative researchers wrestle with the question of whether validity itself is the appropriate standard to target under the nonpositivist epistemologies that typically underlie qualitative inquiry. Whereas quantitative research traditionally relies on notions of validity meant to help researchers create the most accurate representations possible of a "true" reality, many approaches in qualitative research focus on subjective lived experience and/or the coconstruction of meaning between researcher and researched (Willig, 2013). As such, qualitative researchers have moved away from validity and toward notions of "authenticity," wherein " 'truth' not only means 'corresponding to the facts,' but also 'trustworthy' . . . i.e., 'does it persuade us that we might helpfully rely on the insights it presents about that particular situation to guide our thinking about other situations?' " (Winter, 2002, pp. 144–45).

Portraiture's standard of authenticity aligns with Winter's (2002) framing of the concept. Gazing at a successful portrait is "not like looking in the mirror" but, rather, coming to "recognize, appreciate, respect, scrutinize" oneself through a portraitist's "generous and tough" eyes (Lawrence-Lightfoot & Davis, 1997, p. 4). In portraiture, the rationale for seeking participant response is therefore less centered on validation of component parts to ensure the integrity of the final product; it is more about the aesthetic whole achieving "resonance" for participants. Of course, accuracy is still an important prerequisite for achieving resonance; a participant who has been misquoted is not likely to feel "seen." Beyond this rational appraisal and verification of the written report, though, the portraitist seeks a more instinctual response as a methodological check on the quality of her portrait, a reflexive identification that is described as a "click" of self-recognition (Lawrence-Lightfoot & Davis, 1997, p. 247). Portraitists seek the same automaticity that enables us to put a finger immediately on our own face in a group photo even when the faces are tiny or the photo is blurry. We recognize ourselves in a way that others cannot.

The methodological aims of participant response in portraiture therefore expand on traditional approaches to member checking in qualitative research in that the participant holds the unique authority to affirm the research report, not only factually or intellectually, but at a gut level. Contrary to English's (2000) critique of authenticity as a standard that imbues the portraitist with "totalizing power" and "omniscience" in "posturing to present a single, grand, encompassing truth . . . an authentic view of reality" (p. 23), the pursuit of authenticity requires a humble, receptive stance from the portraitist, awaiting the "click" of self-recognition that can *only* come from the participant herself.

Ethical Rationale

The notion of trustworthiness bound up in authenticity also inherently centralizes the relationship between researcher and participant, of which the quality of the research report is both a component and a product. Consideration of these interpersonal dynamics lies at the heart of the ethical rationale for soliciting participant response. Qualitative researchers have long wrestled with ethical concerns over voice and representation in research (Fine & Weis, 2010; Luttrell, 2000; Rodriguez & Brown, 2009; Tuck, 2009; Villenas, 1996). These concerns center on inherent power differentials in the researcher-participant relationship, what Fine (1994) calls the "Self-Other" dynamic, in which researchers are inherently asserting the power to speak " 'of' and 'for' Others" (p. 70). This paternalistic and colonialist perspective on participants is a common critique of seminal anthropological studies of indigenous populations by Western researchers (Crapanzano, 1996; Rosaldo, 1993). However, even when a researcher identifies with her participants (Villenas, 1996) or is "studying up" rather than "down" societal hierarchies (Gaztambide-Fernandez, 2009), she still holds a privileged status in key areas of the research enterprise—notably, the final research report. By authoring the product of the research, the researcher gets the final word on how a participant is depicted.

Soliciting participant response is one method a researcher can employ to confront the potentially uncomfortable truths about how she has represented the Other in the final research report. While the process can also serve methodological functions, Luttrell (2000) cautions against retreating into rationales of validation that serve primarily to "bind [researchers'] anxieties" over ethical complexities (p. 515), advocating instead that researchers actively engage with the messy questions and relational challenges inherent in qualitative research. Inviting the participant to comment on the researcher's rendering places "Self" and "Other" in an active dialogue around the ethical tensions inherent in third-party representation.

Related to, but distinct from, the ethical challenges of representation is the risk of participants' study involvement feeling or becoming exploitative. Included in this tension are questions of who benefits from the research and what researchers "owe" their participants in return for participants' time and investment. In traditional models of inquiry, the fact that the researcher initiates, frames, and concludes the study often makes her the primary beneficiary: the study is done to satisfy her curiosity, on her terms, for her purposes. While institutional review boards and the process of informed consent are meant to safeguard a baseline of ethical treatment of human subjects (Nelson-Marten & Rich, 1999), researchers must negotiate for themselves the nature and extent of their ethical obligation to share study findings with participants and to nurture reciprocity in the research relationship (Lather, 1986; Maiter et al., 2008; Trainor & Bouchard, 2013). To prompt researchers to reflect on these ethical issues, recent models of qualitative research design place relationships at the core (Luttrell, 2010; Maxwell, 2005). Within these frameworks, seeking participant response can function not just as a check on validity/authenticity and the wielding of researcher power in representation but also as a relational gesture of reciprocity—giving something back to the participant for her study involvement.

Portraiture likewise faces "complex and vexing interpersonal and ethical challenges" as it seeks to "become more participatory, collaborative, symmetric, dialectic" (Lawrence-Lightfoot, 2005, pp. 8–9). Inviting the participant's response to a complex portrait can be seen as a linchpin of the relationships portraitists must cultivate with their participants, in which both parties receive opportunities to challenge the other and the researcher avoids a one-sided, exploitative voyeurism (Lawrence-Lightfoot, 2016). By temporarily reversing the lens of scrutiny, a participant response process restores some symmetry to the research relationship, though it can never fully equalize it; the participant, as the subject of depiction, is inherently more vulnerable than the portraitist. Soliciting participant response in the study aftermath therefore offers researchers an opportunity to continue negotiating key ethical tensions: how to wield one's power in representing the Other and strive for reciprocity *and* rigor in inherently unequal research relationships.

Interventionist Rationale

Attending to the methodological and ethical rationales for sharing a portrait does not necessarily translate into the participant liking what she sees. The work of the portraitist is to look not only for "strength, resilience, and creativity" but also for "the weakness, imperfection, and vulnerability that inevitably compromise the goodness" (Lawrence-Lightfoot & Davis, 1997, p. 158), in part because of an interventionist goal of catalyzing reflective change in the participant.

While an implicit goal of all research is to produce knowledge that can inform scholarship, policy, or practice, methodological writings have not focused as extensively on the potential role of the research report in altering *participant* behavior specifically. Scholars have debated whether researchers' energies are better spent seeking to explain study effects on specific individual participants or extrapolating from granular findings to the broader population (Hostetler, 2005). Among empirical approaches, the field of action research, which seeks to "effect desired change as a path to generating knowledge and empowering stakeholders" (H. B. Huang, 2010, p. 93), probably engages most deeply in questions about the direct impact of research on participants, particularly in its youth participatory models, where the experience of research involvement itself is intended to be trans-formative (Rodriguez & Brown, 2009).

With its goal of illuminating universal themes through individual stories (Lawrence-Lightfoot, 2016), portraiture likewise seeks to influence audiences beyond the immediate orbit of a specific study, but it is also unusual among even qualitative methods in its explicit attention to the desired impact on participants. From their inception, portraits have been conceptualized as "documents of inquiry *and* intervention, hopefully lead-ing toward new understandings and insights, as well as instigating change" (Lawrence-Lightfoot & Davis, 1997, pp. 4–5). These change-instigating insights often arrive in a third and final stage of participant reaction, after initial anxiety and then a period of denial have faded (Lawrence-Lightfoot, 1983). Thus, the interventionist goal is in some ways the desired terminus for the process of soliciting participant response in portraiture.

Yet, the attainment of the interventionist goal is rarely depicted. In one of the few examples of portraitists publishing their participants' responses alongside the original portraits, Quigley and colleagues (2015) describe a participant stating that reading the portrait allowed her to "see the girls working together in different ways," giving her "a new understanding of experiences and episodes" in her classroom (pp. 42–43). Even this account, however, is limited in its description of what changes may arise from this teacher's increased awareness and insight. Bloom and Erlandson (2003) solicited more detailed third-party reader responses to portraits to explore whether and how a reader uses a portrait "to make meaning for his or her own purposes" (p. 876), but to my knowledge, analogous work has not been done on the responses of participants themselves.

The interventionist rationale foments the tensions and paradoxes among the coexisting rationales for seeking participant response. A portraitist may ask participants to affirm the "click" of self-recognition for methodological purposes, but also to recognize—and, hopefully, ultimately accept—a complex and potentially critical representation as part of a rigorous and respectful research relationship and for interventionist aims. Meanwhile, ethical challenges could surface in the interventionist rationale related to whether the participant feels agency in acknowledging the need for change and deciding what those changes will be or if the intervention is perceived as an assertion of researcher authority and dominance. These paradoxes present the portraitist with a highly complex puzzle as she nears the completion of her work.

CHALLENGES IN NEGOTIATING PARTICIPANT AND PORTRAITIST RESPONSE

The tensions inherent in the rationales for *why* a portraitist would seek participant response hold practical implications for *how* she chooses to solicit and then respond to that response. In the limited writings on participant response procedures, a common recommendation is for researchers to convey clear expectations and set parameters for the desired response (Carlson, 2010; Lawrence-Lightfoot, 1983), but the coexisting rationales can create multiple and contradictory aims, as well as conflicting paradigms for researcher behavior. For example, a participant may initially dispute the authenticity of a portrait and only later come to understand and appreciate it through an interventionist lens; under this logic, the portraitist, as the facilitator of the change process, need not act in response to the initial dispute and accepts that she may never see the change occur. Yet, there are ethical and methodological risks in assuming that a participant's repudiation of parts or all of a portrait is simply part of *the participant's* necessary growth trajectory, a temporary stage of denial en route to self-reflective enlightenment. Meanwhile, the methodological rationale recognizes the participant's unique ability to endorse the portrait's resonance and authenticity but has not clarified whether and how a portraitist might alter a portrait based on the participant's response versus positioning herself as an artist whose creative endeavor is complete, a stance that may inadequately address ethical tensions over voice and representation.

Methodological writings on portraiture have not provided much clarity or guidance on negotiating these challenges. Lawrence-Lightfoot (1983) argues that the portraitist should not take participant reactions "at face value" or view them as "evidence of his or her goodness or maliciousness" but rather must "find an unswerving, confident position that listens and accepts, but is not controlled, enhanced, or diminished by others' perceptions and judgments" (p. 377). In this description of "unswerving confiden[ce]" I see some basis for English's (2000) critique of the portraitist asserting "totalizing power," a potential problem for the methodological and ethical goals of authenticity and reciprocity. Indeed, in two existing models of the participant response process in portraiture, the researchers constrain the potential influence of their participants, first in the rationale(s) they provide to participants for seeking response and then in the rebuffing of participant suggestions that transgress the perceived boundaries of the stated rationale(s). In *The Art and Science of Portraiture,* Davis frames her request for participant response as an opportunity for participants to contest "factual errors" only; her study team "trie[s] to make clear to the actors that the portrait was a finished product—our interpretation was complete" (Lawrence-Lightfoot & Davis, 1997, p. 173). Thus, the stated rationale for soliciting participant response is a limited kind of methodological authentication. The choice to situate this account in a broader discussion about research relationships also belies an ethical rationale for sharing the portrait: it is about "guarding" the research relationship after the study has concluded, though the constraints placed on the acceptable responses potentially make the gesture ring somewhat hollow.

Likewise, when one headmaster in *The Good High School* begins to propose revisions beyond "correcting the errors or softening the sharp edge of several . . . words," Lawrence-Lightfoot (1983) explains to him that the portrait "must maintain the coherence and integrity that I have tried to bring to it . . . I have carefully combed through the data, searched my soul on many questions of interpretation, and take full responsibility for my observations" (pp. 375–76). In doing so, she asserts her methodological authority and frames the response solicitation process as primarily serving an interventionist goal to "catalyze . . . internal conversation and self-criticism at your school" (p. 375). This, in turn, illuminates an ethical conflict in the unequal research relationship: the portraitist can nudge the participants toward change, but not the other way around.

Crucially, however, Lawrence-Lightfoot (1983) includes this detailed account of the participant response process—including verbatim dialogue between herself and this headmaster—in the same volume as the portraits themselves, which invites third-party scrutiny and therefore challenges to her otherwise seemingly monolithic authority. Her decision to do so and its potential effects are consistent with calls for greater transparency from qualitative researchers about their choices (Anfara et al., 2002) and with Luttrell's (2000) conceptualization of "good enough" methods, in which qualitative researchers discuss their "complex choices and decision making . . . in terms of what is lost and what is gained, rather than what might be ideal" (p. 500). Likewise, rather than proposing an "ideal" protocol for soliciting and then responding to participants' responses, I seek to model this increased transparency and contribute to the limited body of literature on participant response by presenting my own experience sharing the portraits in this volume with the participants. I invite the reader's critique of the choices I made and the trade-offs I accepted.

REFLEXIVE SCRUTINY: CASE STUDIES OF PARTICIPANT RESPONSE

Following the conclusion of official data collection in December 2017, I had no further communication with my four focal educators until I sent them the near-final portrait drafts in December 2018. I e-mailed the draft portraits with an explanatory letter that described the portraits as "close to final" and informed participants that I could not make "major changes" to their "structure and substance" but that I welcomed "feedback on my interpretations, as well as any clarifications you want to make or any requests you may have for me to provide more context at particular moments." I offered to meet in person or speak by phone to facilitate communication, but everyone responded via email. I focus here on the responses from Zachary, Liz, and Colin, as Diane provided only a minimal response to her portrait.

Zachary: Methods in Madness

Zachary was a very different kind of high school English teacher than I had been, flexible in all the places where I insisted on structure and consistency. Our different teaching paradigms meant that I had to work diligently throughout the composition process to restrain my own voice in favor of Zachary's when describing incidents where I would have intervened but Zachary chose not to. I wanted to allow the reader—and myself—to view the behavior through Zachary's eyes, to understand the goodness in his perspective on the issue, reasoning that my interpretation was already implicit in my shaping of the narrative and that layering on my voice more explicitly might be an unethical use of my authorial power, tipping the scale of interpretation unequivocally toward my old reflexes and preferences as a teacher.

Methodologically, I was curious about Zachary's feedback on how authentically I had represented his pedagogical perspective, given that it was so different from my own. In particular, I had never directly asked him about ignoring Veronica's high-pitched "Spongebob" noises, which feature in a block-quoted field note excerpt in his portrait. His comments that follow that field note, about getting "really wrapped up" in student conferences, came from an interview about a different class. I hoped that Zachary would view that merge as seamless and accurate. I also wondered how he would feel about his own comments on reading them; even though he had said the words, I wondered if they might feel different reflected back to him on the page and contextualized within the overall portrait narrative. I thought that if I had gotten the balance right, Zachary would feel that the portrait authentically depicted his pedagogy but also gently challenged him to consider whether his permissiveness in class was always beneficial for the students.

Zachary was the first of my participants to respond to his portrait, replying the next morning, a mere thirteen hours after I had e-mailed him:

> Thank you for sending this to me—I was actually thinking about it the other day.
>
> I loved reading this—it was nice that someone saw some kind of method to my madness. I'm not sure I could articulate why I do what I do as well as you do, but it certainly made me feel better about my teaching. I showed it to my girlfriend who found my circular and unfinished thoughts/quotes amusing. I'm glad I was able to help you with your research—I was worried that you weren't going to find what you were looking for in my class.

He concluded by asking me to incorporate some information about his school's approach to ability-level tracking and also requested a copy of the final completed study.

I was gratified that Zachary responded so positively and that he felt seen and validated as a teacher by my interpretation of the "method to [his] madness." Ethically, I felt that sharing the portrait had served as a reciprocal act, giving him something in return for his generosity during data collection. I wondered, though, how satisfied I was that one of Zachary's main takeaways from his portrait was that it made him "feel better" about his teaching. While I certainly preferred that to making him feel *worse* about his teaching, it did not necessarily provide me with methodological reassurance about the authenticity of the portrait. I interpreted Zachary's relaying to me of his girlfriend's response to be an implicit endorsement of the authenticity of his "circular and unfinished thoughts/quotes" in the portrait, but he might otherwise have been disinclined to challenge what he saw as a positive portrayal overall. Primarily, though, I wondered whether sharing this portrait had served the interventionist goal of instigating self-reflection and change—indeed, I can see how feeling better about one's teaching could have the opposite effect—and, if not, how I should assess my own work in crafting the portrait. What I did, however, was simply reply to Zachary to thank him for his response and pledge to incorporate his minor addition and send him the final document.

Liz: Writing Thoughts

Liz's portrait was the only one that underwent more than minimal changes or corrections after the draft I sent her to review, though the change did not stem from a direct request on her part but rather a synergy between her and my own dissatisfaction. The major revision was the addition of this paragraph near the end of the portrait:

> Despite sometimes expressing fixed perspectives on her teaching ability and impact, Liz simultaneously holds a powerful growth orientation toward this work that she "love[s] so much." She is unquestionably committed to improving as an instructor; she sometimes pauses during our interviews when a question prompts her to reflect in a new way, saying this is "exactly" why she signed up for the study, and in our last interview, she tells me that she participated because she "just felt like it would be good for me to think about the same things you're thinking about, and to feel sort of accountable, and to get better."

The process leading up to this addition began with my worries about how Liz would respond to her portrait's depiction of her messy and contradictory mixture of fixed and growth mindsets toward her own teaching that paralleled her students' mixed mindsets about their writing ability, hampering development in both cases. I had so much evidence of this paradoxical pattern in Liz's data that I felt confident that it was methodologically sound, but I had many ethical concerns about sharing it with her. Depicting the paradox in the portrait narrative required a quite explicit interpretive voice from me to juxtapose Liz's espoused beliefs and her behaviors, her words to students in class about writing, and her words to me in private about teaching. It was not hard for me to imagine someone reacting negatively to having these contradictions illuminated; it seemed to tread dangerously close to being a "gotcha!" moment antithetical to portraiture's ethos (Lawrence-Lightfoot, 2016, p. 22). I feared that Liz might view the portrait as an assertion of my critical power as researcher and as a betrayal of the quite amiable relationship that had developed between us, as women of a similar age, during data collection.

At the same time, it felt unethical *not* to share my true analysis with Liz, who had repeatedly stated that she was participating in the study because she wanted to grow as a teacher and spoke about our interviews as a valuable opportunity for her to reflect on her practice. Withholding my honest interpretation of a key tension in her pedagogy would have meant denying her the main interventionist benefit she was seeking and further unbalancing our research relationship.

Liz took a couple weeks to respond to her portrait draft, further inflaming my trepidation, but when her e-mail finally arrived, I breathed a sigh of relief at the first paragraph: "This is the single most helpful thing that's happened for my teaching since the two-week training six years ago! I don't have anyone to talk to about how what I'm doing is or is not achieving what I want and what to do differently anymore. Thank you so much."

She identified specific themes and findings from the portrait that had resonated with her and helped her "see the connection" between her different instructional choices, particularly around establishing explicit criteria for students' writing: "I realize the problem is that I haven't articulated the components even to myself, that my approach is also mysterious to me, and I need to know what I'm doing so that I can articulate to [students] what I'm doing . . . Anyway, I'm going to make a rubric. :)"

However, she voiced some concern over the ending of the portrait, particularly my interpretation of the block interview quote about students not being "done cooking" yet:

> The tone of that exchange, or maybe the position of it at the
> end, sort of makes it sound like I'm totally letting myself off the

hook for students' outcomes! That's the only thing that I didn't think represented my position accurately. Or maybe it makes me uncomfortable because I do think about that to comfort myself around failure!

. . . Sorry for all the thinking-through-writing. I would love to see the analytical introduction and discussion related to my narrative, as well as the whole dissertation! This is so, so helpful for me. I am so grateful!!

Even while pushing back against my reading of her quote, Liz was willing to entertain the possibility that her reflexive denial of my interpretation was, in fact, a validation of that very interpretation—that my distance as a researcher may have enabled me to recognize something that was hidden and mysterious to her in the same way that her assessment criteria had been. She was essentially member checking and, simultaneously, critiquing her own member checking, which could have left me with quite the methodological conundrum if her response had not converged with some of my own thinking.

Indeed, I had been dissatisfied with Liz's portrait ending for similar reasons and had continued working on it while awaiting her response. That process resulted in the paragraph quoted at the beginning of this section, which I used to soften the implications of the block quote we had both found problematic. Thus, not only did Liz's response validate my independent decision to add to the portrait ending, but the gratitude and desire to improve that she expressed throughout her response e-mail was consistent with the content I had already added. In this way, her gentle pushback on my interpretation of her quote provided me with multifaceted feedback to achieve a more resonant authenticity in her portrait.

I therefore replied to Liz with the new paragraph and offered to send her another revision in the event of any further tweaks, or just to supply her with additional reflection time. She thanked me and accepted the paragraph as adding helpful nuance to that moment in the portrait. She also assured me that she did not need to see another interim draft, just "the whole thing when you're done" to "check out what the other teachers are doing and read your thoughts."

While I have some lingering questions about Liz's response to her portrait, I admire and appreciate how fully she embraced the interventionist goal in a manner that affirms the inherent goodness in her teaching, even as that goodness is "laced with imperfections" (Lawrence-Lightfoot &

Davis, 1997, p. 9). I am gratified that my portrait of her practice allowed her to regard its complexity and see a path to change. I also see evidence in Liz's response of the importance of enacting Lawrence-Lightfoot's (2000) multifaceted notion of respect in research relationships. My ethical responsibility toward Liz in this case was not to protect her feelings but to treat her with respectful challenge and rigor; this was what ultimately created greater reciprocity and mutual benefit in our relationship.

Colin: Grade Deflation

Colin's portrait, like Liz's, showed parallels between himself and his students that I was fairly certain were hidden to him even as he knowingly solicited my assessment of his teaching multiple times. Whenever this happened, I tried to avoid directly answering Colin's questions; it was important to me not to cast an evaluative lens during data collection. His anxiety also surprised me because I found him to be an excellent teacher; my search for goodness in his classroom was not difficult at all. His inability to see or acknowledge that goodness, however, was so pervasive in our interactions that it ultimately manifested in his portrait.

I therefore had a methodological goal in seeking Colin's authentication of the portrait's depiction of his and the students' parallel search for the way to "win" at teaching and writing, respectively. However, I also harbored some ethical concerns about how Colin would react to my representation of him—even if he affirmed its resonance—given how his personality differed from Liz's. Specifically, I worried about giving Colin additional fodder for his trademark self-deprecation. However, he was such an obviously skilled teacher, in my mind, that I hoped the portrait would simultaneously force him to acknowledge his pedagogical strengths. Having deliberately withheld many of my thoughts about his teaching during data collection, I also hoped that the completed portrait would help Colin achieve the interventionist goal that he, like Liz, frequently stated as a reason for his study participation.

Colin's response to his portrait resembled Liz's in its length and the apparent "thinking through writing" that he was engaging in, but his tone was starkly different.

> I like your writing style, and I support your conclusions whole-heartedly. It's quite uncanny to read so much about myself, and I feel vulnerable after having read it all. I appear as a motley character—part sad clown, part symptom of institutional policies,

> and part looming executioner. It confirms my worst suspicions, though it makes for an interesting story.
>
> I was struck by your descriptions of the peculiar institutional game of grades, and all the [students'] pre-class conversations on that topic. And I think you're right about how I have failed to make clear expectations and clear benchmarks for success along the way. Honestly, I don't know how to do that with writing . . . I hate the obsession with grades and I wish there was a way to get done with it.
>
> . . . I'm feeling more and more the ineffectiveness of the class, or the ineffectiveness of me. It's frustrating. I don't know where to go next, but it's clear that I need to figure out some stuff. Back to the drawing board, I guess.

He concluded by correcting "one tiny detail" in the portrait about ungraded assignments before expressing his interest in reading the final study to "learn more about what your other respondents do in the classroom and with their assignments."

I mulled over this e-mail for some time, concerned about the negative language that permeated Colin's response and yet diverged so starkly from how I saw his teaching and what I thought I had expressed in his portrait. At the same time, though, this negativity was consistent with his manner of engaging with me throughout the study. I wrestled, therefore, with the question of to what extent Colin's perception of failure in his portrait reflected my possible methodological and ethical failures as the portraitist versus a manifestation of precisely the performance insecurities I was trying to portray, akin to Liz's questioning of her own pushback on my quote interpretation. I was uncomfortable with leaving this ambiguity unresolved and felt obligated to write Colin a more extensive reply than what I had sent Liz or Zachary. In it, I also tried to speak more directly at last to his persistent questions about the quality of his teaching.

> I'm grateful that you shared your thoughts so honestly, and I'd like to address some of them here . . . I was a little concerned to read your response because it seems your takeaways from it about your own teaching are quite negative, which leaves me wondering if there are ways for me to frame parts of your narrative to convey more clearly that my takeaways absolutely are

not negative. Quite the contrary—I consistently found you a thoughtful and skillful teacher, and I think your students learned a great deal in your class . . . you enacted so many practices that are consistent with the theoretical literature, and you did so mostly intuitively, and yet with great skill.

However, alongside those effective instructional enactments, my goal is to highlight the pedagogical tensions and challenges that can be found in any classroom—even those of exemplary teachers—when trying to wrangle something as intangible as student mindsets. In pointing out these challenges, I'm not so much critiquing your "failures" as trying to invite the reader to reflect on what we can learn from your case about the relationships between teachers and their students, and between teachers and their institutions, and what this all means for how we should be better supporting teachers in achieving their pedagogical goals and supporting student mindset development.

That said . . . I feel a responsibility to try to compose a text that strikes a better balance for you as the subject. I do think the sections of my dissertation that you haven't read provide a bit more of the context and framing I describe above, but I also don't want your narrative itself to leave you feeling so bummed out! . . . I would welcome your input—written or verbal, if you want to talk or meet up—about whether and how this narrative could be improved in that respect.

Colin wrote back within a few hours.

Thanks for your response. I didn't mean in any way to criticize your findings—I think your portrait is extremely generous, detailed, and well-reasoned.

My response is more about my own sense that I'm "not there yet," and my own frustrations about teaching day to day. Your portrait makes it clearer to me why students feel confused about assignments and frameworks in my class—and they do—and it comes in a season full of small arguments about grades. It's been a rough week, and I'm mostly inclined to focus on negative aspects of my classes because that's what keeps me up at night.

I need your text to be just the way it is—it's honest and right, and that's going to help my teaching more than anything else (don't inflate my grade, please!). I wouldn't have you change anything.

I remain conflicted over Colin's response. Although he appears to endorse the authenticity of the portrait, I worry that he might simply be deferring to what he perceives to be my pedagogical expertise, presenting both an ethical tension over the sustained power differential between us and a related methodological tension over how his deference might bias his authentication of my report. Despite calling the portrait "generous," he also speaks only to the authenticity of the negative impressions he has drawn from it, which provides me with little methodological feedback on whether I achieved the balance I sought. Sharing the portrait does seem to have fulfilled an interventionist rationale in persuading Colin that some change is needed, but he "do[esn't] know where to go next" other than nihilistically "back to the drawing board," as if all of his pedagogy has been invalidated. I recognize the ethical soundness in having Colin arrive at his own enactment of change, rather than unduly leveraging my power as researcher to prescribe an intervention, but his enduring dissatisfaction with himself also leaves me with ethical concerns about my role in surfacing and/or reinforcing his discontent. Given all this, I chose not to respond to Colin's final e-mail, not wanting to compel him into further reassurances about my portrait. In this case, I felt my most respectful course of action was, as Lawrence-Lightfoot (1983) writes, simply to "accept" his response and allow him to have the final word in our interaction, rather than continuing to probe in order to resolve my own nagging insecurities.

CASE SYNTHESIS: ENDURING QUESTIONS

I focus here on two key tensions that emerged from the intersection of the methodological, ethical, and interventionist rationales across the three cases. One is the variability in how the "click" of self-recognition manifests depending on the circumstances, participant individuality, and research relationships in each case. Given this variability, how should the portraitist assess the portrait's authenticity? The second tension concerns the ways in which the interventionist rationale and related expectations of participants as well as portraitists can complicate the ethical challenges already present in portraiture. In a methodology that aspires to instigate change, what is our ethical responsibility as portraitists in relation to that change? As I briefly discuss each in turn, I do not set out to answer these questions—in fact, engaging with them seems only to beget more questions—but, rather, to convey the importance of wrestling with them openly as portraitists.

Variable "Clicks"

While all three of my participants either affirmed the authenticity of their portraits or at least raised no major objections about them, Zachary's and Colin's responses lay at opposite ends of a spectrum of self-recognition. Zachary found his portrait revelatory in a complimentary way—the pleasant surprise you feel when you unexpectedly look really good in a candid photograph—whereas Colin accepted his portrait as a third-party confirmation of all his own perceived weaknesses. As I told Colin, his reaction made me worry that my portrait was methodologically flawed in not adequately portraying the goodness of his teaching. Zachary's reaction, though more positive and gratifying, was potentially equally limited in its methodological utility if it made him disinclined to identify overly generous interpretations I might have made about the "methods in his madness." I am also aware of how their differing professional backgrounds and prior experience and comfort level with observation may have influenced their responses. How much were their portrait responses a reflection of my methodology versus their different personalities and/or prior experience with viewing their teaching practice through an interpretive lens?

Meanwhile, Liz was the only participant to question any part of her portrait as not "represent[ing] my position accurately," but she was willing to consider that her resistance was a manifestation of the very pattern of behavior I was identifying in that moment. I also shared her opinion of the excerpt in question. That these two convergences occurred and we were able to agree on a revised portrait ending may be evidence of a sound methodological process and research relationship, but it also may have been fortuitous. What if we had not agreed about the tone of the ending, or what if Liz had not been willing to question her own challenging of my interpretation? Would I have modified the portrait anyway, in deference to Liz's self-expertise, or would I have asked her to defer to my authority as portraitist to see patterns that she could not recognize in her own life, categorizing her response as part of the self-reflexive denial that precedes change?

The Ethics of Intervention

Both Colin and Liz articulated their own interventionist rationales for participating in the study and recognized the necessity of change after reading their portraits. Sharing their portraits would therefore seem to have fulfilled not only an interventionist goal but also an ethical goal by giving them what they said they wanted from their study involvement. However, I feel quite differently about the reciprocity achieved in each case. Liz seemed to identify both that a change was warranted and also some specific changes she could make; she also seemed motivated and inspired to implement her new ideas. By contrast, Colin registered a general sense of "ineffectiveness" that prompted him to go "back to the drawing board."

While I think individual personality is certainly a factor here, I wonder about my own role in prompting these divergent responses, whether through representational choices in the portraits themselves or my interactions with each participant during the study. As a former teacher educator, I often struggled to restrain my coaching instincts in favor of the disciplined, probingly descriptive pen of a portraitist; this was especially true when Colin repeatedly appealed to my professional experience even as he understood that I was occupying the role of researcher in his classroom. There are ethical concerns around a researcher wielding her authority to impose prescriptive change on study participants, yet I cannot help wondering if providing Colin with more concrete feedback and suggestions—woven into the portrait itself, possibly, or in my response to his response—might have been more ethical than leaving him with a perceived need to change but no sense of how to do so.

Likewise, I continue to question whether I missed opportunities to prompt change in Zachary's practice, perhaps because my past experience as a high school English teacher—but a very different one stylistically from Zachary's—made me acutely aware and overly cautious of the ethical challenges in my role as researcher. However, Zachary's response also illuminates the important question of whether and how portraitists should interpret participants' responses through an interventionist rationale given that the change might be subtle or unarticulated even to the participant himself at the moment of his response; further time for reflection may be necessary to arrive at self-critical change (Lawrence-Lightfoot, 1983). How much, then, should portraitists expect to be privy to the interventionist outcomes of their portraits? Accordingly, how much should an interventionist rationale factor into a portraitist's decisions about sharing the portrait and reengaging with participants in the study aftermath?

These questions persist in part because, in addition to the multiple, intersecting, and potentially conflicting rationales for doing so, soliciting participants' responses to their portraits is inherently an interpretive act, a continuation of the "research enterprise." Whatever rationale(s) the portraitist is seeking to address, she is dependent on what a participant chooses to articulate in the response, and how. Rather than being taken at "face value" (Lawrence-Lightfoot, 1983, p. 377), these words are part of and should be contextualized within the research record, despite technically occurring after data collection has concluded. While treating participant response as still more data may seem unduly complicated, doing so affords the researcher potential tools for more intentionally soliciting, interpreting, and disseminating those responses.

NEW COMMITMENTS, FINAL REFLECTIONS

Lawrence-Lightfoot and Davis (1997) selected Picasso's *Girl before a Mirror* as the cover image for *The Art and Science of Portraiture* because it depicts an actor confronting not a mirror-image reflection but rather "a more penetrating image—one that is both revelatory and disturbing . . . a deeper, more authentic reflection of who she is" (p. xvii). However, the entire scene is filtered through Picasso's interpretive lens; there is no indication that the girl had any influence on this representation of her reaction, and she has no avenue for sharing her impressions directly with the viewer. The notion of a portrait subject making demands of Picasso—or potentially taking her own brush to his canvas—may seem unthinkable, even laughable. But a methodology that seeks to blend art and aesthetics with empirical, scientific rigor while becoming "more participatory, collaborative, symmetric, dialectic" (Lawrence-Lightfoot, 2005, p. 8) *should* engage with questions about the role of participant response in the study aftermath. For my part in this engagement, I make three interrelated commitments for my future portraiture work.

First, I commit to continuing to highlight verbatim participant responses to their portraits as a "transgressive" data source in my future work, as I have done in this book (St. Pierre, 1997). These data are transgressive in that they sit outside the typical boundaries that we envision on what is subject to analysis and documentation in the final research report. Yet, we may cite the existence of these response data in our methods sections to persuade our readers of our trustworthiness and the integrity of our research enterprise (Harvey, 2015), even as we withhold the specific content of the responses. We would enact our trustworthiness more fully by allowing third-party scrutiny of these data as well as what we traditionally consider our "study data." In each of the three cases discussed, I feel the participant responses help illuminate challenges and tensions that readers should be aware of and consider in their independent appraisals of my work. But each response also, in my judgment, enriches the original portrait by giving the participants a coda of sorts, allowing us to hear their reflections that, in many cases, affirm and add texture to the representations and interpretations in the portraits. For both reasons, these responses deserve our regard and consideration.

My second commitment builds on the first by leveraging existing tools within portraiture's methodology to accomplish the goal of integrating participant response as transgressive data. Specifically, I commit to extending the concept of "voice in dialogue" to the portrait response process. As one of the five dimensions of a portraitist's voice, voice in dialogue is meant to "chronicle . . . the emerging trust" and "symmetry of voice" between researcher and researched as the portraitist makes herself "more evident and more visible" as a coparticipant in dialogue, rather than an omniscient narrator, giving readers potential insight into the portraitist's "methodology, her questions, her interpretations, her interventions" (Lawrence-Lightfoot & Davis, 1997, p. 103). I contend that the concept of voice in dialogue can and should be extended to include the transgressive postproduction dialogue between portraitist and participant over the portrait itself, allowing reader scrutiny of our methodological and ethical negotiations in the study aftermath.

Finally, I commit to exploring ways to incorporate this transgressive postproduction dialogue alongside the portraits themselves in my future work. Seminal sources in qualitative social science research advocated for the inclusion of participant response in research publications (Colaizzi, 1978), and yet it is researcher voices still that are privileged in raising these issues, reinforcing the ongoing ethical challenges in seeking greater symmetry and reciprocity in research relationships and participant representation. How often are study participants allowed to be seen speaking directly to researchers, reacting to their findings and interpretations, in research publications where scholars routinely question and evaluate the work of those they view as "peers"? It seems that we as individual researchers, as well as the academy as a whole, have not yet found the appropriate mechanism, or plucked up the courage, to confront voices other than those traditionally accepted and valued in the academic gatekeeping process (Van Galen & Eaker, 1995). In keeping with the advocacy around transparency in qualitative methodologies more broadly (Fine & Weis, 2010; Luttrell, 2000), individual portraitists as well as editors, mentors, and disciplinary thought leaders can strive to be more intentional about finding publication space for researchers to articulate the choices they have made and the trade-offs they have accepted in the process of soliciting participant response and then acting—or not—on the feedback received. Doing so would gradually shift existing norms about what can be included in scholarly publication and strengthen our work overall by substantiating reflexivity as not just a hollow catchphrase but a productively discomfiting process that contributes to rigorous and quality work (Pillow, 2003).

Indeed, I confess that, just like participants awaiting their portraits, I experienced my own "terror of exposure" (Lawrence-Lightfoot, 1983, p. 378) prior to the unveiling of my work, the product of over a year of intensive labor. Yet, I could not help feeling that it was ethically fitting that I share my participants' feelings in this way. I often wonder how the "research enterprise" might change if researchers conducted and wrote up their studies with the expectation that they would have to present and defend it not only to an audience of peer scholars but directly to the participants themselves. In addition to holding up our portraits as interpretive mirrors to prompt others to confront their reflections, we might do well to allow others to spin the reflective lens and force us to regard ourselves.

Notes

Introduction

1. Massachusetts Comprehensive Assessment System, the accountability exam in Massachusetts public schools, taken for the first time in tenth grade, with retesting options offered in subsequent years for students who do not pass the first time.

2. Because high school students in Boston can choose any open-enrollment public school in the city, representatives from the high schools typically visit middle schools each year to introduce their school as an option to eighth-grade students and their parents.

3. Throughout this book, I use "college" and "postsecondary" interchangeably to describe undergraduate education. Reflecting differences in professional pathways and identities across sectors, I use "teacher(s)" for high school and "instructor(s)" for college, while "educator(s)" refers to both/either population.

4. I use pseudonyms for focal participants, their students, and any institution whose practices are subject to analysis/critique. In this chapter, I use quotation marks when introducing pseudonyms for the first time, but remove the quotation marks in all subsequent mentions.

5. School-related statistics are approximated throughout this book to mask the identity of the institutions.

6. The State Department of Education defines "economically disadvantaged" as participating in one or more state food assistance programs, foster care, or Medicaid.

Chapter 1

1. EL Education. (2018). Redefining and raising student achievement. Retrieved from https://eleducation.org/who-we-are/our-approach

2. Ultimately, 94 percent of Riverside's Class of 2017 cohort graduates on time, compared to 77 percent of the district.

3. Janie is either referring to the scoring scale of 1 through 5 for the criterion-referenced AP exam, where a 3 designates a student as "qualified" for college-level work (according to the College Board, the creators of the exam), or the scale of 1 through 4 used for Riverside's standards-based assessment, where a 3 is equivalent to meeting the learning target. In either case, a 1 is the lowest possible score.

4. Two hours of the AP English Literature exam are devoted to three essays worth 55% of the total score. The first two essay questions ask students to perform a textual analysis on a poem (Q1) and a prose or drama passage (Q2) supplied by the exam. The third question (Q3) is a thematic analysis prompt that students apply to a book of their choice that they have read previously.

5. The habits of work are: 1) I come to class ready to learn; 2) I actively and collaboratively participate in class; 3) I assess and revise my own work; 4) I complete daily homework.

6. The State Department of Education provides racial demographic data only for full-time equivalency (FTE) staff at a school, which includes staff members who are not classroom teachers. The proportion of White teachers is likely higher than 70 percent.

7. District-wide, 71 percent of FTE staff are White; state-wide for public school teachers, the figure is 90 percent. Nationally, about 80 percent of all teachers (public and private school) are White (National Center for Education Statistics, 2018).

8. AP English Literature has much more curricular flexibility than most other AP courses; many educators I talk to are surprised to learn, for example, that there is no set reading list.

9. Anderson, N. (2018, June 18). Several well-known private schools in the DC area are scrapping Advanced Placement classes. *The Washington Post*. Retrieved from https://www.washingtonpost.com/news/grade-point/wp/2018/06/18/several-well-known-private-schools-in-the-d-c-area-are-scrapping-advanced-placement-classes/

Chapter 2

1. AP is a curricular "track" at OBS in terms of the designated level of the course but not any top-down student sorting or assignment process; any eleventh- or twelfth-grade student who wants to take AP can do so.

Chapter 3

1. In the past, Liz has also taught "low-income students, often from immigrant families, from the surrounding area," who are eligible for a local scholarship at Mayfield. Her class this year does not include any such students.

2. The conceit of Liz's final reflection assignment is to compose a letter to your beginning-of-semester self, so some students write it in second person. I

have converted most other reflection excerpts in this portrait to first person for clarity (but do not otherwise edit them); the tone of this one, however, is lost if converted.

3. Liz assumed the placement essays were largely judged on grammar and relevance to the supplied prompt. In reality, the rubric comprises four categories—Argument, Organization, Evidence, and Style and Usage—each evaluated on a scale from 1 through 6. Two Mayfield faculty from different disciplines read and score each student essay. Additionally, students complete a short questionnaire about themselves, including their perceived strengths and weaknesses as a writer, typical weekly reading load, favorite and least favorite assignments from high school, and the number of drafts they typically write before submitting a final. The writing director emphasized to me the department's effort to be holistic in evaluating students' writing placement.

4. The "polishing categories" are: *1) An opening that engages the readers; 2) an overall sense of purpose; 3) sufficient context/background/support of ideas; 4) a blend of discussion of the text and writer's own thinking/experiences; 5) liveliness!; 6) quotes/ signal phrases.*

Chapter 4

1. Bök, C. (2001). *Eunoia* (1ˢᵗ ed.). Coach House Books.

2. Students must score at least a 4 on the AP English Literature exam, a 6 on the IB Higher-Level English exam, or a B on a British A-Level Language exam to place out of English 101.

3. Williams, J. M. (1995). *Style: Toward clarity and grace*. Chicago: University of Chicago Press.

4. After Colin dismisses the students, he follows up with Tony about juul: "I assumed it was something smokeable?" Tony explains that "it's like a vape," to which Colin replies, "Well, that's much cleaner than I thought."

5. Mattel & Fisher-Price. (n.d.). *Apples to Apples instruction sheet*. Retrieved from https://service.mattel.com/instruction_sheets/N1488-0920.pdf.

6. The only Abbott students who are automatically exempt from English 102 are those with top scores on the eligible qualifying exams (a 5 on the AP, a 7 on the IB, or an A on the A-Level) and engineering students.

7. All of Colin's reading quizzes are announced on the syllabus.

8. During first-year orientation, my cohort was instructed to repeat the Swarthmore mantra that we were to invoke when we inevitably performed below expectations (our professors', or our own): "No matter what you say or do to me, I am still a worthwhile person." The campus bookstore also sold a t-shirt bearing another popular slogan: *Anywhere else, it would've been an A.*

9. Anderson, S. (2012, April 4). Just one more game: Angry Birds, Farmville and other hyperaddictive "stupid games." *New York Times Magazine*.

Chapter 5

1. However, both colleges accepted a score of 4 or above on the AP English Literature exam as some form of course exemption, so Diane was not totally off base.

Appendixes

1. The only unscheduled disruptions to my college observations were class cancellations due to instructor illness: Liz cancelled one class and Colin, two.

2. This appendix is an abridged version of the article: Liu, P. (2020). Afterwords: Negotiating participant and portraitist response in the study "aftermath." *Harvard Educational Review*, *90*(1), 102–126. Reprinted with permission.

References

Acker, S. R., & Halasek, K. (2008). Preparing high school students for college-level writing: Using ePortfolio to support a successful transition. *The Journal of General Education, 57*(1), 1–14. https://doi.org/10.1353/jge.0.0012.

ACT. (2014). *The Condition of College & Career Readiness 2014.* ACT, Inc.

ACT. (2016). *ACT National Curriculum Survey 2016: Education and Work in a Time of Change.*

Addison, J., & McGee, S. J. (2010). Writing in high school/writing in college: Research trends and future directions. *College Composition and Communication, 62*(1), 147–179.

Adler-Kassner, L., & Wardle, E. (Eds.). (2016). *Naming what we know: Threshold concepts of writing studies.* Utah State University Press.

Ahn, H. S., Bong, M., & Kim, S. (2017). Social models in the cognitive appraisal of self-efficacy information. *Contemporary Educational Psychology, 48*, 149–166. https://doi.org/10.1016/j.cedpsych.2016.08.002.

Alder, N. (2002). Interpretations of the meaning of care: Creating caring relationships in urban middle school classrooms. *Urban Education, 37*(2), 241–266. https://doi.org/10.1177/0042085902372005.

Alford, B., Rudolph, A., Olson Beal, H., & Hill, B. (2014). A school-university math and science P-16 partnership: Lessons learned in promoting college and career readiness. *Planning & Changing, 45*(1/2), 99–119.

Allen, D. W., & Eve, A. W. (1968). Microteaching. *Theory into Practice, 7*(5), 181–185.

Alliance for Excellent Education. (2007). *High School Teaching for the Twenty-First Century: Preparing Students for College. Issue Brief.* Alliance for Excellent Education.

Ames, C. (1992). Classrooms: Goals, structures, and student motivation. *Journal of Educational Psychology, 84*(3), 261–271. https://doi.org/10.1037/0022-0663.84.3.261.

Anderman, E. M., Austin, C. C., & Johnson, D. M. (2002). The development of goal orientation. In A. Wigfield & J. S. Eccles (Eds.), *Development of achievement motivation* (pp. 197–220). Academic.

238 | References

Anderman, L. H., Andrzejewski, C. E., & Allen, J. (2011). How do teachers support students' motivation and learning in their classrooms? *Teachers College Record, 113*(5), 969–1003.

Anfara, V. A., Brown, K. M., & Mangione, T. L. (2002). Qualitative analysis on stage: Making the research process more public. *Educational Researcher, 31*(7), 28–38. https://doi.org/10.3102/0013189X031007028.

Applebee, A. N., & Langer, J. A. (2011). A snapshot of writing instruction in middle schools and high schools. *The English Journal, 100*(6), 14–27.

Arunkumar, R., Midgley, C., & Urdan, T. (1999). Perceiving high or low home-school dissonance: Longitudinal effects on adolescent emotional and academic well-being. *Journal of Research on Adolescence, 9*(4), 441–466. https://doi.org/10.1207/s15327795jra0904_4.

Assor, A., Kaplan, H., & Roth, G. (2002). Choice is good, but relevance is excellent: Autonomy-enhancing and suppressing teacher behaviours predicting students' engagement in schoolwork. *British Journal of Educational Psychology, 72*(2), 261–278. https://doi.org/10.1348/000709902158883.

Baier, S. T., Markman, B. S., & Pernice-Duca, F. M. 3. (2016). Intent to persist in college freshmen: The role of self-efficacy and mentorship. *Journal of College Student Development, 57*(5), 614–619. https://doi.org/10.1353/csd.2016.0056.

Ballenger, B., & Myers, K. (2019). The emotional work of revision. *College Composition and Communication, 70*(4), 590–614.

Bandura, A. (1986). *Social foundations of thought and action: A social cognitive theory*. Prentice-Hall.

Bandura, A. (1991). Social cognitive theory of self-regulation. *Organizational Behavior and Human Decision Processes, 50*(2), 248–287. https://doi.org/10.1016/0749-5978(91)90022-L.

Bandura, A. (1997). *Self-efficacy: The exercise of control*. W. H. Freeman.

Bardach, L., Yanagida, T., Schober, B., & Lüftenegger, M. (2019). Students' and teachers' perceptions of goal structures—Will they ever converge? Exploring changes in student-teacher agreement and reciprocal relations to self-concept and achievement. *Contemporary Educational Psychology, 59*, 101799. https://doi.org/10.1016/j.cedpsych.2019.101799.

Battle, A. A., & Looney, L. (2014). Teachers' intentions to stay in teaching: The role of values and knowledge of adolescent development. *Education, 134*(3), 369–379.

Baum, S., & McPherson, M. (2019). Improving teaching: Strengthening the college learning experience. *Daedalus, 148*(4), 5–13. https://doi.org/10.1162/daed_e_01757.

Baumeister, R. F., & Leary, M. R. (1995). The need to belong: Desire for interpersonal attachments as a fundamental human motivation. *Psychological Bulletin, 117*(3), 497–529. https://doi.org/10.1037/0033-2909.117.3.497.

Bazerman, C., & Tinberg, H. (2016). Writing is an expression of embodied cognition. In L. Adler-Kassner & E. Wardle (Eds.), *Naming what we know: Threshold concepts of writing studies* (pp. 74–75). Utah State University Press.

Beachboard, M., Beachboard, J., Li, W., & Adkison, S. (2011). Cohorts and relatedness: Self-determination theory as an explanation of how learning communities affect educational outcomes. *Research in Higher Education, 52*(8), 853–874.

Beaufort, A. (2016). Reflection: The metacognitive move towards transfer of learning. In K. B. Yancey (Ed.), *A rhetoric of reflection* (pp. 23–41). University Press of Colorado.

Beymer, P. N., Rosenberg, J. M., & Schmidt, J. A. (2020). Does choice matter or is it all about interest? An investigation using an experience sampling approach in high school science classrooms. *Learning and Individual Differences, 78*, 101812. https://doi.org/10.1016/j.lindif.2019.101812.

Blackwell, L. S., Trzesniewski, K. H., & Dweck, C. S. (2007). Implicit theories of intelligence predict achievement across an adolescent transition: A longitudinal study and an intervention. *Child Development, 78*(1), 246–263. https://doi.org/10.1111/j.1467-8624.2007.00995.x.

Bloom, C. M., & Erlandson, D. A. (2003). Three voices in portraiture: Actor, artist, and audience. *Qualitative Inquiry, 9*(6), 874–894. https://doi.org/10.1177/1077800403254730.

Bong, M. (2001). Role of self-efficacy and task-value in predicting college students' course performance and future enrollment intentions. *Contemporary Educational Psychology, 26*(4), 553–570. https://doi.org/10.1006/ceps.2000.1048.

Bonner, E. P. (2014). Investigating practices of highly successful mathematics teachers of traditionally underserved students. *Educational Studies in Mathematics, 86*(3), 377–399. https://doi.org/10.1007/s10649-014-9533-7.

Boscolo, P., & Gelati, C. (2018). Motivating writers. In S. Graham, C. A. MacArthur, & M. Hebert (Eds.), *Best Practices in Writing Instruction* (3rd ed; pp. 51–80). Guilford Publications.

Boscolo, P., & Hidi, S. E. (2006). The multiple meanings of motivation to write. In S. E. Hidi & P. Boscolo (Eds.), *Writing and motivation* (pp. 1–14). Elsevier.

Bottiani, J. H., Bradshaw, C. P., & Mendelson, T. (2016). Inequality in Black and White high school students' perceptions of school support: An examination of race in context. *Journal of Youth and Adolescence, 45*(6), 1176–1191. https://doi.org/10.1007/s10964-015-0411-0.

Bradbury-Jones, C., Irvine, F., & Sambrook, S. (2010). Phenomenology and participant feedback: Convention or contention? *Nurse Researcher, 17*(2), 25–33. https://doi.org/10.7748/nr2010.01.17.2.25.c7459.

Brewster, A. B., & Bowen, G. L. (2004). Teacher support and the school engagement of Latino middle and high school students at risk of school failure. *Child and Adolescent Social Work Journal*, *21*(1), 47–67. https://doi. org/10.1023/B:CASW.0000012348.83939.6b.

Bronfenbrenner, U. (1977). Toward an experimental ecology of human development. *American Psychologist*, July, 513–531.

Brooke, C., & Carr, A. (2016). Failure can be an important part of writing development. In L. Adler-Kassner & E. Wardle (Eds.), *Naming what we know: Threshold concepts of writing studies* (pp. 62–64). Utah State University Press.

Brophy, J. (2008). Developing students' appreciation for what is taught in school. *Educational Psychologist*, *43*(3), 132–141. https://doi. org/10.1080/00461520701756511.

Brown, M. R., Higgins, K., Pierce, T., Hong, E., & Thoma, C. (2003). Secondary students' perceptions of school life with regard to alienation: The effects of disability, gender and race. *Learning Disability Quarterly*, *26*(4), 227–238.

Bryk, A. S., & Schneider, B. (2002). *Trust in schools*. Russell Sage Foundation.

Buehl, M. M., Alexander, P. A., & Murphy, P. K. (2002). Beliefs about schooled knowledge: Domain specific or domain general? *Contemporary Educational Psychology*, *27*(3), 415–449. https://doi.org/10.1006/ceps.2001.1103.

Butz, A. R., & Usher, E. L. (2015). Salient sources of early adolescents' self-efficacy in two domains. *Contemporary Educational Psychology*, *42*, 49–61. https://doi. org/10.1016/j.cedpsych.2015.04.001.

Callahan, M. K., & Chumney, D. (2009). "Write like college": How remedial writing courses at a community college and a research university position "at-risk" students in the field of higher education. *Teachers College Record*, *111*(7), 1619–1664.

Carr, P. B., & Walton, G. M. (2014). Cues of working together fuel intrinsic motivation. *Journal of Experimental Social Psychology*, *53*, 169–184. https:// doi.org/10.1016/j.jesp.2014.03.015.

Charmaz, K. (2006). Coding in grounded theory practice. In *Constructing grounded theory: A practical guide through qualitative analysis* (pp. 42–71). Sage.

Chatzisarantis, N. L. D., Nilay Ada, E., Bing, Q., Papaioannou, A., Prpa, N., & Hagger, M. S. (2016). Clarifying the link between mastery goals and social comparisons in classroom settings. *Contemporary Educational Psychology*, *46*, 61–72. https://doi.org/10.1016/j.cedpsych.2016.04.009.

Chemers, M. M., Hu, L., & Garcia, B. F. (2001). Academic self-efficacy and first-year college student performance and adjustment. *Journal of Educational Psychology*, *93*(1), 55–64.

Chmielewski, A. K., Dumont, H., & Trautwein, U. (2013). Tracking effects depend on tracking type: An international comparison of students' mathematics self-concept. *American Educational Research Journal*, *50*(5), 925–957. https:// doi.org/10.3102/0002831213489843.

Ciani, K. D., Middleton, M. J., Summers, J. J., & Sheldon, K. M. (2010). Buffering against performance classroom goal structures: The importance of autonomy support and classroom community. *Contemporary Educational Psychology*, *35*(1), 88–99. https://doi.org/10.1016/j.cedpsych.2009.11.001.

Cimpian, A., Arce, H.-M. C., Markman, E. M., & Dweck, C. S. (2007). Subtle linguistic cues affect children's motivation. *Psychological Science*, *18*(4), 314–316. https://doi.org/10.1111/j.1467-9280.2007.01896.x.

Colaizzi, P. F. (1978). Psychological research as the phenomenologist views it. In R. S. Valle & M. King (Eds.), *Existential-phenomenological alternatives for psychology* (pp. 48–71). Oxford University Press.

Conley, C. S. (2015). SEL in higher education. In J. A. Durlak, C. E. Domitrovich, R. P. Weissberg, & T. P. Gullotta (Eds.), *Handbook of social and emotional learning: Research and practice* (pp. 197–212). Guilford Press.

Cook, J., & Caouette, B. (2013). All hands on deck: Bringing together high school teachers and adjunct instructors for professional development in the teaching of writing. *Teaching/Writing: The Journal of Writing Teacher Education*, *2*(1).

Cornelius-White, J. (2007). Learner-centered teacher-student relationships are effective: A meta-analysis. *Review of Educational Research*, *77*(1), 113–143. https://doi.org/10.3102/003465430298563.

Coutinho, S. A., & Neuman, G. (2008). A model of metacognition, achievement goal orientation, learning style and self-efficacy. *Learning Environments Research*, *11*(2), 131–151.

Cowan, M. (2020). A legacy of grading contracts for composition. *Journal of Writing Assessment*, *13*(2).

Cox, R. (2009). *The college fear factor: How students and professors misunderstand one another*. Harvard University Press.

Crank, V. (2012). From high school to college: Developing writing skills in the discipline. *The WAC Journal*, *23*, 49–64.

Crapanzano, V. (1996). "Self"-centering narratives. In M. S. Silverstein & G. Urban (Eds.), *Natural histories of discourse* (pp. 106–127). University of Chicago Press.

Darling-Hammond, L., & Hammerness, K. (2002). Toward a pedagogy of cases in teacher education. *Teaching Education*, *13*(2), 125–135. https://doi.org/10.1080/1047621022000007549.

De Hei, M. S. A., Strijbos, J.-W., Sjoer, E., & Admiraal, W. (2015). Collaborative learning in higher education: Lecturers' practices and beliefs. *Research Papers in Education*, *30*(2), 232–247. https://doi.org/10.1080/02671522.2014.908407.

Deci, E. L., Koestner, R., & Ryan, R. M. (1999). A meta-analytic review of experiments examining the effects of extrinsic rewards on intrinsic motivation. *Psychological Bulletin*, *125*(6), 627–668. https://doi.org/10.1037/0033-2909.125.6.627.

Deci, E. L., & Ryan, R. M. (2002). *Handbook of self-determination research*. University of Rochester Press.

Decker, D. M., Dona, D. P., & Christenson, S. L. (2007). Behaviorally at-risk African American students: The importance of student–teacher relationships for student outcomes. *Journal of School Psychology*, *45*(1), 83–109. https://doi.org/10.1016/j.jsp.2006.09.004.

Deemer, S. (2004). Classroom goal orientation in high school classrooms: Revealing links between teacher beliefs and classroom environments. *Educational Research*, *46*(1), 73–90. https://doi.org/10.1080/0013188042000178836.

DeFreitas, S. C. (2012). Differences between African American and European American first-year college students in the relationship between self-efficacy, outcome expectations, and academic achievement. *Social Psychology of Education: An International Journal*, *15*(1), 109–123.

Destin, M. (2018). Leveraging psychological factors. In F. M. Hess & L. E. Hatalsky (Eds.), *Elevating college completion*. American Enterprise Institute.

Dja'far, V. H., Cahyono, B. Y., & Bashtomi, Y. (2016). EFL teachers' perception of university students' motivation and ESP learning achievement. *Journal of Education and Practice*, *7*(14), 28–37.

D'Lima, G. M., Winsler, A., & Kitsantas, A. (2014). Ethnic and gender differences in first-year college students' goal orientation, self-efficacy, and extrinsic and intrinsic motivation. *Journal of Educational Research*, *107*(5), 341–356.

Downs, D. (2016). Revision is central to developing writing. In L. Adler-Kassner & E. Wardle (Eds.), *Naming what we know: Threshold concepts of writing studies* (pp. 66–67). Utah State University Press.

Downs, D., & Robertson, L. (2015). Threshold concepts in first-year composition. In L. Adler-Kassner & E. Wardle (Eds.), *Naming what we know: Threshold concepts of writing studies* (pp. 105–121). Utah State University Press.

Durden, T., Mcmunn Dooley, C., & Truscott, D. (2016). Race still matters: Preparing culturally relevant teachers. *Race Ethnicity and Education*, *19*(5), 1003–1023. https://doi.org/10.1080/13613324.2014.969226.

Dweck, C. S. (1999). *Self-theories: Their role in motivation, personality and development*. Taylor and Francis/Psychology Press.

Dweck, C. S., & Leggett, E. L. (1988). A social-cognitive approach to motivation and personality. *Psychological Review*, *95*(2), 256–273. http://doi.org/10.1037/0033-295X.95.2.256.

Dweck, C. S., & Molden, D. C. (2017). Mindsets: Their impact on competence motivation and acquisition. In A. J. Elliot, C. S. Dweck, & D. S. Yeager (Eds.), *Handbook of competence and motivation* (2nd edition, pp. 135–154). Guilford Press.

Dweck, C. S., Walton, G. M., & Cohen, G. L. (2014). *Academic tenacity: Mindsets and skills that promote long-term learning* [White paper]. Gates Foundation.

Eccles, J. S., & Wigfield, A. (2002). Motivational beliefs, values, and goals. *Annual Review of Psychology*, *53*(1), 109–132. https://doi.org/10.1146/annurev.psych.53.100901.135153.

Eccles, J. S., & Wigfield, A. (2020). From expectancy-value theory to situated expectancy-value theory: A developmental, social cognitive, and sociocultural perspective on motivation. *Contemporary Educational Psychology*, 101859. https://doi.org/10.1016/j.cedpsych.2020.101859.

Elbow, P. (1997). Taking time out from grading and evaluating while working in a conventional system. *Assessing Writing*, 4(1), 5–27. https://doi.org/10.1016/S1075-2935(97)80003-7.

Emerson, R. M., Fretz, R., & Shaw, S. S. (2011). Fieldnotes in ethnographic research. In *Writing ethnographic fieldnotes* (pp. 3–20). University of Chicago Press.

English, F. W. (2000). A critical appraisal of Sara Lawrence-Lightfoot's portraiture as a method of educational research. *Educational Researcher*, 29(7), 21–26. https://doi.org/10.3102/0013189X029007021.

Ericcson, K. A., Krampe, R. T., & Tesch-Römer, C. (1993). The role of deliberate practice in the acquisition of expert performance. *Psychological Review*, 100(3), 363–406.

Fanetti, S., Bushrow, K. M., & DeWeese, D. L. (2010). Closing the gap between high school writing instruction and college writing expectations. *The English Journal*, 99(4), 77–83.

Farber, J. (1990). Learning how to teach: A progress report. *College English*, 52(2), 135–141. https://doi.org/10.2307/377440.

Farrington, C. A., Roderick, M., Allensworth, E., Nagaoka, J., Keyes, T. S., Johnson, D. W., & Beechum, N. O. (2012). *Teaching Adolescents to Become Learners: The Role of Noncognitive Factors in Shaping School Performance—A Critical Literature Review*. Consortium on Chicago School Research.

Feltham, M., & Sharen, C. (2015). "What do you mean I wrote a C paper?" Writing, revision, and self-regulation. *Collected Essays on Learning and Teaching*, 8, 111–138.

Ferguson, A. A. (2001). *Bad boys: Public schools in the making of black masculinity*. University of Michigan Press.

Fine, M. (1994). Working the hyphens: Reinventing self and other in qualitative research. In N. K. Denzin & Y. S. Lincoln (Eds.), *Handbook of qualitative research* (pp. 70–82). Sage.

Fine, M., & Weis, L. (2010). Writing the "wrongs" of fieldwork: Confronting our own research/writing dilemmas in urban ethnographies. In W. Luttrell (Ed.), *Qualitative educational research: Readings in reflexive methodology and transformative practice* (pp. 448–466). Routledge.

Fisher, B. A., Dufault, C. L., Repice, M. D., & Frey, R. F. (2013). Fostering a growth mind-set. *To Improve the Academy*, 32(1), 39–56. https://doi.org/10.1002/j.2334-4822.2013.tb00697.x.

Flower, L., Hayes, J. R., Carey, L., Schriver, K., & Stratman, J. (1986). Detection, diagnosis, and the strategies of revision. *College Composition and Communication*, 37(1), 16–55. https://doi.org/10.2307/357381.

Ford, A. C., & Sassi, K. (2014). Authority in cross-racial teaching and learning: (Re)considering the transferability of warm demander approaches. *Urban Education*, 49(1), 39–74. https://doi.org/10.1177/0042085912464790.

Forsythe, A., & Johnson, S. (2017). Thanks, but no thanks for the feedback. *Assessment & Evaluation in Higher Education, 42*(6), 850–859.

Francis, B., Skelton, C., Carrington, B., Hutchings, M., Read, B., & Hall, I. (2008). A perfect match? Pupils' and teachers' views of the impact of matching educators and learners by gender. *Research Papers in Education, 23*(1), 21–36. https://doi.org/10.1080/02671520701692510.

Fredricks, J. A., Blumenfeld, P. C., & Paris, A. H. (2004). School engagement: Potential of the concept, state of the evidence. *Review of Educational Research, 74*(1), 59–109. https://doi.org/10.3102/00346543074001059.

Freeman, T. M., Anderman, L. H., & Jensen, J. M. (2007). Sense of belonging in college freshmen at the classroom and campus levels. *The Journal of Experimental Education, 75*(3), 203–220. https://doi.org/10.3200/JEXE.75.3.203-220.

Frost, J. H., Coomes, J., & Lindeblad, K. (2012). Partnership paves the way to college success: High school and college math teachers collaborate to improve instruction. *Journal of Staff Development, 33*(5), 24–26.

Furrer, C., & Skinner, E. (2003). Sense of relatedness as a factor in children's academic engagement and performance. *Journal of Educational Psychology, 95*, 148–162.

Garcia-Reid, P., Reid, R. J., & Peterson, N. A. (2005). School engagement among Latino youth in an urban middle school context: Valuing the role of social support. *Education and Urban Society, 37*(3), 257–275.

Garner, J. K., & Kaplan, A. (2019). A complex dynamic systems perspective on teacher learning and identity formation: An instrumental case. *Teachers & Teaching, 25*(1), 7–33. https://doi.org/10.1080/13540602.2018.1533811.

Garza, R. (2009). Latino and white high school students' perceptions of caring behaviors: Are we culturally responsive to our students? *Urban Education, 44*(3), 297–321. https://doi.org/10.1177/0042085908318714.

Gaspard, H., Dicke, A.-L., Flunger, B., Schreier, B., Häfner, I., Trautwein, U., & Nagengast, B. (2015). More value through greater differentiation: Gender differences in value beliefs about math. *Journal of Educational Psychology, 107*(3), 663–677. https://doi.org/10.1037/edu0000003.

Gaztambide-Fernandez, R. A. (2009). *The best of the best: Becoming elite at an American boarding school.* Harvard University Press.

Goldblatt, H., Karnieli-Miller, O., & Neumann, M. (2011). Sharing qualitative research findings with participants: Study experiences of methodological and ethical dilemmas. *Patient Education and Counseling, 82*(3), 389–395. https://doi.org/10.1016/j.pec.2010.12.016.

Goodenow, C. (1993). The psychological sense of school membership among adolescents: Scale development and educational correlates. *Psychology in the Schools, 30*(1), 79–90. https://doi.org/10.1002/1520-6807(199301)30:1<79::AID-PITS2310300113>3.0.CO;2-X.

Gordon, E. W., & Bridglall, B. L. (2007). *Affirmative development: Cultivating academic ability.* Rowman & Littlefield.

Gordon, S. C., Dembo, M. H., & Hocevar, D. (2007). Do teachers' own learning behaviors influence their classroom goal orientation and control ideology? *Teaching and Teacher Education, 23*(1), 36–46. https://doi.org/10.1016/j.tate.2004.08.002.

Graham, S., MacArthur, C. A., & Hebert, M. (Eds.). (2018). *Best practices in writing instruction* (3rd edition). Guilford Publications.

Gravett, S., de Beer, J., Odendaal-Kroon, R., & Merseth, K. K. (2017). The affordances of case-based teaching for the professional learning of student-teachers. *Journal of Curriculum Studies, 49*(3), 369–390. https://doi.org/10.1080/002 20272.2016.1149224.

Gray, D. L., Hope, E. C., & Matthews, J. S. (2018). Black and belonging at school: A case for interpersonal, instructional, and institutional opportunity structures. *Educational Psychologist, 53*(2), 97–113. https://doi.org/10.1080/00461520.2017.1421466.

Green, S. K. (2002). Using an expectancy-value approach to examine teachers' motivational strategies. *Teaching & Teacher Education, 18*(8), 989.

Greenfield, G. M. (2013). *Developing and sustaining successful first-year programs: A guide for practitioners.* Wiley.

Grossman, P., Hammerness, K., & McDonald, M. (2009). Redefining teaching, reimagining teacher education. *Teachers and Teaching, 15*(2), 273–289. https://doi.org/10.1080/13540600902875340.

Hafen, C. A., Allen, J. P., Mikami, A. Y., Gregory, A., Hamre, B., & Pianta, R. C. (2011). The pivotal role of adolescent autonomy in secondary school classrooms. *Journal of Youth and Adolescence, 41*(3), 245–255. https://doi.org/10.1007/s10964-011-9739-2.

Haimovitz, K., & Dweck, C. S. (2016). Parents' views of failure predict children's fixed and growth intelligence mind-sets. *Psychological Science, 27*(6), 859–869. https://doi.org/10.1177/0956797616639727.

Han, C., Farruggia, S. P., & Moss, T. P. (2017). Effects of academic mindsets on college students' achievement and retention. *Journal of College Student Development, 58*(8), 1119–1134.

Harackiewicz, J. M., Smith, J. L., & Priniski, S. J. (2016). Interest matters: The importance of promoting interest in education. *Policy Insights from the Behavioral and Brain Sciences, 3*(2), 220–227. https://doi.org/10.1177/2372732216655542.

Hardré, P. L., & Hennessey, M. N. (2013). What they think, what they know, what they do: Rural secondary teachers' motivational beliefs and strategies. *Learning Environments Research, 16*(3), 411–436. http://doi.org./10.1007/s10984-013-9131-0.

Hardré, P. L., & Sullivan, D. W. (2008). Teacher perceptions and individual differences: How they influence rural teachers' motivating strategies. *Teaching and Teacher Education: An International Journal of Research and Studies, 24*(8), 2059–2075. https://doi.org/10.1016/j.tate.2008.04.007.

Harris, J. (2006). Undisciplined writing. In K. B. Yancey (Ed.), *Delivering college composition: The fifth canon* (pp. 155–167). Boynton/Cook.

Harvey, L. (2015). Beyond member-checking: A dialogic approach to the research interview. *International Journal of Research & Method in Education, 38*(1), 23–38. https://doi.org/10.1080/1743727X.2014.914487.

Hastie, P. A., Martin, E., & Buchanan, A. M. (2006). Stepping out of the norm: An examination of praxis for a culturally-relevant pedagogy for African-American children. *Journal of Curriculum Studies, 38*(3), 293–306. https://doi.org/10.1080/00220270500296630.

Hayes, C. B., Ryan, A., & Zseller, E. B. (1994). The middle school child's perceptions of caring teachers. *American Journal of Education, 103*(1), 1–19. https://doi.org/10.1086/444087.

Haynes, T. L., Perry, R. P., & Daniels, L. M. (2009). A review of attributional retraining treatments: Fostering engagement and persistence in vulnerable college students. In J. C. Smart (Ed.), *Higher education: Handbook of theory and research* (Vol. 24, pp. 227–272). Springer.

Hecht, C. A., Yeager, D. S., Dweck, C. S., & Murphy, M. C. (2021). Beliefs, affordances, and adolescent development: Lessons from a decade of growth mindset interventions. In J. J. Lockman (Ed.), *Advances in Child Development and Behavior* (Vol. 61, pp. 169–197). JAI. https://doi.org/10.1016/bs.acdb.2021.04.004.

Heitzmann, R. (2008). Case study instruction in teacher education: Opportunity to develop students' critical thinking, school smarts and decision making. *Education, 128*(4), 523–542.

Henson, R. K. (2002). From adolescent angst to adulthood: Substantive implications and measurement dilemmas in the development of teacher efficacy research. *Educational Psychologist, 37*(3), 137–150. https://doi.org/10.1207/S15326985EP3703_1.

Hidi, S., & Boscolo, P. (2006). *Writing and motivation.* Elsevier.

Hill, K. D. (2012). We're actually comfortable with diversity: Affirming teacher candidates for culturally relevant reading pedagogy in urban practicum. *Action in Teacher Education, 34*(5–6), 420–432. https://doi.org/10.1080/01626620.2012.729472.

Hillocks, G. (1995). *Teaching writing as reflective practice.* Teachers College Press.

Hostetler, K. (2005). What is "good" education research? *Educational Researcher, 34*(6), 16–21. https://doi.org/10.3102/0013189X034006016.

Howard, T. C. (2003). Culturally relevant pedagogy: Ingredients for critical teacher reflection. *Theory Into Practice, 42*(3), 195–202. https://doi.org/10.1207/s15430421tip4203_5.

Huang, C. (2011). Achievement goals and achievement emotions: A meta-analysis. *Educational Psychology Review, 23*(3), 359–388.

Huang, H. B. (2010). What is good action research? Why the resurgent interest? *Action Research, 8*(1), 93–109. https://doi.org/10.1177/1476750310362435.

Hudley, C., Moschetti, R., Gonzalez, A., Cho, S.-J., Barry, L., & Kelly, M. (2009). College freshmen's perceptions of their high school experiences. *Journal of Advanced Academics, 20*(3), 438–471.

Hulleman, C. S., Godes, O., Hendricks, B. L., & Harackiewicz, J. M. (2010). Enhancing interest and performance with a utility value intervention. *Journal of Educational Psychology, 102*(4), 880–895. https://doi.org/10.1037/a0019 506.

Hulleman, C. S., Kosovich, J. J., Barron, K. E., & Daniel, D. B. (2017). Making connections: Replicating and extending the utility value intervention in the classroom. *Journal of Educational Psychology, 109*(3), 387–404. https://doi.org/10.1037/edu0000146.

Hurtado, S., Eagan, M. K., Tran, M. C., Newman, C. B., Chang, M. J., & Velasco, P. (2011). "We do science here": Underrepresented students' interactions with faculty in different college contexts. *Journal of Social Issues, 67*(3), 553–579. https://doi.org/10.1111/j.1540-4560.2011.01714.x.

Hyers, A. D., & Joslin, M. N. (1998). The first year seminar as a predictor of academic achievement and persistence. *Journal of the Freshman Year Experience & Students in Transition, 10*(1), 7–30. eric.

Hyland, N. E. (2005). Being a good teacher of black students? White teachers and unintentional racism. *Curriculum Inquiry, 35*(4), 429–459. https://doi.org/10.1111/j.1467-873X.2005.00336.x.

Imbrenda, J.-P. (2018). Developing academic literacy: Breakthroughs and barriers in a college-access intervention. *Research in the Teaching of English, 52*(3), 317–341.

Inman, J. O., & Powell, R. A. (2018). In the absence of grades: Dissonance and desire in course-contract classrooms. *College Composition and Communication, 70*(1), 30–56.

Inoue, A. B. (2019). How do we language so people stop killing each other, or what do we do about White language supremacy? *College Composition and Communication, 71*(2), 352–369.

Inoue, A. B. (2020). Stories about grading contracts, or how do I like through the violence I've done? *Journal of Writing Assessment, 13*(2).

Jackson, M. C., Galvez, G., Landa, I., Buonora, P., & Thoman, D. B. (2016). Science that matters: The importance of a cultural connection in underrepresented students' science pursuit. *CBE-Life Sciences Education, 15*(3), ar42. https://doi.org/10.1187/cbe.16-01-0067.

Jacobs, J. E., Lanza, S., Osgood, D. W., Eccles, J. S., & Wigfield, A. (2002). Changes in children's self-competence and values: Gender and domain differences across grades one through twelve. *Child Development, 73*(2), 509–527. https://doi.org/10.1111/1467-8624.00421.

Jang, H. (2008). Supporting students' motivation, engagement, and learning during an uninteresting activity. *Journal of Educational Psychology, 100*(4), 798–811. https://doi.org/10.1037/a0012841.

Jansen, W. S., Otten, S., van der Zee, K. I., & Jans, L. (2014). Inclusion: Conceptualization and measurement. *European Journal of Social Psychology, 44*(4), 370–385. https://doi.org/10.1002/ejsp.2011.

Johnson, D. R., Soldner, M., Leonard, J. B., Alvarez, P., Inkelas, K. K., Rowan-Kenyon, H. T., & Longerbeam, S. D. (2007). Examining sense of belonging among first-year undergraduates from different racial/ethnic groups. *Journal of College Student Development, 48*(5), 525–542. https://doi.org/10.1353/csd.2007.0054.

Johnson, S. M., Kraft, M. A., & Papay, J. P. (2012). How context matters in high-need schools: The effects of teachers' working conditions on their professional satisfaction and their students' achievement. *Teachers College Record, 114*(10).

Jones, B. D., Paretti, M. C., Hein, S. F., & Knott, T. W. (2010). An analysis of motivation constructs with first-year engineering students: Relationships among expectancies, values, achievement, and career plans. *Journal of Engineering Education, 99*(4), 319–336. https://doi.org/10.1002/j.2168-9830.2010.tb01066.x.

Jones, E. (2008). Predicting performance in first-semester college basic writers: Revisiting the role of self-beliefs. *Contemporary Educational Psychology, 33*(2), 209–238. https://doi.org/10.1016/j.cedpsych.2006.11.001.

Jones, J. (2007). Muted voices: High school teachers, composition, and the college imperative. *Writing Instructor.* https://eric.ed.gov/?id=EJ824634.

Jones, S. (2014). From ideas in the head to words on the page: Young adolescents' reflections on their own writing processes. *Language and Education, 28*(1), 52–67.

Joram, E., Gabriele, A. J., & Walton, K. (2020). What influences teachers' "buy-in" of research? Teachers' beliefs about the applicability of educational research to their practice. *Teaching and Teacher Education, 88*, 102980. https://doi.org/10.1016/j.tate.2019.102980.

Kafkas, S. S., Schmidt, J. A., Shumow, L., & Durik, A. M. (2017, April 30). Be specific: Science teachers' utility value statements and students' immediate and global science utility perceptions. *The Influence of Teachers on Students' Motivation and Metacognition.* Annual meeting of the American Educational Research Association, San Antonio, Texas.

Kaplan, A., Middleton, M., Urdan, T., & Midgley, C. (2002). Achievement goals and goal structures. In C. Midgley (Ed.), *Goals, goal structures, and patterns of adaptive learning* (pp. 21–54). Lawrence Erlbaum.

Kazemi, E., & Stipek, D. (2009). Promoting conceptual thinking in four upper-elementary mathematics classrooms. *Journal of Education, 189*(1–2), 123–137. https://doi.org/10.1177/0022057409189001-209.

Kennett, D. J., & Keefer, K. (2006). Impact of learned resourcefulness and theories of intelligence on academic achievement of university students: An integrated approach. *Educational Psychology, 26*(3), 441–457. https://doi.org/10.1080/01443410500342062.

Kesner, J. E. (2000). Teacher characteristics and the quality of child–teacher relationships. *Journal of School Psychology, 38*(2), 133–149. https://doi.org/10.1016/S0022-4405(99)00043-6.

Kirst, M. W., & Venezia, A. (2004). *From high school to college: Improving opportunities for success in postsecondary education.* Jossey-Bass.

Kosovich, J. J., Flake, J. K., & Hulleman, C. S. (2017). Short-term motivation trajectories: A parallel process model of expectancy-value. *Contemporary Educational Psychology, 49*, 130–139. https://doi.org/10.1016/j.cedpsych.2017.01.004.

Krumrei-Mancuso, E. J., Newton, F. B., Kim, E., & Wilcox, D. (2013). Psychosocial factors predicting first-year college student success. *Journal of College Student Development, 54*(3), 247–266. https://doi.org/10.1353/csd.2013.0034.

Kumar, R., Zusho, A., & Bondie, R. (2018). Weaving cultural relevance and achievement motivation into inclusive classroom cultures. *Educational Psychologist, 53*(2), 78–96. https://doi.org/10.1080/00461520.2018.1432361.

Kvale, S., & Brinkmann, S. (2009). *InterViews: Learning the craft of qualitative research interviewing* (2nd ed.). Sage.

Ladson-Billings, G. (1994). *The dreamkeepers: Successful teachers of African American children.* Jossey-Bass.

Ladson-Billings, G. (1995a). But that's just good teaching! The case for culturally relevant pedagogy. *Theory into Practice, 34*(3), 159–165.

Ladson-Billings, G. (1995b). Toward a theory of culturally relevant pedagogy. In *American Educational Research Journal, 32*(3).

Lai, Y. (2018). Accounting for mathematicians' priorities in mathematics courses for secondary teachers. *The Journal of Mathematical Behavior.* https://doi.org/10.1016/j.jmathb.2018.08.001.

Lather, P. (1986). Research as praxis. *Harvard Educational Review, 56*(3), 257–278. https://doi.org/10.17763/haer.56.3.bj2h231877069482

Lawrence-Lightfoot, S. (2000). *Respect: An exploration.* Perseus Books.

Lawrence-Lightfoot, S. (2005). Reflections on portraiture: A dialogue between art and science. *Qualitative Inquiry, 11*(1), 3–15. https://doi.org/10.1177/1077800404270955

Lawrence-Lightfoot, S. (2009). *The third chapter: Passion, risk, and adventure in the 25 years after 50.* Sarah Crichton Books.

Lawrence-Lightfoot, S. (2012). *Exit.* Sarah Creighton Books.

Lawrence-Lightfoot, S. (2016). *Growing each other up: When our children become our teachers.* University of Chicago Press.

Lawrence-Lightfoot, S., & Davis, J. H. (1997). *The art and science of portraiture.* Jossey-Bass.

Leibbrand, J. A., & Watson, B. H. (2010). *The Road Less Traveled: How the Developmental Sciences Can Prepare Educators to Improve Student Achievement—Policy Recommendations.* National Council for Accreditation of Teacher Education.

Lillge, D. (2019). Uncovering conflict: Why teachers struggle to apply professional development learning about the teaching of writing. *Research in the Teaching of English*, *53*(4), 340–362.

Lincoln, Y. S., & Guba, E. G. (1985). *Naturalistic inquiry*. Sage.

Lindenman, H., Camper, M., Jacoby, L. D., & Enoch, J. (2018). Revision and reflection: A study of (dis)connections between writing knowledge and writing practice. *College Composition and Communication*, *69*(4), 581–611.

Linnenbrink-Garcia, L., & Patall, E. A. (2015). Motivation. In L. Corno & E. M. Anderman (Eds.), *Handbook of Educational Psychology* (3rd ed., pp. 91–103). Taylor and Francis.

Liu, P., McKinney, D., Lee, A. A., Schmidt, J. A., Marchand, G. C., & Linnenbrink-Garcia, L. (2023). A mixed-methods exploration of mastery goal support in 7th-grade science classrooms. *Cognition and Instruction*, *41*(2), 201–247. https://doi.org/10.1080/07370008.2022.2140807.

Liu, P., Savitz-Romer, M., Perella, J., Hill, N. E., & Liang, B. (2018). Student representations of dyadic and global teacher-student relationships: Perceived caring, negativity, affinity, and differences across gender and race/ethnicity. *Contemporary Educational Psychology*, *54*, 281–296. https://doi.org/10.1016/j.cedpsych.2018.07.005.

Luttrell, W. (2000). "Good enough" methods for ethnographic research. *Harvard Educational Review*, *70*(4), 499–523. https://doi.org/10.17763/haer.70.4.5333230502744141.

Luttrell, W. (2010). Interactive and reflexive models of qualitative research design. In W. Luttrell (Ed.), *Qualitative educational research: Readings in reflexive methodology and transformative practice* (pp. 159–163). Routledge.

MacArthur, C. A., & Graham, S. (2016). Writing research from a cognitive perspective. In *Handbook of writing research, 2nd ed* (pp. 24–40). Guilford.

MacArthur, C. A., Philippakos, Z. A., & Graham, S. (2016). A multicomponent measure of writing motivation with basic college writers. *Learning Disability Quarterly*, *39*(1), 31–43.

Maehr, M. L., & Midgley, C. (1991). Enhancing student motivation: A schoolwide approach. *Educational Psychologist*, *26*(3–4), 399–427. https://doi.org/10.1080/00461520.1991.9653140.

Maiter, S., Simich, L., Jacobson, N., & Wise, J. (2008). Reciprocity: An ethic for community-based participatory action research. *Action Research*, *6*(3), 305–325. https://doi.org/10.1177/1476750307083720.

Mangels, J. A., Butterfield, B., Lamb, J., Good, C., & Dweck, C. S. (2006). Why do beliefs about intelligence influence learning success? A social cognitive neuroscience model. *Social Cognitive and Affective Neuroscience*, *1*(2), 75–86. https://doi.org/10.1093/scan/nsl013.

Marchand, G. C., Schmidt, J. A., Linnenbrink-Garcia, L., Harris, C. J., McKinney, D., & Liu, P. (2022). Lessons from a co-design team on supporting student motivation in middle school science classrooms. *Theory into Practice, 61*(1), 113–128. https://doi.org/10.1080/00405841.2021.1932155.

Marsh, H. W., & Hau, K.-T. (2003). Big-fish-little-pond effect on academic self-concept: A cross-cultural (26-country) test of the negative effects of academically selective schools. *American Psychologist, 58*(5), 364–376. https://doi.org/10.1037/0003-066X.58.5.364.

Marsh, H. W., Martin, A. J., & Cheng, J. H. S. (2008). A multilevel perspective on gender in classroom motivation and climate: Potential benefits of male teachers for boys? *Journal of Educational Psychology, 100*(1), 78–95.

Marzano, R. J. (2000). *Transforming classroom grading.* Association for Supervision and Curriculum Development.

Matias, C. E. (2013). Check yo'self before you wreck yo'self and our kids: Counter-stories from culturally responsive White teachers? . . . to culturally responsive White teachers! *Interdisciplinary Journal of Teaching & Learning, 3*(2), 68–81.

Maxwell, J. A. (2005). *Qualitative research design: An interactive approach* (2nd ed., Vol. 41). Sage.

Maxwell, J. A. (2010). Validity: How might you be wrong? In W. Luttrell (Ed.), *Qualitative educational research: Readings in reflexive methodology and transformative practice* (pp. 279–287). Routledge.

McAninch, A. R. (1993). *Teacher thinking and the case method: Theory and future directions.* Teachers College Press.

McGrath, K. F., & Van Bergen, P. (2015). Who, when, why and to what end? Students at risk of negative student–teacher relationships and their outcomes. *Educational Research Review, 14*, 1–17. https://doi.org/10.1016/j.edurev.2014.12.001.

Melzer, D. K., & Grant, R. M. (2016). Investigating differences in personality traits and academic needs among prepared and underprepared first-year college students. *Journal of College Student Development, 57*(1), 99–103.

Menges, R. J., & Weimer, M. (1996). *Teaching on solid ground: Using scholarship to improve practice* (1st ed.). Jossey-Bass.

Merseth, K. K. (1991). *The case for cases in teacher education.* AACTE.

Meyer, J. H. F., & Land, R. (2006). Threshold concepts and troublesome knowledge: An introduction. In *Overcoming barriers to student learning* (pp. 3–18). Routledge.

Midgley, C., Anderman, E., & Hicks, L. (1995). Differences between elementary and middle school teachers and students: A goal theory approach. *The Journal of Early Adolescence, 15*(1), 90–113. https://doi.org/10.1177/0272431695015001006.

Midgley, C., Kaplan, A., & Middleton, M. (2001). Performance-approach goals: Good for what, for whom, under what circumstances, and at what cost? *Journal of Educational Psychology, 93*(1), 77–86. https://doi.org/10.1037/0022-0663.93.1.77.

Miles, M. B., & Huberman, A. M. (1994). *Qualitative data analysis: An expanded sourcebook* (2nd ed.). Sage.

Moje, E. B., & Wade, S. E. (1997). What case discussions reveal about teacher thinking. *Teaching and Teacher Education, 13*(7), 691–712. https://doi.org/10.1016/S0742-051X(97)00015-2.

Morrison, K. A., Robbins, H. H., & Rose, D. G. (2008). Operationalizing culturally relevant pedagogy: A synthesis of classroom-based research. *Equity & Excellence in Education, 41*(4), 433–452. https://doi.org/10.1080/10665680802400006.

Morse, J. M., Barrett, M., Mayan, M., Olson, K., & Spiers, J. (2002). Verification strategies for establishing reliability and validity in qualitative research. *International Journal of Qualitative Methods, 1*(2), 13–22. https://doi.org/10.1177/160940690200100202.

Mueller, C. M., & Dweck, C. S. (1998). Praise for intelligence can undermine children's motivation and performance. *Journal of Personality and Social Psychology, 75*(1), 33–52. https://doi.org/10.1037/0022-3514.75.1.33.

Musu-Gillette, L. E., Wigfield, A., Harring, J. R., & Eccles, J. S. (2015). Trajectories of change in students' self-concepts of ability and values in math and college major choice. *Educational Research and Evaluation, 21*(4), 343–370.

Nakkula, M. J., & Toshalis, E. (2006). Risk taking and creativity. In *Understanding youth: Adolescent development for educators* (pp. 41–60). Harvard Education Press.

Nakkula, M. J., & Toshalis, E. (2006). *Understanding youth: Adolescent development for educators.* Harvard Education Press.

National Center for Education Statistics. (2018). *Digest of Education Statistics, 2017.*

National Research Council Committee on Increasing High School Students' Engagement and Motivation to Learn. (2004). The nature and conditions of engagement. In *Engaging schools: Fostering high school students' motivation to learn.* National Academies Press.

NCTE. (2013). *First-Year Writing: What Good Does It Do? A Policy Research Brief.* National Council of Teachers of English.

Neal, J. W., Neal, Z. P., Kornbluh, M., Mills, K. J., & Lawlor, J. A. (2015). Brokering the research-practice gap: A typology. *American Journal of Community Psychology, 56*(3–4), 422–435. https://doi.org/10.1007/s10464-015-9745-8.

Nelson-Marten, P., & Rich, B. A. (1999). A historical perspective of informed consent in clinical practice and research. *Seminars in Oncology Nursing, 15*(2), 81–88. https://doi.org/10.1016/S0749-2081(99)80065-5.

Nieto, S. (2004). *Affirming diversity* (4th ed.). Pearson, Allyn & Bacon.

Noddings, N. (2005). *The challenge of care in schools: An alternative approach to education* (2nd ed.). Teachers College Press.

Nowacek, R. S. (2011). *Agents of integration: Understanding transfer as a rhetorical act.* Southern Illinois University Press.

Nussbaum, A. D., & Dweck, C. S. (2008). Defensiveness versus remediation: Self-theories and modes of self-esteem maintenance. *Personality and Social Psychology Bulletin, 34*(5), 599–612. https://doi.org/10.1177/0146167207312960.

O'Neill, P., Adler-Kassner, L., Fleischer, C., Hall, A.-M., Severino, C., McComiskey, B., Hansen, K., Summerfield, J., Anderson, P. M., & Sullivan, P. (2012). Symposium: On the "Framework for Success in Postsecondary Writing." *College English, 74*(6), 520–553.

Onwuegbuzie, A. J., & Leech, N. L. (2007). Validity and qualitative research: An oxymoron? *Quality & Quantity, 41*(2), 233–249. https://doi.org/10.1007/s11135-006-9000-3.

Oyserman, D., & Fryberg, S. A. (2006). The possible selves of diverse adolescents: Content and function across gender, race and national origin. In C. Dunkel & J. Kerpelman (Eds.), *Possible selves: Theory, research, and applications* (pp. 17–39). Nova.

Pajares, F., Johnson, M. J., & Usher, E. L. (2007). Sources of writing self-efficacy beliefs of elementary, middle, and high school students. *Research in the Teaching of English, 42*(1), 104–120.

Panadero, E., & Jonsson, A. (2013). The use of scoring rubrics for formative assessment purposes revisited: A review. *Educational Research Review, 9*, 129–144. https://doi.org/10.1016/j.edurev.2013.01.002.

Park, D., Gunderson, E. A., Tsukayama, E., Levine, S. C., & Beilock, S. L. (2016). Young children's motivational frameworks and math achievement: Relation to teacher-reported instructional practices, but not teacher theory of intelligence. *Journal of Educational Psychology, 108*(3), 300–313. http://doi.org/10.1037/edu0000064.

Parrott, H. M., & Cherry, E. (2015). Process memos: Facilitating dialogues about writing between students and instructors. *Teaching Sociology, 43*(2), 146–153.

Patall, E. A. (2013). Constructing motivation through choice, interest, and interestingness. *Journal of Educational Psychology, 105*(2), 522–534. https://doi.org/10.1037/a0030307.

Patall, E. A., Linnenbrink-Garcia, L., Liu, P., Zambrano, J., & Yates, N. (2022). Instructional practices that support adaptive motivation, engagement, and learning. In A. M. O'Donnell, N. C. Barnes, & J. Reeve (Eds.), *The Oxford Handbook of Educational Psychology*. Oxford University Press.

Patrick, H., Anderman, L. H., & Ryan, A. M. (2002). Social motivation and the classroom social environment. In C. Midgley (Ed.), *Goals, goal structures, and patterns of adaptive learning* (pp. 85–108). Lawrence Erlbaum Associates.

Patrick, H., Kaplan, A., & Ryan, A. M. (2011). Positive classroom motivational environments: Convergence between mastery goal structure and classroom social climate. *Journal of Educational Psychology, 103*(2), 367–382. https://doi.org/10.1037/a0023311.

Patterson, J. P., & Duer, D. (2006). High school teaching and college expectations in writing and reading. *English Journal, 95*(3), 81–87.

Perez, T., Dai, T., Kaplan, A., Cromley, J. G., Brooks, W. D., White, A. C., Mara, K. R., & Balsai, M. J. (2019). Interrelations among expectancies, task values, and perceived costs in undergraduate biology achievement. *Learning and Individual Differences*, *72*, 26–38. https://doi.org/10.1016/j.lindif.2019.04.001.

Phillippo, K. L., & Stone, S. (2013). Teacher role breadth and its relationship to student-reported teacher support. *High School Journal*, *96*(4), 358–379.

Piaget, J. (1972). Intellectual evolution from adolescence to adulthood. *Human Development*, *15*(1), 1–12. https://doi.org/10.1159/000271225.

Pianta, R. C., Hitz, R., & West, B. (2010). *Increasing the Application of Developmental Sciences Knowledge in Educator Preparation: Policy Issues and Recommendations.* National Council for Accreditation of Teacher Education.

Pillow, W. (2003). Confession, catharsis, or cure? Rethinking the uses of reflexivity as methodological power in qualitative research. *International Journal of Qualitative Studies in Education*, *16*(2), 175–196. https://doi.org/10.1080/0951839032000060635.

Priess-Groben, H., & Hyde, J. (2017). Implicit theories, expectancies, and values predict mathematics motivation and behavior across high school and college. *Journal of Youth & Adolescence*, *46*(6), 1318–1332. https://doi.org/10.1007/s10964-016-0579-y.

Pruchnic, J., Barton, E., Trimble, T., Primeau, S., Weiss, H., Varty, N. G., & Moore, T. F. (2021). The effects of student-fashioning and teacher-pleasing in the assessment of first-year writing reflective essays. *Journal of Writing Assessment*, *14*(1). https://doi.org/10.5070/W414155459.

Pugh, K. J., Bergstrom, C. M., & Spencer, B. (2017). Profiles of transformative engagement: Identification, description, and relation to learning and instruction. *Science Education*, *101*(3), 369–398. https://doi.org/10.1002/sce.21270.

Pugh, K. J., & Phillips, M. M. (2011). Helping students develop an appreciation for school content. *Theory Into Practice*, *50*(4), 285–292. https://doi.org/10.1080/00405841.2011.607383.

Quigley, C., Trauth-Nare, A., & Beeman-Cadwallader, N. (2015). The viability of portraiture for science education research: Learning from portraits of two science classrooms. *International Journal of Qualitative Studies in Education (QSE)*, *28*(1), 21–49. https://doi.org/10.1080/09518398.2013.847507.

Quin, D. (2017). Longitudinal and contextual associations between teacher-student relationships and student engagement: A systematic review. *Review of Educational Research*, *87*(2), 345–387. https://doi.org/10.3102/0034654316669434.

Ransdell, D. R., & Glau, G. R. (1996). Articulation and student voices: Eliminating the perception that "high school English doesn't teach you nothing." *English Journal*, *85*(1), 17–21.

Rattan, A., Good, C., & Dweck, C. S. (2012). "It's ok—Not everyone can be good at math": Instructors with an entity theory comfort (and demotivate) students. *Journal of Experimental Social Psychology*, *48*(3), 731–737.

Raufelder, D., Kittler, F., Braun, S. R., Lätsch, A., Wilkinson, R. P., & Hoferichter, F. (2014). The interplay of perceived stress, self-determination and school engagement in adolescence. *School Psychology International, 35*(4), 405–420. https://doi.org/10.1177/0143034313498953.

Reeve, J., & Jang, H. (2006). What teachers say and do to support students' autonomy during a learning activity. *Journal of Educational Psychology, 98*(1), 209–218.

Renninger, K. A., & Hidi, S. (2002). Student interest and achievement: Developmental issues raised by a case study. In A. Wigfield & J. S. Eccles (Eds.), *Development of achievement motivation* (pp. 173–195). Academic.

Richardson, V. (1996). The role of attitudes and beliefs in learning to teach. In J. P. Sikula, T. J. Buttery, & E. Guyton (Eds.), *Handbook of research on teacher education* (2nd ed., pp. 102–117). Macmillan.

Robinson, C. D., Gallus, J., Lee, M. G., & Rogers, T. (2021). The demotivating effect (and unintended message) of awards. *Organizational Behavior and Human Decision Processes, 163*, 51–64. https://doi.org/10.1016/j.obhdp.2019.03.006.

Rodriguez, L. F., & Brown, T. M. (2009). From voice to agency: Guiding principles for participatory action research with youth. *New Directions for Youth Development, 123*, 19–34.

Roozen, K., Adler-Kassner, L., & Wardle, E. (2016). Writing is a social and rhetorical activity. In *Naming what we know: Threshold concepts of writing studies* (pp. 17–19). Utah State University Press.

Rosaldo, R. (1993). *Culture & truth: The remaking of social analysis.* Beacon.

Rosenzweig, E. Q., & Wigfield, A. (2017). What if reading is easy but unimportant? How students' patterns of affirming and undermining motivation for reading information texts predict different reading outcomes. *Contemporary Educational Psychology, 48*, 133–148. https://doi.org/10.1016/j.cedpsych.2016.09.002.

Roseth, C. J., Johnson, D. W., & Johnson, R. T. (2008). Promoting early adolescents' achievement and peer relationships: The effects of cooperative, competitive, and individualistic goal structures. *Psychological Bulletin, 134*(2), 223–246. https://doi.org/10.1037/0033-2909.134.2.223.

Rubin, H. J., & Rubin, I. S. (2012). *Qualitative interviewing: The art of hearing data* (3rd ed.). Sage.

Ryan, R. M., & Deci, E. L. (2020). Intrinsic and extrinsic motivation from a self-determination theory perspective: Definitions, theory, practices, and future directions. *Contemporary Educational Psychology, 61*, 101860. https://doi.org/10.1016/j.cedpsych.2020.101860.

Saft, E. W., & Pianta, R. C. (2001). Teachers' perceptions of their relationships with students: Effects of child age, gender, and ethnicity of teachers and children. *School Psychology Quarterly, 16*(2), 125–141.

Salanova, M., Llorens, S., & Schaufeli, W. B. (2011). "Yes, I can, I feel good, and I just do it!" On gain cycles and spirals of efficacy beliefs, affect, and engagement. *Applied Psychology: An International Review, 60*(2), 255–285.

Santagata, R. (2005). Practices and beliefs in mistake-handling activities: A video study of Italian and US mathematics lessons. *Teaching and Teacher Education, 21*(5), 491–508. https://doi.org/10.1016/j.tate.2005.03.004.

Schell, E. E. (2017). The new faculty majority in writing programs: Organizing for change. In S. Kahn, W. B. Lalicker, & A. Lynch-Biniek (Eds.), *Contingency, exploitation, and solidarity: Labor and action in English composition* (pp. ix–xx). The WAC Clearinghouse and University Press of Colorado.

Schmidt, J. A., Kafkas, S. S., Maier, K. S., Shumow, L., & Kackar-Cam, H. Z. (2018). Why are we learning this? Using mixed methods to understand teachers' relevance statements and how they shape middle school students' perceptions of science utility. *Contemporary Educational Psychology.* https://doi.org/10.1016/j.cedpsych.2018.08.005.

Schön, D. (1983). *The reflective practitioner.* Basic Books.

Schunk, D. H., Meece, J. L., & Pintrich, P. R. (2014). *Motivation in education: Theory, research, and applications* (4th ed.). Pearson.

Schunk, D. H., & Pajares, F. (2005). Competence perceptions and academic functioning. In A. J. Elliot & C. S. Dweck (Eds.), *Handbook of competence and motivation* (pp. 85–104). Guilford.

Seidman, I. (2006). *Interviewing as qualitative research: A guide for researchers in education and the social sciences* (3rd ed.). Teachers College.

Senko, C., Durik, A. M., Patel, L., Lovejoy, C. M., & Valentiner, D. (2013). Performance-approach goal effects on achievement under low versus high challenge conditions. *Learning & Instruction, 23,* 60–68.

Senko, C., Hulleman, C. S., & Harackiewicz, J. M. (2011). Achievement goal theory at the crossroads: Old controversies, current challenges, and new directions. *Educational Psychologist, 46*(1), 26–47. https://doi.org/10.1080/0 0461520.2011.538646.

Shaughnessy, M. (1975). Basic writing. In G. Tate (Ed.), *Teaching composition: Ten bibliographical essays* (pp. 142–167). Texas Christian University Press.

Shepherd, R. P., Mauck, C. A., Barber, C. J., & Fletcher, S. (2021). Beyond osmosis: Developing teaching for transfer pedagogy for graduate classes in composition. *Composition Forum, 46.*

Shulman, L. S. (1986). Those who understand: Knowledge growth in teaching. *Educational Researcher, 15*(2), 4–14. https://doi.org/10.3102/0013189X015002004.

Silva, K. M., Spinrad, T. L., Eisenberg, N., Sulik, M. J., Valiente, C., Huerta, S., Edwards, A., Eggum, N. D., Kupfer, A. S., Lonigan, C. J., Phillips, B. M., Wilson, S. B., Clancy-Menchetti, J., Landry, S. H., Swank, P. R., Assel, M. A., Taylor, H. B., & Consortium, S. R. (2011). Relations of children's effortful control and teacher-child relationship quality to school attitudes in a low-income sample. *Early Education and Development, 22*(3), 434–460. https://doi.org/10.1080/10409289.2011.578046.

Sleeter, C. E. (2008). Preparing White teachers for diverse students. In M. Cochran-Smith, S. Feiman-Nemser, D. J. McIntyre, & Association of Teacher Educators (Eds.), *Handbook of research on teacher education: Enduring questions in changing contexts.* (3rd ed., pp. 559–582). Routledge.

Smith, J. A. (1999). Contracting English composition: It only sounds like an illness. *Teaching English in the Two Year College, 26*, 427–430.

Smith, T., Brumskill, R., Johnson, A., & Zimmer, T. (2018). The impact of teacher language on students' mindsets and statistics performance. *Social Psychology of Education: An International Journal, 21*(4), 775–786.

Sommers, N., & Saltz, L. (2004). The novice as expert: Writing the freshman year. *College Composition and Communication, 56*(1), 124–149. https://doi.org/10.2307/4140684.

Spinath, B., & Steinmayr, R. (2008). Longitudinal analysis of intrinsic motivation and competence beliefs: Is there a relation over time? *Child Development, 79*(5), 1555–1569. https://doi.org/10.1111/j.1467-8624.2008.01205.x.

St. Pierre, E. A. (1997). Methodology in the fold and the irruption of transgressive data. *International Journal of Qualitative Studies in Education, 10*(2), 175–189. https://doi.org/10.1080/095183997237278.

Stäbler, F., Dumont, H., Becker, M., & Baumert, J. (2017). What happens to the fish's achievement in a little pond? A simultaneous analysis of class-average achievement effects on achievement and academic self-concept. *Journal of Educational Psychology, 109*(2), 191–207. https://doi.org/10.1037/edu0000135.

Steele, C. (2003). Stereotype threat and African-American student achievement. In T. Perry, C. Steele, & A. Hilliard III, *Young, gifted, and Black: Promoting high achievement among African-American students* (pp. 109–130). Beacon.

Sternglass, M. S. (1997). *Time to know them: A longitudinal study of writing and learning at the college level.* Lawrence Erlbaum.

Strachan, W. (2002). Talking about the transition: Dialogues between high school and university teachers. In T. C. Thompson (Ed.), *Teaching writing in high school and college: Conversations and collaborations* (pp. 136–149). National Council of Teachers of English.

Sun, K. L. (2018a). Beyond rhetoric: Authentically supporting a growth mindset. *Teaching Children Mathematics, 24*(5), 280–284.

Sun, K. L. (2018b). The role of mathematics teaching in fostering student growth mindset. *Journal for Research in Mathematics Education, 49*(3), 330–355. https://doi.org/10.5951/jresematheduc.49.3.0330.

Taczak, K. (2016). Reflection is critical for writers' development. In L. Adler-Kassner & E. Wardle (Eds.), *Naming what we know: Threshold concepts of writing studies* (pp. 78–81). Utah State University Press.

Thompson, G. L. (2004). *Through ebony eyes: What teachers need to know but are afraid to ask about African American students.* Jossey-Bass.

Timmermans, A. C., Boer, H. de, & Werf, M. P. C. van der. (2016). An investigation of the relationship between teachers' expectations and teachers' perceptions of student attributes. *Social Psychology of Education, 19*(2), 217–240. https://doi.org/10.1007/s11218-015-9326-6.

Tosolt, B. (2010). Gender and race differences in middle school students' perceptions of caring teacher behaviors. *Multicultural Perspectives, 12*(3), 145–151. https://doi.org/10.1080/15210960.2010.504484.

Trainor, A., & Bouchard, K. A. (2013). Exploring and developing reciprocity in research design. *International Journal of Qualitative Studies in Education, 26*(8), 986–1003. https://doi.org/10.1080/09518398.2012.724467.

Tuck, E. (2009). Suspending damage: A letter to communities. *Harvard Educational Review, 79*(3), 409–428. https://doi.org/10.17763/haer.79.3.n001 6675661t3n15.

Turner, J. C., Gray, D. L., Anderman, L. H., Dawson, H. S., & Anderman, E. M. (2013). Getting to know my teacher: Does the relation between perceived mastery goal structures and perceived teacher support change across the school year? *Contemporary Educational Psychology, 38*(4), 316–327. https://doi.org/10.1016/j.cedpsych.2013.06.003.

Turner, J. C., Midgley, C., Meyer, D. K., Gheen, M., Anderman, E. M., Kang, Y., & Patrick, H. (2002). The classroom environment and students' reports of avoidance strategies in mathematics: A multimethod study. *Journal of Educational Psychology, 94*(1), 88–106. http://doi.org/10.1037/0022-0663.94.1.88.

Urdan, T., & Bruchmann, K. (2018). Examining the academic motivation of a diverse student population: A consideration of methodology. *Educational Psychologist, 53*(2), 114–130. https://doi.org/10.1080/00461520.2018.1440234.

Urdan, T., & Kaplan, A. (2020). The origins, evolution, and future directions of achievement goal theory. *Contemporary Educational Psychology*, 101862. https://doi.org/10.1016/j.cedpsych.2020.101862.

Urdan, T., Kneisel, L., & Mason, G. (1999). Interpreting messages about motivation in the classroom: Examining the effects of achievement goal structures. In T. Urdan (Ed.), *Advanced in motivation and achievement* (Vol. 11, pp. 123–158). JAI.

Urdan, T., & Schoenfelder, E. (2006). Classroom effects on student motivation: Goal structures, social relationships, and competence beliefs. *Journal of School Psychology, 44*(5), 331–349. https://doi.org/10.1016/j.jsp.2006.04.003.

Usher, E. L., & Pajares, F. (2008). Sources of self-efficacy in school: Critical review of the literature and future directions. *Review of Educational Research, 78*(4), 751–796. https://doi.org/10.3102/0034654308321456.

Valverde, L. A. (2006). *Creating new schools for Mexican Latinos*. Rowman & Littlefield.

Van Galen, J., & Eaker, D. (1995). Beyond settling for scholarship: On defining the beginning and ending points of postmodern research. In W. Pink & G. Noblit (Eds.), *Continuity and contradiction: The futures of the sociology of education* (pp. 113–131). Hampton.

Vander Kloet, M., Frake-Mistak, M., McGinn, M. K., Caldecott, M., Aspenlieder, E. D., Beres, J. L., Fukuzawa, S., Cassidy, A., & Gill, A. (2017). Conditions for contingent instructors engaged in the scholarship of teaching and learning. *The Canadian Journal for the Scholarship of Teaching and Learning*, *8*(2). https://doi.org/10.5206/cjsotl-rcacea.2017.2.9.

Varpio, L., Ajjawi, R., Monrouxe, L. V., O'Brien, B. C., & Rees, C. E. (2017). Shedding the cobra effect: Problematising thematic emergence, triangulation, saturation and member checking. *Medical Education*, *51*(1), 40–50. https://doi.org/10.1111/medu.13124.

Vega, D., Moore, J. L., III, & Miranda, A. H. (2015). In their own words: Perceived barriers to achievement by African American and Latino high school students. *American Secondary Education*, *43*(3), 36–59.

Venezia, A., Callan, P. M., Finney, J. E., Kirst, M. W., & Usdan, M. D. (2005). *The Governance Divide: A Report on a Four-State Study on Improving College Readiness and Success*. National Center for Public Policy and Higher Education.

Venezia, A., & Jaeger, L. (2013). Transitions from high school to college. *Future of Children*, *23*(1), 117–136.

Venezia, A., Kirst, M. W., & Antonio, A. L. (2003). *Betraying the College Dream: How Disconnected K–12 and Postsecondary Education Systems Undermine Student Aspirations*. Bridge Project, Stanford Institute for Higher Education Research.

Villegas, A. M., & Davis, D. E. (2008). Preparing teachers of color to confront racial/ethnic disparities in educational outcomes. In M. Cochran-Smith, S. Feiman-Nemser, D. J. McIntyre, & Association of Teacher Educators (Eds.), *Handbook of research on teacher education: Enduring questions in changing contexts*. (3rd ed., pp. 583–605). Routledge.

Villegas, A. M., & Lucas, T. (2002). Developing fundamental orientations for teaching a changing student population: Gaining sociocultural consciousness. In *Educating culturally responsive teachers: A coherent approach* (pp. 27–39). State University of New York Press.

Villenas, S. (1996). The colonizer/colonized Chicana ethnographer: Identity, marginalization, and co-optation in the field. *Harvard Educational Review*, *66*(4), 711–732. https://doi.org/10.17763/haer.66.4.3483672630865482.

Voelkl, K. E. (2012). School identification. In S. L. Christenson, A. L. Reschly, & C. Wylie (Eds.), *Handbook of research on student engagement* (pp. 193–218). Springer.

Walker, V. S. (2001). African American teaching in the South: 1940–1960. *American Educational Research Journal*, *38*(4), 751–779. https://doi.org/10.3102/00028 312038004751.

Wallace, S. (2014). When you're smiling: Exploring how teachers motivate and engage learners in the further education sector. *Journal of Further and Higher Education*, *38*(3), 346–360.

Wardle, E. (2013). Intractable writing program problems, "Kairos," and writing about writing: A profile of the university of central Florida's first-year composition program. *Composition Forum*, *27*.

Ware, F. (2006). Warm demander pedagogy: Culturally responsive teaching that supports a culture of achievement for African American students. *Urban Education, 41*(4), 427–456.

Watt, H. M. G. (2004). Development of adolescents' self-perceptions, values, and task perceptions according to gender and domain in 7th- through 11th-grade Australian students. *Child Development, 75*(5), 1556–1574. https://doi.org/10.1111/j.1467-8624.2004.00757.x.

Weimer, M. (2012). Learner-centered teaching and transformative learning. In E. W. Taylor & P. Cranton (Eds.), *The handbook of transformative learning: Theory, research, and practice* (pp. 439–454). John Wiley & Sons.

Weiner, B. (1986). An attributional theory of achievement motivation and emotion. In *An Attributional Theory of Motivation and Emotion* (pp. 159–190). Springer.

Wentzel, K. R. (1997). Student motivation in middle school: The role of perceived pedagogical caring. *Journal of Educational Psychology, 89*(3), 411–419.

Wentzel, K. R. (2000). What is it that I'm trying to achieve? Classroom goals from a content perspective. *Contemporary Educational Psychology, 25*(1), 105–115. https://doi.org/10.1006/ceps.1999.1021.

Wentzel, K. R. (2021). *Motivating students to learn* (5th ed.). Routledge.

White, E. M. (2010). College-level writing and the liberal arts tradition. In P. Sullivan, H. Tinberg, & S. Blau (Eds.), *What is "college-level" writing?* (Vol. 2, pp. 295–299). National Council of Teachers of English.

Wiersema, J. A., Licklider, B., Thompson, J. R., Hendrich, S., Haynes, C., & Thompson, K. (2015). Mindset about intelligence and meaningful and mindful effort: It's not my hardest class any more! *Learning Communities: Research & Practice, 3*(2). https://eric.ed.gov/?id=EJ1112509.

Wigfield, A., & Eccles, J. S. (1992). The development of achievement task values: A theoretical analysis. *Developmental Review, 12*(3), 265–310.

Wigfield, A., Eccles, J. S., Fredricks, J. A., Simpkins, S., Roeser, R. W., & Schiefele, U. (2015). Development of achievement motivation and engagement. In W. F. Overton, P. C. M. Molenaar, & R. M. Lerner (Eds.), *Handbook of child psychology and developmental Science* (Vol. 1, pp. 1–44). Wiley. https://doi.org/10.1002/9781118963418.childpsy316.

Wigfield, A., Tonks, S. M., & Klauda, S. L. (2016). Expectancy-value theory. In K. R. Wentzel & D. B. Miele (Eds.), *Handbook of motivation in school* (2nd ed., pp. 55–74). Routledge.

Willig, C. (2008). Quality in qualitative research. In *Introducing qualitative research in psychology: Adventures in theory and method* (pp. 149–161). McGraw-Hill Education.

Willig, C. (2013). *Introducing qualitative research in psychology* (3rd ed.). McGraw-Hill Education.

Wingard, J., & Geosits, A. (2014). Effective comments and revisions in student writing from WAC courses. *Across the Disciplines, 11*(1), 1–16.

Winter, R. (2002). Truth or fiction: Problems of validity and authenticity in narratives of action research. *Educational Action Research, 10*(1), 143–154. https://doi.org/10.1080/09650790200200178.

Wollenschläger, M., Hattie, J., Machts, N., Möller, J., & Harms, U. (2016). What makes rubrics effective in teacher-feedback? Transparency of learning goals is not enough. *Contemporary Educational Psychology, 44–45,* 1–11. https://doi.org/10.1016/j.cedpsych.2015.11.003.

Wolters, C. A. (2004). Advancing achievement goal theory: Using goal structures and goal orientations to predict students' motivation, cognition, and achievement. *Journal of Educational Psychology, 96*(2), 236–250.

Wormington, S. V., & Linnenbrink-Garcia, L. (2017). A new look at multiple goal pursuit: The promise of a person-centered approach. *Educational Psychology Review, 29*(3), 407–445. http://doi.org/10.1007/s10648-016-9358-2.

Wright, S. L., Jenkins-Guarnieri, M. A., & Murdock, J. L. (2013). Career development among first-year college students: College self-efficacy, student persistence, and academic success. *Journal of Career Development, 40*(4), 292–310.

Yancey, K. B. (2016a). Introduction: Coming to terms: Composition/rhetoric, threshold concepts, and a disciplinary core. In L. Adler-Kassner & E. Wardle (Eds.), *Naming what we know: Threshold concepts of writing studies* (pp. xvii–xxxi). Utah State University Press.

Yancey, K. B. (2016b). Introduction: Contextualizing reflection. In *A rhetoric of reflection* (pp. 3–20). University Press of Colorado.

Yancey, K. B. (2016c). Learning to write effectively requires different kinds of practice, time, and effort. In L. Adler-Kassner & E. Wardle (Eds.), *Naming what we know: Threshold concepts of writing studies* (pp. 64–65). Utah State University Press.

Yeager, D. S., Carroll, J. M., Buontempo, J., Cimpian, A., Woody, S., Crosnoe, R., Muller, C., Murray, J., Mhatre, P., Kersting, N., Hulleman, C., Kudym, M., Murphy, M., Duckworth, A. L., Walton, G. M., & Dweck, C. S. (2022). Teacher mindsets help explain where a growth-mindset intervention does and doesn't work. *Psychological Science, 33*(1), 18–32. https://doi.org/10.1177/09567976211028984.

Yeager, D. S., & Dweck, C. S. (2012). Mindsets that promote resilience: When students believe that personal characteristics can be developed. *Educational Psychologist, 47*(4), 302–314. https://doi.org/10.1080/00461520.2012.722805.

Yeager, D. S., Henderson, M. D., Paunesku, D., Walton, G. M., D'Mello, S., Spitzer, B. J., & Duckworth, A. L. (2014). Boring but important: A self-transcendent purpose for learning fosters academic self-regulation. *Journal of Personality and Social Psychology, 107*(4), 559–580. https://doi.org/10.1037/a0037637.

Yeager, D. S., Purdie-Vaughns, V., Garcia, J., Apfel, N., Brzustoski, P., Master, A., Hessert, W. T., Williams, M. E., & Cohen, G. L. (2014). Breaking the cycle of mistrust: Wise interventions to provide critical feedback across the racial divide. *Journal of Experimental Psychology: General, 143*(2), 804–824. https://doi.org/10.1037/a0033906.

Yin, R. K. (2009). *Case study research: Design and methods* (4th ed.). Sage.

Zuidema, L. A., & Fredricksen, J. E. (2016). Resources preservice teachers use to think about student writing. *Research in the Teaching of English, 51*(1), 12–36.

Zumbrunn, S., Carter, Y. M., & Conklin, S. (2014). Unpacking the value of writing: Exploring college students' perceptions of writing. *Journal of Research in Education, 24*(2), 18–33.

Zumwalt, K., & Craig, M. (2008). Who is teaching? Does it matter? In M. Cochran-Smith, S. Feiman-Nemser, D. J. McIntyre, & Association of Teacher Educators (Eds.), *Handbook of research on teacher education: Enduring questions in changing contexts.* (3rd ed., pp. 404–423). Routledge.

Index

Milton Keynes UK
Ingram Content Group UK Ltd.
UKHW010730050624
443777UK00004B/211

9 781438 495781